Special Education Series
Peter Knoblock, *Editor*

Achieving the Complete School: Strategies for Effective Mainstreaming
Douglas Biklen with Robert Bogdan, Dianne L. Ferguson, Stanford J. Searl, Jr., and Steven J. Taylor

Stress in Childhood: An Intervention Model for Teachers and Other Professionals
Gaston E. Blom, Bruce D. Cheney, and James E. Snoddy

Curriculum Decision Making for Students with Severe Handicaps: Policy and Practice
Dianne L. Ferguson

Helping the Visually Impaired Child with Developmental Problems: Effective Practice in Home, School, and Community
Sally M. Rogow

Progress Without Punishment: Effective Approaches for Learners with Behavioral Problems
Anne M. Donnellan, Gary W. LaVigna, Nanette Negri-Shoultz, and Lynette L. Fassbender

Issues and Research in Special Education, Volumes 1 and 2
Robert Gaylord-Ross, Editor

Cultural Diversity, Families, and the Special Education System: Communication and Empowerment
Beth Harry

Interpreting Disability: A Qualitative Reader
Philip M. Ferguson, Dianne L. Ferguson, and Steven J. Taylor, Editors

On Being L.D.: Perspectives and Strategies of Young Adults
Stephen T. Murphy

Toward Effective Public School Programs for Deaf Students: Context, Process, and Outcomes
Thomas N. Kluwin, Donald F. Moores, and Martha Gonter Gaustad, Editors

Communication Unbound: How Facilitated Communication Is Challenging Traditional Views of Autism and Ability/Disability
Douglas Biklen

Facilitated Communication Training
Rosemary Crossley

The Social Meaning of Mental Retardation: Two Life Stories
Robert Bogdan and Steven J. Taylor

Toward Inclusive Schools?
Catherine Clark, Alan Dyson, and Alan Millward, Editors

Disability and Democracy: Reconstructing (Special) Education for Postmodernity
Thomas M. Skrtic, Editor

Curriculum Trends, Special Education, and Reform: Refocusing the Conversation
Marleen C. Pugach and Cynthia L. Warger, Editors

Curriculum Trends, Special Education, and Reform

REFOCUSING THE CONVERSATION

EDITED BY

Marleen C. Pugach and Cynthia L. Warger

FOREWORD BY MICHAEL FULLAN

Teachers College, Columbia University
New York and London

Published by Teachers College Press, 1234 Amsterdam Avenue, New York, NY 10027

Library of Congress Cataloging-in-Publication Data

Curriculum trends, special education, and reform : refocusing the conversation / edited by Marleen C. Pugach and Cynthia L. Warger ; foreword by Michael Fullan.
p. cm.—(Special education series)
Includes bibliographical references and index.
ISBN 0-8077-3563-9 (alk. paper)—ISBN 0-8077-3562-0 (pbk. : alk. paper)
1. Special education—United States—Curricula. 2. Curriculum change—United States. I. Pugach, Marleen Carol, 1949– . II. Warger, Cynthia L. III. Series: Special education series (New York, N.Y.)
LC3981.C87 1996
375′.001—dc20 96-9469

ISBN 0-8077-3562-0 (paper)
ISBN 0-8077-3563-9 (cloth)

Printed on acid-free paper
Manufactured in the United States of America

03 02 01 00 99 98 97 96 8 7 6 5 4 3 2 1

That is the happiest conversation, where there is no competition, no vanity, but a calm quiet interchange of sentiments.

—Samuel Johnson

Contents

Foreword

I doubt if there is a book on special education that speaks to so many audiences. While retaining the compassion and advocacy for the place of special education, CURRICULUM TRENDS, SPECIAL EDUCATION, AND REFORM provides a comprehensive theoretical and practical analysis of curriculum reform across the disciplines. Each curriculum chapter is a gem in its own right. Science, mathematics, social studies, literacy, early childhood are all addressed with concise, up-to-date analyses of where the subfields are going and how they connect to one another. These chapters represent a curriculum text that is accessible and boundary pushing, giving us a clear picture of curriculum reform.

The response sections of each chapter provide insightful and practical descriptions of reform trends in special education as they interrelate with developments in the basic subject disciplines themselves. The reader is treated to a clear and convincing picture of how general and special education have implications for each other.

What is most exciting about this book is how it is based on the premise that general curriculum reform and special education curriculum reform must be deeply interrelated. From Chapter 1, which poses the question "Can Special and General Education Learn from Each Other?" to the last chapter, "Challenges for the Special Education–Curriculum Reform Partnership," the mutual dependency between developments in special education and curriculum more generally is compellingly portrayed. There is no other book focusing on special education that I know of that uses curriculum reform across the disciplines as the "glue" and that so clearly demonstrates that progress is intimately tied to how we address the education of all students.

This book does not present easy answers. It does provide clarity about curriculum trends and dilemmas. It leaves the reader with a sense of hope and promising lines of thought and action. It also shows how much work remains to be done, and how complex the challenges will be. But it leaves no doubt that the future of special education cannot be conceived as a separate problem. Nor does it argue for abstract ideological inclusion. It says that the hard, but rewarding work of the future lies in "building bridges of mutual reform" between special and general curriculum reform—and it establishes a clear and comprehensive agenda for this work.

Michael Fullan
University of Toronto

Preface

Two decades have passed since the passage of The Education for All Handicapped Children Act (PL 94–142) and, while great advances have been made in accommodating the needs of diverse learners, educators are still throwing up their hands in frustration. Why is it so hard to educate children and youth with mild disabilities alongside their peers in the public schools? What makes it so difficult to include children in regular classrooms who learn at slightly different rates, or who bring to the learning situation different learning styles, or who react to instruction and schooling with less than positive attitudes? Special and general educators alike have struggled for years to answer these questions. And, while we seem to inch closer to our goal with new techniques and approaches that come along, somehow we just cannot seem to get out in front—and stay there.

It is the contention in this book that until we begin to look seriously at the standard curriculum—what students are expected to know and be able to do as a result of their schooling—we will continue this back-pedaling from the goal of successfully including students with mild disabilities in least restrictive educational settings. We will continue to plan alternative routes and design new and better vehicles, without having a clear sense of where we are going or whether it is worth the effort of getting there.

In trying to understand what makes it so hard to educate children with disabilities in general education programs, we believe curriculum must be—but has not been—at the forefront of all discussions. Curriculum stands at the core of schooling. As the systematic structure or plan of learning experiences in school, the curriculum anchors what children do, how they are instructed to do it, and how they are assessed. Curriculum also dictates how the instructional environment is organized to support students in reaching outcomes. It is no minor coincidence that students with mild disabilities are so labeled as a result of having failed in the prevailing curriculum.

We are currently at a point in general education reform efforts where curriculum has become a prominent focus for discussion. Over a decade's work exists in revamping curriculum standards in the various subject areas. New curriculum frameworks have been articulated, as well as new ways to organize curriculum that reflect outcomes identified by work force and consumer studies as essential for a productive life in the twenty-first century. At the same time, we have an emerging body of knowledge that calls for rethinking the place of special education as a system separate and distinct from its general education counterpart. With the convergence of these factors, we explore in this book opportunities to forge new alliances and create new answers to the age-old question: What is worth knowing and being able to do? And, in so answering, we also address whether these skills and knowledge should differ for students with mild disabilities.

The purpose of the book is to describe new curriculum trends and the impact those trends will have on providing equitable educational programs to all students, especially students with mild disabilities. We focus on describing how special and general educators can use both the opportunities and the challenges presented by these trends as a jumping-off point for rethinking how students are educated and with what results. The book explores current curriculum debates within general education, characterizes current states of reform, and then situates those debates within questions of reform in special education. As such, it falls in the intersection between special and general education and is designed to bridge the two current debates—which often seem much more separate than they indeed are. Our purpose is to provoke discussion around these pertinent curriculum issues. We will not prescribe or even endorse one approach for ensuring that all students receive a high-quality educational program; nor do we plan to judge the merits of each new curriculum thrust. We will present the current state of curriculum work and consider how special and general educators can best use that information in renewing their programs.

Our intent is to explore curriculum reform as it relates to *mild disabilities.* We have chosen to focus on mild disabilities for three reasons. First, children in these categories continue to form the largest proportion of students in special education. Second, the curriculum reform issues for students in general education and the curriculum needs of students now labeled as having mild disabilities are much more similar than different. Third, if curriculum reform is successful to the degree that students now labeled as having mild disabilities can succeed academically in much greater numbers, the implications for the organization and delivery of special education are great indeed.

To achieve our goal, we have organized the book in the following way. First we set the context for a curriculum emphasis in special education. We describe current curriculum renewal efforts and common themes that have emerged. The impact of major trends is considered in the context of special education programming and the current reform movement.

Next we take a closer look at specific curriculum trends in the major academic subject areas and their potential impact on special education. Experts in the content areas of mathematics, science, literacy, and social studies each present a synthesis of major curriculum trends affecting their subject domain. We also have encouraged them to identify promising instructional practices from their perspectives. These curriculum chapters are followed by a series of commentaries prepared by special educators or by general educators who have attempted to draw on these trends with special education students. The commentaries are intended to raise issues concerning the impact these curriculum trends will have on serving the educational needs of students with mild disabilities. A section on early childhood education is included separately, as the organization of curriculum at this level treats subject areas in an integrated manner. We conclude with a summary of the opportunities and challenges facing special and general educators in planning curriculum for a diverse student population according to these new trends, and offer a series of suggestions for how educators can take the next steps forward in addressing the issues.

For whom might this volume be appropriate? We would hope that prospective and practicing special education teachers who are interested in inclusion will use it to gain an understanding of the role curriculum plays in their efforts. Conversely, we hope that prospective and practicing general education teachers find it helpful in linking their understanding of curriculum to the practice of special education. Finally, we encourage administrators, policy makers, and teacher educators to use these ideas in developing plans for school-wide or program-wide reform.

Because both of us believe in the need for much greater interaction between special and general education, we are especially pleased to bring together in one volume the thinking of many prominent persons in both fields. We are grateful to these authors, who enthusiastically agreed to write and who also saw this as an important bridge to build. To support the work of the contributors, Cathymae Nelson of the University of Wisconsin–Milwaukee did a masterful job of preparing the manuscript, and we thank her for her fine technical and editorial skills. Our editors at Teachers College Press, Brian Ellerbeck and Sarah Biondello, provided us with guidance and good judgment throughout the process and showed great patience as we wrestled with some of the difficult decisions that inevitably accompany cross-disciplinary projects.

No one familiar with the educational scene as we end the millennium can dispute that the future of special education hangs in the balance. As we move into the twenty-first century, many questions loom large in the picture. In what form will special education exist? Will there be targeted services for students with lifelong disabilities? If there is less special education, will enough people demonstrate the commitment needed to ensure that all students—no matter the range of their differences—have a good chance of being successful in life as a result of their schooling? As supporters of greater collegial interaction, we are no less concerned about these issues than are our colleagues who would prefer that the status of special education remain much as it always has been. However, we believe that the answers are to be found in the intersection of general and special education and will emerge from an honest, mutually well-informed dialogue about the relevant issues. We hope this volume is one step in that direction.

Curriculum Trends, Special Education, and Reform

REFOCUSING THE CONVERSATION

∗ CHAPTER 1 ∗

Treating Curriculum as a Target of Reform: Can Special and General Education Learn from Each Other?

Marleen C. Pugach and Cynthia L. Warger

American education is in the midst of a curriculum revolution designed to bring schooling into line with society's most pressing needs. However, as we all know, curriculum reform is not a new venture. As far back as the nineteenth century, we have had documented accounts of efforts to bring the curriculum more in line with current societal needs and requirements (Kliebard, 1994). Within our present frame of reference, most of us can remember such curriculum revolutions as "new" math, environmental education, and a revamping of history to allow for coverage beyond the exploits of males of European descent. We may even have experienced the cheers and protests that accompanied sex education and drug use prevention curriculums into classrooms, or found ourselves logged on to a PC network where we learned what the technology ruckus was all about. But few of us have ever witnessed personally the kind of transformation that is currently taking place in school curriculum nationwide.

Unlike recent attempts to address curriculum reform through add-ons or band-aids in the form of "electives"—attempts that often have been lost in political rhetoric or budgetary crunches—present-day curriculum reform is ushering in new frameworks and new philosophies for determining what is worth knowing and being able to do. Spawned by a growing urgency to stop widespread problems of illiteracy, poverty, and violence threatening the very fabric of society, the school curriculum has become the last hope for ensuring a better future for the nation's children.

In the current context of education reform, the question is one of effecting congruence between what is taught and what is needed to ensure a cadre of productive citizens at the end of formal schooling. The issues

Curriculum Trends, Special Education, and Reform: Refocusing the Conversation. ISBN 0-8077-3562-0 (pbk), ISBN 0-8077-3563-9 (cloth).

tend to focus on the inadequacy of what children in this country are expected to know and be able to do, as well as on how to guarantee success for *all* children, regardless of their advantages or disadvantages (Lewis, 1990). Although both issues resonate equally well with special and general educators, each comes to the discussion from a different tradition and a seemingly incompatible mind-set. How to bring special and general education together for the goal of school improvement for a broad range of students has been an enduring problem in the schools.

Historically, special education has carved out a well-identified, advocacy-based role for itself and has had difficulty figuring out exactly how to participate effectively in the wider educational community and its reform. Conversely, general education has been comfortable allowing special education to pull off as many students as possible and to be conducted separately from the everyday dynamics of schooling. As convenient as this arrangement has been, it is finally coming to an end as evidence mounts to show that it is not serving students well. The students this system serves least well are those with mild disabilities.

Traditional general education has not served students well either. The rationale for reforming the regular education curriculum is twofold. Advantaged students are not well served because they are not adequately challenged. Less advantaged students who come to school less well prepared for academics are not well served because they are placed in a curriculum context that (1) ignores their backgrounds, (2) minimizes their motivation for academic work, and (3) prepares them neither for advanced education nor for the technological demands of new vocational options. These students, who often are members of minority groups, frequently end up in the special education system (Artiles & Trent, 1994; Heller, Holtzman, & Messick, 1982) or leave school (Wyman, 1993).

These two streams of concern about schooling converge on the issue of curriculum. Historically, curriculum has been one of the least likely places for joint conversations and joint action to occur. With the advent of inclusion, special education, willingly or not, has been thrust into the midst of the setting in which curriculum reform is being played out, namely, the general education classroom. Whether one buys into inclusion as a full- or part-time practice (and this debate is far from resolved, as evidenced by the continuing surge of articles for and against in nearly every major special education journal and many prominent general education journals as well), the reality of schooling as the century draws to a close is that inclusion has forced special education teachers and students into general education classrooms in greater numbers and for more sustained periods of time than ever before. How special education responds to this challenge for students with mild disabilities is crucial.

Significant changes will continue to occur in the general education curriculum. We may need a decade or more to implement the curriculum trends described in this volume; during that time, general education will not be doing business as usual. The rules regarding curriculum and its implementation will surely change. Exactly how they change will depend, to a great extent, on the support educators receive in their efforts to improve learning for all children.

Whether special educators will choose simply to import traditional special education practice into the general education setting or begin instead to participate as full members of the curriculum reform debate and subsequent implementation remains speculative. If special educators fail to participate in curriculum reform, they also will fail to develop a good sense of what the new curriculum practices might mean for students labeled as having disabilities. Moreover, they will not be in a position either to support these new trends where support will help students who previously have failed, or to challenge these new trends when such challenges are warranted. Without sustained curriculum dialogue between special and general educators, we may see yet another generation of special education students go without having their needs met in school.

Inclusion, then, provides the opportunity for special educators to consider their role in the schools from an entirely new vantage point, and the vantage point we believe to be most valuable is that of curriculum reform—even though curriculum has been the point of least interaction to date. For students with severe disabilities, curriculum reform is not nearly so central a goal as reform that enables students to be accepted as full members of the classroom community; separate, distinguishable curriculum goals will always be needed for this population. For students with mild disabilities, whose failure typically appears only when they come into contact with the curriculum in the first place, reforming the curriculum—with all the implications such reform has for redefining instruction as well as norms of professional interaction—holds great promise for improving their educational futures. As a foundation for our efforts to encourage this link between special education and the reform of the general education curriculum, we begin with a description of how both general and special education have arrived at their respective positions in relationship to curriculum, and thus to its reform.

THE ORIGINS OF CURRENT CURRICULUM REFORM IN GENERAL EDUCATION

Curriculum change follows no predictable schedule. Rather, it occurs when trends in society, in our understanding of students, or in the subject area itself force a reconsideration of the status quo. In 1949, Tyler espoused a model that showed that the origins of curriculum change could be traced to one or more of the following sources: students, contemporary societal needs, and the integrity of the subject matter. From Tyler's perspective, curriculum change usually reflects a compromise among these elements (Brandt & Tyler, 1983).

The curriculum reform effort we currently find ourselves embroiled in can best be traced to the early 1980s, with the issuance of *A Nation at Risk* (National Commission on Excellence in Education, 1983) and the many reform reports that preceded and followed it. During the 1980s, reform was driven primarily by the needs of society, changing demographics, and new knowledge about how children grow and learn, not by advances in curriculum subject areas. The sentiments consistently expressed throughout this wave of public commentary attacked school systems for failing to produce competent students who could top their Japanese and European peers on standardized tests, and encouraged educators to rid schools of an old and tired curriculum that through neglect had fallen out of sync with the changing global economy (President's Commission on Time and Learning, 1994).

The needs of an industrial society had been replaced seemingly overnight by those of a new, knowledge-intensive economic order. Whereas for years children had been disciplined in a rigid curriculum that fostered conformity and compliance—the graded school concept in toto (Goodlad & Anderson, 1987)—calls were made to switch over to a flexible curriculum that would result in children who could think analytically and creatively, communicate effectively across diverse settings, work together to solve problems and finish tasks, and participate as citizens in a multicultural society (Darling-Hammond, 1993).

Integrally tied to this curriculum reform agenda was the growing exodus of students from the general education curriculum—and in some cases, the school itself, prior to graduation (Flores, 1991; Wehlage, 1989). The national drop-out rate for the 1980s hovered at 25–28% overall, with some urban centers facing rates of 50% or higher (National Association of State Boards of Education, 1988). Increasing poverty, psychological and physical abuse, substance abuse, and violence in the homes of many American children (Knitzer, Steinberg, & Fleisch, 1990) resulted in a host of school- and neighborhood-based problems that curriculum frameworks in use did not seem capable of affecting. Added to this scenario was the growing diversity within and across minority groups with regard to language, dialect, cultural background, arts, and values (Hodgkinson, 1987). Making schools more attractive for students from diverse backgrounds or who were at risk became once again a national and local priority (Glatthorn, 1985).

At the same time, leaders in special education began to acknowledge the overlap between the large number of students labeled as "at risk" and the growing population of students in mild categories of disability. This was published in a document that came to be known as the Regular Education Initiative (see Will, 1986, and the numerous commentaries publication on this document spawned). However, the relationship between these two populations did not capture the interest of those who promoted reform in general education, and the link was not pursued vigorously either on the part of special or general education.

Nevertheless, the work force and society had spoken. The schools got the message—continue as you are and the legacy you leave to those entering the twenty-first century will be one fraught with poverty, violence in the streets, and the inability of workers to compete in the world economy. Given this heavy dose of Armageddon prophecy, it is not surprising that calls for reform, and specifically curriculum reform, hit a chord with policy makers, educators, and the general public, who desperately needed solutions to the problems they were facing. The reasoning was clear: Change what schools teach and what students learn and we have a chance of fixing what ails our society and of ensuring our economic standing worldwide. From a curriculum perspective, this message translated into heavy demands for an emphasis on rigorous content and increased academic standards for all students.

However, as we look back on this time of hope and dissect the rhetoric, the notion of who constituted "all" students seems limited; "all" referred to the students who were dropping out of school and to disadvantaged students—often members of minority groups—who were at risk for failure in the educational system. At summit meetings and in response to national blue-ribbon task forces, educators directed their attention primarily to capable students who could, with the right reforms, succeed in school. Special education was not part of this "at-risk" dialogue, not with respect to the overlap between students labeled as "at risk" and those labeled as having mild disabilities, or with respect to the need for clear demarcations between the educational demands of the larger population of students in categories of mild disability and the smaller population of students whose disabilities were more enduring and who would always require specialized services. Furthermore, on the whole, special education chose not to address the growing number of minority students being referred to its programs, despite compelling reports (e.g., Heller, Holtzman, & Messick, 1982) documenting the problem (Pugach, 1995). It was against this complex backdrop that national subject-area organizations were hit with mounting pressure to develop "world-class standards" that would define for the twenty-first century what schools should teach and what all students should learn.

SUBJECT-AREA GROUPS RESPOND TO PRESSURE FOR REFORM

Subject-area organizations responded by attempting to bring their curriculum standards into line with the realities facing students and the world they would face upon graduation, while simultaneously rethinking curriculum to make it more attractive to disaffected youth (American Association for the Advancement of Science, 1989; Bradley Commission on History in the Schools, 1988; Mathematical Sciences Education Board, 1989; National Center for History in the Schools, 1992; National Commission on Social Studies in the Schools, 1989; National Council of Teachers of Mathematics, 1989). Proposed subject-area reform agendas emerging from this work generally suggested that the school curriculum should be revised to emphasize the following (Lewis, 1990):

- In-depth coverage of content, with less review of facts
- Students' abilities to think critically and creatively and to solve problems
- Identification and integration into the curriculum of concepts that are connected across subject areas
- Increased curriculum standards for all students
- Students' abilities to work cooperatively together to solve problems and complete tasks

As Darling-Hammond (1993) summarized, the new curriculum reform changes signaled a new mission for schools—one in which teachers no longer simply cover the curriculum, but in which students are enabled to construct their own knowledge and to develop their own talents in effective and powerful ways.

Today we have moved beyond a discussion of the merits of such curriculum reform efforts and have eased into confronting what those reforms mean to subject-matter pedagogy and outcomes for the nation's children. Each day we are presented with suggestions. Most dramatic, perhaps, has been the rush to adopt the National Council for Teachers of Mathematics (NCTM) standards into state mathematics frameworks; as of 1993, 41 states had undertaken such action (O'Neil, 1993). One has only to have read *Education Week* over the past few years to know that national subject-area standards are on an upswing. Despite the fact that such standards may be used as political footballs (recall the brouhaha in 1994–95 over history standards), the issue of what children will learn in school and how worthwhile it may be remains a dominant concern (Ravitch, 1993).

The prospect of subject-area standards has opened the door for discussion regarding establishment of a national curriculum—a discussion that focuses on curriculum as a key mechanism for improving student performance, measured against national goals and international standards of achievement (O'Neil, 1991; Orrill, 1994; Smith, Fuhrman, & O'Day, 1994). The Goals 2000: Educate America Act, signed into law in March 1994, takes this movement a step further by encouraging states to set standards based on those identified at the national level. The lure of a national "fix-all" curriculum is strong; a recent example is yet another federally funded blue-ribbon panel, the National Educational Standards and Assessment Council, whose charge is to certify content and student performance standards as well as criteria for assessments linked to national standards.

We are still not at the crossroads of making a momentous decision about whether a national curriculum will be prescribed. However, as the field of education continues to move forward in creating national standards that ensure that *all* children have access to challenging subject matter, these questions, which have particular relevance for special education, are being asked with little, if any, input from special educators. Yet, as Newman (1993) asserts, significant tension exists between the desire for uniform outcomes across large numbers of schools and the differentiation of schooling due to cultural diversity, vocational specialization, individual differences, and local political control.

In some ways special education's absence from these conversations strikes a familiar chord. Consider the first wave of reform reports in 1983, beginning with the publication of *A Nation at Risk,* when special education was not identified as part of either the problem or the solution (Pugach & Sapon-Shevin, 1987) and in fact was not mentioned in a significant way at all. Again, when equity issues burst onto the scene during the curriculum debates, issues of disability were rarely raised. Yet, variability among students' opportunity to learn, as reflected by the learning characteristics of students with disabilities, makes the prospect of educational equity seem daunting.

Except for a brief outcry questioning the feasibility of demanding higher academic standards for students with disabilities without first addressing the inequities in the current system (see, for example, Algozzine, Ysseldyke, Kauffman, & Landrum, 1991; National Joint Committee on Learning Disabilities, 1991), special educators have been remarkably quiet on the curriculum reform front. To understand this phenomenon, we must address the question: How has special education framed issues of curriculum for students with mild disabilities, and what has special education been doing about curriculum while the rest of the educational profession has been traveling down the national standards route full speed ahead?

INTERPRETING CURRICULUM FROM A SPECIAL EDUCATION PERSPECTIVE

Traditionally, it is the standard school curriculum that poses problems for students with mild disabilities or for students in the categories of learning disability, behavior disorders, and mild mental retardation. The general education curriculum is the place where their failure or lack of achievement marks them as having a mild disability in the first place.

There are numerous reasons why the traditional curriculum is problematic for students with disabilities. To a large extent, these are the very same reasons it also has failed to meet the needs of so many other students in schools. At the root of the problem, as those who advocate broad-based curriculum reform have contended, is the graded school, with its rigid, lock-step curriculum. Such a curriculum is far too inflexible to accommodate the real and fluid nature of student learning (Cuban, 1989; Goodlad & Anderson, 1987). The acquisition of fragmented pieces of academic content, which has been the dominant curriculum framework for nearly the past century, leaves out the learner and the society as central curriculum considerations; in this paradigm, subject-area facts and their memorization are paramount. These observations about the limitations of the curriculum presently in use are not new; indeed, as we have suggested, the general failure of current conceptions of curriculum to provide acceptable outcomes accounts, in large part, for the curriculum upheaval we continue to witness as the millennium comes to a close.

Interestingly enough, many special educators agree that the standard curriculum could use a major overhaul. However, their criticisms of the general education curriculum did not originate in the general education reform discussion. Instead, they have come to the forefront as a result of discussions within the special education community. This is an important distinction, since the source of the special education discourse about the failure of curriculum resides in a more philosophical debate regarding the merits of *individualization.* When special educators argue that the problems many students exhibit—particularly those of students with mild disabilities—could be prevented or greatly diminished if only the general education curriculum were totally redesigned, they usually base their solutions on the philosophical premise that *all* educational programs should be tailored (that is, individualized) for individual students. Indeed, this is a departure from the group orientation in general education, which holds that education is a public good and that there is a set of knowledge and skills that should be held in common by all children. In practice, however, it is questionable whether special education has lived up to its mission of providing an individualized curriculum. Individually tailored programs of instruction that have been developed for students with mild disabilities and carried out in resource room programs have been remarkably similar to one another (Wesson & Deno, 1989; Ysseldyke, O'Sullivan, Thurlow, & Christenson, 1989). In reality, individualization of the curriculum to meet the educational deficits of each student in special education has not occurred, calling into question the feasibility of relying on the argument for individualization as a curriculum goal.

It is this individualized, deficit approach to the identification and remediation of all disabilities that has dominated special education and has tended to characterize nearly all of its programs and practices, focusing attention on individual students and not on the curriculum. It is also this mind-set that has, for all practical purposes, kept special education out of the curriculum debates.

Given the central role the standard curriculum plays in the initial identification of mild disabilities and considering that the majority of students with mild disabilities spend more time in general education than special education classrooms, the standard curriculum presents a natural context in which to target the reform energies of special education. Whether the debate focuses on a more general issue, such as whether what all children are being asked to do is worth doing and knowing (which is, after all, the central curriculum question), or on a more specific one, such as whether the standard curriculum is designed to foster or squelch the diverse learning needs of students who carry labels of mild disability, the direct involvement of special education is demanded.

From our perspective, special education has always had a major part to play in the curriculum debates. It has been only in recent years, when special education program outcomes have come under internal as well as external scrutiny (Edgar, 1988; Macmillan, Widaman, Balow, Borthwick-Duffy, Hendrick, & Hemsley, 1992; National Longitudinal Transition Study, 1994; SRI International, 1993; Wagner, D'Amico, Marder, Newman, & Blackorby, 1992), that the role was catapulted into the limelight. For students with mild disabilities, special educators seldom have worried about the general education curriculum other than to lament its lack of attention to the needs of individual students. In fact, the special education collaboration literature indicates that one of the primary problems special educators, serving in a collaborative or consultative role, face when establishing their credibility is their *lack of knowledge* of general educators' subject matter (Aldinger, Warger, & Eavy, 1992; Pugach, 1992). For most special educators, the answer to limited curriculum knowledge has not been to race out and complete a masters degree in content area. Instead, for students with mild disabilities special educators have approached curriculum from an *access* perspective.

Approaching Curriculum for Students with Mild Disabilities: The Press for Access

Over the years, special educators have addressed this persistent general education curriculum dilemma from a child deficit perspective: fix the child, fix the instruction, offer basic skills instruction when it is clear that the child has not learned the prerequisite skills—but never fix the curriculum. Consistent with its roots in a medical model of disability, special educators have based their relationship with the standard curriculum on this deficit philosophy, which holds that as long as the problem resides within the individual student, efforts to overcome the difficulties students experience likewise need to be tailored to the individual, and not to the curriculum itself (Case, 1992). Even in some of the most current descriptions of early, faltering attempts at inclusion (see Zigmond & Baker, 1995), the individual, within-student problem model continues to be the focal point of reform efforts. The message has been stated explicitly, over and over again: With adaptation and support suited to the needs of the individual, all students can be successful in achieving the same curriculum goals (Van Dyke, Stallings, & Colley, 1995).

As a result of defining their relationship with curriculum in this within-child manner, special educators have been successful in teaching students learning strategies to help them engage in classroom lessons, in helping teachers modify their instructional approaches to accommodate a wide variance of student learning styles, and in adapting materials, textbooks, and instructional tools for greater utilization (for a summary see Gable, Hendrickson, & Lyon, 1987; Nolet & Tindal, 1993; Schiller, Coutinho, & Kaufman, 1993). Additionally, special educators have applied task analysis to lessons, and using the information gleaned, have taught students the prerequisite skills for participating in specific activities. All in all, special educators have made these accommodations to ensure *access* to the standard curriculum. Once students gained access and were thought to be equipped to step back into the general education classroom, special educators left worries about the basic form and content of the standard curriculum to classroom teachers.

At one level it is not hard to understand this overriding concern with access. After all, educating students in less restrictive environments was a cornerstone of the 1975 special education reform. The very real goal of getting students with more severe disabilities out of either their homes or segregated facilities and into public schools to begin with, as well as getting students out of segregated public school programs and into general classrooms for even part of the day, dominated the special education landscape.

Enabling students to participate in the general curriculum to any extent represented real progress. However, for the most part, special education's attention to the actual curriculum stopped at the point of gaining student access to classroom lessons and activities.

The access problem is made even more complex by the pragmatics of translating curriculum goals into lessons and activities. For many general education classroom teachers, lessons and activities are treated as the curriculum. Both general and special education teachers routinely write student outcome objectives that focus on *what students are asked to do in the particular activity,* rather than on what students should be learning as a result of those activities. As Howell and Evans (1995) comment, "It is easy to find IEPS [individualized education plans] that contain objectives with wording like this: 'The student will read book 7 of the series.' However, this is not an objective; it is an instructional procedure" (p. 395). Yet in reality, the activities are merely vehicles to reach the skills and knowledge mandated in the curriculum.

In classrooms across the country, activities reign supreme. From an access perspective, the emphasis on activities can send a confusing message to special educators. Does one teach the student the skills and knowledge necessary to access the teacher's lesson, even if it is imperfect, *or* does one focus on finding radically different routes to accessing the curriculum? Framing the dilemma from an access perspective allows us an entry point into addressing the curriculum delivery flaw.

For students with disabilities, access to the curriculum occurs through the teacher's lessons and activities, or through instruction. In some cases, the particular way the teacher chooses to deliver instruction or implement activities will make access impossible for some students. For example, as the authors in this volume point out, new curricula tend to emphasize collaboration and social discourse. Many teachers have responded to these trends by presenting curriculum content in lessons that make use of cooperative learning strategies (Slavin, 1995). Note, however, that the outcome is not cooperative learning (except in cases where cooperation is the primary objective), but *better learning of the subject matter.* The cooperative learning activity is the entry point to the subject matter—whether it be mathematics, science, social studies, or language arts. However, the cooperative activity itself requires getting along with others, listening, waiting one's turn, and so on—all social skills that many students with mild learning and behavioral difficulties have never been taught. In this scenario, the special education teacher, committed to ensuring access for the student, typically will come to the conclusion that the student needs remediation or basic skills instruction in the social skills area. This is not to say that the particular student does not also need social skills instruction. In fact, many students do need social skills instruction to be successful in general education classrooms (Fad & Ryser, 1993; Warger & Rutherford, 1993). However, the target of this remediation is access to the teacher's lesson rather than access to the curriculum skills and knowledge, which requires much broader reform than simply appending cooperative learning to the traditional curriculum.

From this example, and countless others that have similar themes, we can see how easy it is to criticize special education for teaching little more than a hodgepodge of fragmented basic skills and for not producing better *outcomes* in its students. The de-emphasis of complex academics in favor of these basic skills, along with social skills and strategy learning, has been promoted in the context of "enabling" the learner's participation in the classroom (Adams & Cessna, 1993; Ysseldyke, Thurlow, & Shriner, 1992).

The model of gaining accessibility to the standard curriculum assumes a congruence between what is taught and how it is taught, a congruence that, in reality, may not exist. Special educators have been busy ensuring access—but this access may not necessarily lead to improved learning of the curriculum. As students move from the elementary to the secondary level, the general education curriculum becomes more specialized and less dependent on basic skills as an end, allowing the achievement gap to grow wider (Nolet & Tindal, 1993).

The Cumulative Impact of an "Acurricular" Stance

The combined effect of (1) working from a child deficit model of disability and (2) focusing on access to the standard curriculum as opposed to working toward a new, more accessible curriculum, has resulted, over time, in a largely "acurricular" orientation within special education. This habit of being acurricular has meant, among other things, that most special educators are unfamiliar with the workings of the standard curriculum and have had little experience with curriculum development. This stance has been institutionalized in one of two ways.

First, the IEP—the flagship instrument of curriculum negotiation within special education—has not been successful in moving toward a transformation of the standard curriculum. Instead, it has been used to adapt the standard curriculum via instruction or basic skills instruction. So although the IEP was conceptualized to accommodate wide departures from the existing curriculum, this function has been largely replaced by lesson modification and by making fewer demands in terms of what students are expected to achieve. Most often, in the name of individualization, students have been taught a watered-down version of the curriculum that their nondisabled peers are taught. As Goldstein (1982) observed early on in the recent history of special education, however, a sound knowledge of the curriculum should form the basis of any differentiation that appears on the IEP. Without a grounding in curriculum knowledge, those who formulate IEPs use them primarily as tools of instructional, rather than curricular, adaptation. The IEP itself, conceived as an instrument of curriculum reform, has failed to play that role, further distancing special education from taking an active part in curriculum reform efforts, while at the same time absorbing undue amounts of precious teacher time that might otherwise be spent in curriculum redesign work.

Second, adapting curriculum continues to be one of the most explicit, identifiable contributions a special education teacher can make when students are being educated in general education classrooms. It is a rare special education teacher who has ventured into a collaborative effort with general education subject counterparts to *change* what is taught and expected to be learned. Rather, special educators have crafted a support role that promises assistance in understanding and meeting the individual needs of students by way of adaptation. The need for curriculum adaptation supports the case for collaboration and often is cited as one of the most important functions special education teachers play in fostering student success in inclusive classrooms. What this persistent focus on curriculum adaptation, as opposed to curriculum reform, has *not* done is to challenge the possibility that for the large group of students identified as having mild disabilities, a radical reform of the curriculum might actually preclude the necessity for so much adaptation—and thus, so much special education—in the first place, and in fact might be one of the most powerful ways to affect their potential success in school. Had a more sociocultural, rather than an individual deficit, approach prevailed in special education practice, the curriculum itself might have received greater attention over time as a place in which to play out large-scale solutions, particularly for children with mild disabilities.

Without question, adaptation of the standard curriculum will always be a function of special education for students whose disabilities stem from vision, hearing, multiple, or physical impairments. For this smaller population of students, some form of adaptation is always likely to be needed to help them access whatever standard curriculum is used (Pugach & Warger, 1993). Likewise, for children with severe disabilities, differentiated curriculum will always be needed to ensure appropriate educational outcomes. Their participation in general education is designed primarily to force the crucial issue of social integration as a social goal. Within special education, it is for students with mild disabilities that the question of substantive academic curriculum reform is most pivotal.

THE INCLUSION AGENDA: IS THERE A FIT WITH GENERAL CURRICULUM REFORM?

As a result of special education's concern with access to and adaptation of the standard curriculum, professionals in the field have not developed a strong "curriculum consciousness" or a good understanding of the sway the general curriculum—however defined—holds over common teaching practice. The long-term effect of a field that has developed in such an acurricular fashion means that, as inclusion efforts progress, the role of the general education curriculum in fostering the inclusion agenda (whether it be full or partial inclusion) may be vastly understated or not understood at all. For example, available descriptions of the first wave of inclusion classrooms suggest that portraying the content of the general education curriculum simply may not be as important as portraying the role special educators play in curriculum adaptation (McLaughlin, 1995). Problems with the general curriculum may not even be raised as significant issues (Pugach, 1995). Further, special educators who study such classrooms rarely provide descriptions of the general curriculum operating in those classrooms, even as they set the context for experiments with inclusion for students with mild disabilities (e.g., Barry, 1994/1995). This occurs, we believe, precisely because of the longstanding absence of a curriculum consciousness.

Current Responses to Curriculum in a Context of Inclusion

As the preference for general education classrooms increases and more special education takes place in them, one of two things tends to happen relative to the curriculum. Special and general education teachers may team to teach the standard curriculum; having two teachers available may make teaching the traditional curriculum more successful, even though it fails to address the larger issue of why, or whether, the existing curriculum—acknowledged to have many problems—should be preserved (Pugach & Wesson, 1995). Or, special education teachers may provide remediation similar to that traditionally provided in resource rooms, but within the regular classroom (Zigmond & Baker, 1995). In either case, the worth of the existing, traditional curriculum is not questioned as a function of greater integration, and no other larger goal has been entertained; the standard curriculum remains more or less acceptable. Indeed, even when suggestions to tinker with the curriculum have been made to general education classroom teachers—as typically arises when special educators suggest that to compensate for a disability, students should be expected to perform only a portion of what is expected of classmates (e.g., fewer story problems, shorter essays)—cries of fairness abound as the issue of how to grade is addressed (Rojewski, Pollard, & Meers, 1991). Seldom mentioned is the need to rethink what students are cognitively, socially, and physically asked to do in the general education curriculum and whether or not it is worth their effort.

Despite this tentative relationship with curriculum, the inclusion movement has caused many special educators to begin exploring better ways to meet the needs of students with disabilities in age-appropriate environments along with their peers. It is currently in vogue for special educators to reject standard curriculum and content organized by subject matter and to replace it with a planning process around a set of desired learning outcomes (National Association of State Boards of Education, 1992). From this perspective, curriculum is defined as broad areas of knowledge and skills in such areas as literacy, citizenship, interpersonal relations, global participation, and economic well-being (McLaughlin & Warren, 1992; Ysseldyke, Thurlow, & Shriner, 1992). With an outcomes-based model, students work toward the same end result, but in an individualized manner so that students who may have difficulties can work at their own pace (Sage & Burrello, 1994). For example, the Council of Administrators of Special Education (CASE), in its Future Agenda for Special Education (1993), advocates a unified system of educational outcomes for all students but allows for variation in what students are expected to learn (for example, a student will be expected to become literate according to his or her abilities).

This approach to outcomes is consistent with special education's past curriculum practice, in which less of the standard curriculum was expected from students who carried labels of mild disability. Instruction in basic skills or social skills, or decontextualized strategy instruction can be seen from this framework to be "enabling" outcomes that students must master before moving on. However, this link places special education in a precarious camp within the internal outcomes-based education (OBE) debate, denoting a preference for treating subject matter as enabling outcomes related to the performance roles students will play in the future, rather than emphasizing the mastery of academics along with some cross-disciplinary outcomes (even though the latter approach appears to have the best track record to date in the public schools) (Brandt, 1994; Spady, 1994).

Further, as organized parent and fundamentalist religious groups are demanding that OBE be abandoned, it is still not clear to what degree OBE will be embraced by school districts. Witness the 1994 firing of the superintendent of the Littleton, Colorado schools for introducing OBE and the fact that OBE was banished from Pennsylvania as a result of one mother's persistent fight. The point for special education is that alignment with OBE as the main point of entry into the curriculum reform discussion, especially at a time when the future of OBE itself is in question (O'Neil, 1994), may not result in the kinds of changes that will be needed for students with disabilities to be successful in schools. Other points of convergence may hold far greater potential for classroom-based reform.

Our intent here is not to enter into the complex debate over whether OBE is the appropriate approach, but rather to point out that special educators who pursue OBE as "the answer to curriculum" will still need to define what students will be expected to know and be able to do upon graduation. If a common set of outcomes for all students remains a goal, those judged a priori to be less able will be excused from making more significant demonstrations of knowledge (McGhan, 1994). Then we are right back where we started—a separate/alternative curriculum for students who we have predetermined should be prepared for a limited role in society dictated by their perceived level of ability, instead of a curriculum whose fundamental design can begin to absorb wider variations in achievement and the persistently high levels of failure that have resulted from the traditional curriculum.

Closing the Curriculum–Inclusion Gap

The gap between special education's view of "curriculum" as the remediation of basic skills and emerging conceptions of curriculum that emphasize meaning making, learning communities, and the contextualization of the learning of skills (Prawat, 1992) is quite wide. Even as it promotes greater integration, special education has no tradition of curriculum consistent with these current philosophies upon which to draw. As a point of comparison for current trends, its frameworks do not include the experience of, for example, the inquiry method. Special educators traditionally have not been well versed in Deweyan or Vygotskian approaches to curriculum and have had few, if any, historical ties to other than behavioral traditions.

In general, special educators instead have held fast to a view of teaching and learning based on five traditional beliefs, noted by Nolan and Francis (1992):

- Learning is the accumulation of fragments of information.
- Teachers transfer knowledge intact to students.
- The goal of teaching is to change student behavior.
- Classroom process focuses on how teachers and individual students interact.
- Skills transfer across subject areas.

In contrast, contemporary views of teaching and learning that undergird current curriculum reform efforts are based on six very different assumptions (Nolan & Francis, 1992):

- For learning to occur, learners must construct meaning actively.
- Learning is strongly influenced by students' prior knowledge.
- The goal of teaching is to change cognitive structures.
- Students do the work of learning; teachers guide them.
- Learning is a cooperative, collaborative endeavor.
- Content-specific pedagogy is important.

As a result, new curriculum trends may seem particularly remote, distancing special educators even further from curriculum redesign activity precisely when the results of such redesign are likely to have the greatest impact on the growing numbers of special education students whose core program is the general education curriculum. Whether inclusion can proceed as a reform effort will depend in part on how successful special educators are in developing their curricular sophistication.

BUILDING BRIDGES FOR MUTUAL REFORM

Ever since its own momentous changes in 1975, special education has struggled to find an appropriate way to participate in general education. Today, with the simultaneous arrival of both inclusion and curriculum redesign on the educational reform scene, the opportunity for joint efforts finally exists. Whether we will get there together has yet to be determined. One thing is clear: The convergence of reform trends has set an entirely new context for what it means to integrate children with disabilities—perhaps the most promising context since the last major reform of special education 2 decades ago. The basic nature of teaching and learning is poised for redefinition in the schools, and how this redefinition is enacted will have major implications for all children, whether they carry a label of disability or not. This is precisely why it is so critical to address the reform of special and general education together.

The need for joint reform is made even greater because of the clear convergence of the populations we are talking about in terms of which students will benefit most from fundamental curriculum redesign: the large numbers of students who are at risk for school failure but who may or may not be labeled as having a mild disability. The overlap in these populations is unmistakable and is recognized both within and outside of special education. If we are able to make curriculum reform work for this overlapping population of students, we will have tackled one of the most enduring problems facing special education, namely, its function as a "holding zone" for the large number of students who have not been able to handle what most of us already agree is a poorly conceived traditional academic curriculum, a curriculum that is inappropriate for the coming century we face.

As general educators grapple with issues such as "What is worth knowing?" and "How do we move from a curriculum dominated by fragmented, fact-focused subject areas, to an integrated common core of learning that encourages active, thinking learners?" special educators must contribute to the dialogue. They are major stakeholders in curriculum reform, and they need to become well-versed in curriculum issues so that they can become active partners in curriculum reform efforts. Special educators must look not only at recent trends in curriculum renewal in the major academic areas, but also at the impact such trends will have on instruction and assessment in each subject area. Likewise, general educators need to know how special educators assess the curriculum changes being promoted—what their concerns are about how the changes will affect students who have been the responsibility of special education.

The chapters that follow have been designed to provide such understanding. The contributing authors describe new curriculum trends in the major academic subject areas and in early childhood education, and explore how those changes will affect the education of students with mild disabilities. *As these subject-area authors so clearly demonstrate, current curriculum changes are anything but cosmetic; they represent a real change in our understandings of the way teachers teach and students learn.* The changes collectively will affect how general and special education are conceptualized and carried out. As the respondents illustrate, the range of difficulties we may encounter along the way is broad. Once we agree to consider the problem of special education through the window of curriculum reform, we will have identified a common entry point for resolving problems, a place to deal with causes rather than with symptoms.

REFERENCES

Adams, L., & Cessna, K. K. (1993). The expanded curriculum: Individualizing the system. In *Instructionally differentiated programming: A needs-based approach for students with behavioral disorders* (pp. 19–28). Denver: Colorado Department of Education.

Aldinger, L. E., Warger, C. L., & Eavy, P. W. (1992). *Strategies for teacher collaboration.* Ann Arbor, MI: Exceptional Innovations.

Algozzine, B., Ysseldyke, J. E., Kauffman, J. M., & Landrum, T. J. (1991). Implementing school reform in the 1990s for teachers of students with behavior problems. *Preventing School Failure, 35*(2), 6–10.

American Association for the Advancement of Science. (1989). *Science for all Americans: Project 2061.* Washington, DC: Author.

Artiles, A. J., & Trent, S. C. (1994). Overrepresentation of minority students in special education: A continuing debate. *The Journal of Special Education, 27,* 410–437.

Barry, A. (1994/1995). Easing into inclusion classrooms. *Educational Leadership, 52*(4), 4–6.

Bradley Commission on History in the Schools. (1988). *Building a history curriculum: Guidelines for teaching history in the schools.* Washington, DC: Educational Excellence Network.

Brandt, R. (1994). Is outcome-based education dead? *Educational Leadership, 51*(6), 5.

Brandt, R., & Tyler, R. S. (1983). Goals and objectives. In F. W. English (Ed.), *Fundamental curriculum decisions* (pp. 40–52). Alexandria, VA: Association for Supervision and Curriculum Development.

Case, A. D. (1992). The special education rescue: A case for systems thinking. *Educational Leadership, 50*(2), 32–34.

Council of Administrators of Special Education, Inc. (1993). *CASE future agenda for special education: Creating a unified educational system.* Albuquerque, NM: Author.

Cuban, L. (1989). The "at risk" label and the problem of urban school reform. *Phi Delta Kappan, 71,* 780–801.

Darling-Hammond, L. (1993). Reframing the school reform agenda. *Phi Delta Kappan, 74,* 752–761.

Edgar, E. (1988). Employment as an outcome for mildly handicapped students: Current status and future directions. *Focus on Exceptional Children, 21*(1), 1–8.

Fad, K. S., & Ryser, G. R. (1993). Social/behavioral variables related to success in general education. *Remedial and Special Education, 14*(1), 25–35.

Flores, H. (1991). Please do bother them. *Educational Leadership, 49*(4), 58–59.

Gable, R. A., Hendrickson, J. M., & Lyon, S. R. (1987). Materials adaptation for teaching mentally retarded students. *Advances in Mental Retardation and Developmental Disabilities, 3,* 49–86.

Glatthorn, A. A. (1985). *Curriculum reform and at-risk youth.* Philadelphia: Research for Better Schools.

Goldstein, M. T. (1982, May). *Curriculum: The keystone to instructional planning in special education.* Paper presented at the annual meeting of the Association for Educational Communications and Technology, Dallas.

Goodlad, J. I., & Anderson, R. H. (1987). *The non-graded elementary school* (rev. ed.). New York: Teachers College Press.

Heller, K. A., Holtzman, W. H., & Messick, S. (Eds.). (1982). *Placing children in special education: A strategy for equity.* Washington, DC: National Academy Press.

Hodgkinson, H. (1987). Changing society, unchanging curriculum. *National Forum, 67*(3), 8–11.

Howell, K. W., & Evans, D. G. (1995). A comment on "must instructionally useful performance assessment be based in the curriculum?" *Exceptional Children, 61*(4), 394–396.

Kliebard, H. M. (1994). Curriculum ferment in the 1980s. In N. Cobb (Ed.), *The future of education: Perspectives on national standards in America* (pp. 17–39). New York: The College Board.

Knitzer, J., Steinberg, Z., & Fleisch, B. (1990). *At the schoolhouse door: An examination of programs and policies for children with behavioral and emotional problems.* New York: Author and Bank Street College of Education.

Lewis, A. C. (1990). Getting unstuck: Curriculum as a tool of reform. *Phi Delta Kappan, 71*(7), 534–538.

Macmillan, D. L., Widaman, K. F., Balow, I. H., Borthwick-Duffy, S., Hendrick, I. G., & Hemsley, R. E. (1992). Special education students exiting the educational system. *The Journal of Special Education, 26*(1), 20–36.

Mathematical Sciences Education Board. (1989). *Everybody counts: A report to the nation on the future of mathematics education.* Washington, DC: National Academy Press.

McGhan, B. (1994). Responsible outcomes of outcome based education. *Educational Leadership, 51*(6), 70–72.

McLaughlin, M. (1995). What makes inclusion work? *Doubts and Certainties, 9*(3), 1–4.

McLaughlin, M., & Warren, S. (1992). *Issues and options in restructuring schools and special education programs.* College Park: University of Maryland, Center for Policy Options in Special Education and Institute for the Study of Exceptional Children and Youth.

National Association of State Boards of Education. (1988, October). *Rethinking curriculum: A call for fundamental reform.* Alexandria, VA: Author.

National Association of State Boards of Education. (1992). *Winners all: A call for inclusive schools.* Alexandria, VA: Author.

National Center for History in the Schools. (1992). *Lessons from history: Essential understandings and historical perspectives students should acquire.* Los Angeles: Author.

National Commission on Excellence in Education. (1983). *A nation at risk: The imperative for educational reform.* Washington, DC: U.S. Government Printing Office.

National Commission on Social Studies in the Schools. (1989). *Charting a course: Social studies for the 21st century.* Washington, DC: Author.

National Council of Teachers of Mathematics. (1989). *Curriculum and evaluation standards for school mathematics.* Reston, VA: Author.

National Joint Committee on Learning Disabilities. (1991, June 30). School reform: Opportunities for excellence and equity for individuals with learning disabilities. *DLD Times, 9*(1), i–iv.

National Longitudinal Transition Study. (1994, January). *Teaching Exceptional Children, 26*(3, Suppl.).

Newman, F. M. (1993). Beyond common sense in educational restructuring: The issues of content and linkage. *Educational Researcher, 22*(2), 4–13, 22.

Nolan, J., & Francis, P. (1992). Changing perspectives in curriculum and instruction. In C. Glickman (Ed.), *Supervision in transition (1992 Yearbook of the Association for Supervision and Curriculum Development;* pp. 44–60). Alexandria, VA: ASCD.

Nolet, V., & Tindal, G. (1993). Special education in content area classes: Development of a model and practical procedures. *Remedial and Special Education, 14*(1), 36–48.
O'Neil, J. (1991). Drive for national standards picking up steam. *Educational Leadership, 48*(5), 4–9.
O'Neil, J. (1993). Can national standards make a difference? *Educational Leadership, 50*(5), 4–8.
O'Neil, J. (1994). Outcomes-based education comes under attack. *ASCD Update, 36*(3), 1–8.
Orrill, R. (1994). Titanic structure or human scale: School reform at the close of the twentieth century. In N. Cobb (Ed.), *The future of education: Perspectives on national standards in America* (pp. 3–14). New York: The College Board.
Prawat, R. S. (1992). From individual differences to learning communities—Our changing focus. *Educational Leadership, 49*(7), 9–13.
President's Commission on Time and Learning. (1994). *Prisoners of time.* Washington, DC: Author.
Pugach, M. C. (1992). Unifying the preservice preparation of teachers. In W. Stainback & S. Stainback (Eds.), *Controversial issues confronting special education* (pp. 255–269). Boston: Allyn & Bacon.
Pugach, M. C. (1995). The failure of imagination in inclusive schooling. *The Journal of Special Education, 29,* 213–223.
Pugach, M. C., & Sapon-Shevin, M. (1987). New agendas for special education policy: What the national reports haven't said. *Exceptional Children, 53,* 295–299.
Pugach, M. C., & Warger, C. L. (1993). Curriculum considerations. In J. I. Goodlad & T. L. Lovitt (Eds.), *Integrating general and special education* (pp. 125–148). New York: Macmillan.
Pugach, M. C., & Wesson, C. L. (1995). Teachers' and students' views of team teaching of general education and learning-disabled students in two fifth-grade classes. *Elementary School Journal, 95,* 279–295.
Ravitch, D. (1993). Launching a revolution in standards and assessments. *Phi Delta Kappan, 74*(10), 767–772.
Rojewski, J. W., Pollard, R. R., & Meers, G. (1991). Grading mainstreamed special needs students: Determining practices and attitudes of secondary vocational educators using a qualitative approach. *Remedial and Special Education, 12*(1), 7–15.
Sage, D.C., & Burrello, L. C. (1994). *Leadership in educational reform: An administrator's guide to changes in special education.* Baltimore: Brookes.
Schiller, E. P., Coutinho, M., & Kaufman, M. J. (1993). Establishing a unity between regular and special education. In *Integrating students with special needs: Policies and practices that work* (pp. 51–59). Washington, DC: National Education Association.
Slavin, R. E. (1995). *Cooperative learning* (2nd ed.). Boston: Allyn & Bacon.
Smith, M. S., Fuhrman, S. H., & O'Day, J. (1994). National curriculum standards: Are they desirable and feasible? In R. F. Elmore & S. H. Fuhrman (Eds.), *The governance of curriculum* (pp. 12–29). Alexandria, VA: Association for Supervision and Curriculum Development.

Spady, W. G. (1994). Choosing outcomes of significance. *Educational Leadership, 51*(6), 18–23.

SRI International. (1993, December). *Action seminar: The transition experiences of young people with disabilities: Implications for policy and programs. Briefing materials.* Menlo Park, CA: Author.

Van Dyke, R., Stallings, M. A., & Colley, K. (1995). How to build an inclusive school community: A success story. *Phi Delta Kappan, 76*(6), 475–479.

Wagner, M., D'Amico, R., Marder, C., Newman, L., & Blackorby, J. (1992, December). *What happens next? Trends in postschool outcomes of youth with disabilities.* Menlo Park, CA: SRI International.

Warger, C. L., & Rutherford, R. B. (1993). Co-teaching to improve social skills. *Preventing School Failure, 37*(4), 21–27.

Wehlage, G. (1989). Dropping out: Can schools be expected to prevent it? In L. Weiss (Ed.), *Dropouts from school: Issues, dilemmas, and solutions* (pp. 1–22). Albany: State University of New York Press.

Wesson, C. L., & Deno, S. L. (1989). An analysis of long-term instructional plans in reading for elementary resources room teachers. *Remedial and Special Education, 10* (1), 21–28.

Will, M. (1986, November). *Educating students with learning problems—A shared responsibility.* Washington, DC: U.S. Department of Education, Office of Special Education and Rehabilitative Services.

Wyman, S. L. (1993). *How to respond to your culturally diverse student population.* Alexandria, VA: Association for Supervision and Curriculum Development.

Ysseldyke, J. E., O'Sullivan, P. J., Thurlow, M. L., & Christenson, S. L. (1989). Qualitative differences in reading and math instruction received by handicapped students. *Remedial and Special Education, 10* (1), 14–20.

Ysseldyke, J., Thurlow, M., & Shriner, J. (1992). Outcomes are for special educators too. *Teaching Exceptional Children, 25*(1), 36–50.

Zigmond, N., & Baker, J. (1995). Case studies of inclusion for students with learning disabilities [Special issue]. *The Journal of Special Education, 29,* 109–180.

* *CHAPTER 2* *

Trends in Science Education

Audrey B. Champagne, Sigrin T. Newell, and Jacqueline M. Goodnough

Sara Carrese's head was abuzz as she drove home after 3 days at the National Science Teachers Association convention. Listening to science teachers from across the nation enthusiastically describing their success in teaching science in new ways had added a whole new dimension to the constructs she had been exposed to in her education courses at the university. Constructivist approaches to teaching, hands-on science, less is more, interdisciplinary science, themes, STS, authentic assessment, Project 2061, and Scope, Sequence, and Coordination were no longer just slogans. They had become symbols of what some of the best science teachers in the United States were doing in their classrooms.

Ms. Carrese was returning home determined to try out some of these ideas in her own classroom. The plan she was developing for a unit on energy generation was no longer an empty exercise to fulfill a requirement for a course, but an opportunity to test out national recommendations for the reform of school science.

Several weeks later Ms. Carrese introduced the unit called the Archeazoan Project to her eighth graders at Suburban Middle School. She divided her class into several groups and set the task.

The Archeazoan Project

> The town of Archeazoa has no electricity. The town board will hire several consulting firms representing solar, nuclear, chemical, hydro, and wind energy to develop proposals to build a power plant to provide electricity for the town. The class will divide into groups forming consulting firms to advise the citizens. Each firm will advocate a particular kind of power. Your firm is in a budget bind. If you don't get this contract, you might lose your job. Take the task seriously. When your

Curriculum Trends, Special Education, and Reform: Refocusing the Conversation. ISBN 0-8077-3562-0 (pbk), ISBN 0-8077-3563-9 (cloth).

> proposal is developed, you must present it to Archeazoa's planning council. You'll want to appear professional, so you should dress appropriately. Be businesslike as you present your proposal to the citizens of the town [other members of the class]. Tell them the pros and cons of your type of energy. Be honest—they are not stupid but they are naive about electricity. You must explain how your form of energy is converted into electricity. The Archeazoanians will want to know why yours will be most beneficial and if there are any hazards. What will be the cost? How many people will be employed? I'd like you to think of creative names for your firms and get started.
>
> Your grade will be based on the criteria I have outlined in this packet that I am giving to each group. The bottom line is, I am the president of the town board. Basically I will buy the proposals that give me the most thorough information presented in the most professional manner, the ones I am confident with, firms that go the extra mile to show me that they really understand generation of electricity and that will give me my money's worth.

Later Ms. Carrese described her experience with the unit to her colleagues.

> It was great. It was so much fun. The kids got so involved. I wanted them to understand the various ways that solar, water, and wind energy is converted to electricity. They all gave their firms' names. We set the room up with the desks facing each other and put signs with the firm names on the desks. The students phoned Niagara Mohawk, the power plant at Niagara Falls, and a wind plant in Vermont. They got lots of information. The Vermont wind plant even sent information about how the government would purchase excess energy from the town.
>
> It was really neat, they enjoyed it, they got into it, and at the same time I didn't have to give them the whole unit. I didn't have to stand there and say, "This is solar energy, these are the pros and cons." The students looked it up. And it helped too, because when I got to my electricity unit, they already knew a lot.
>
> You should have seen: One group came up with a hydroelectric plant that they made out of cardboard with foil "water" coming down. They talked about safety mechanisms they would actually put into their hydroelectric plant so kids wouldn't get caught in the turbines.
>
> All but one of the 42 projects were excellent. The groups of three or four students were heterogeneously mixed. I had a few basic-skills students that I put with the top students. I tried to mix them. It was a time in the year when I knew what I could expect from them. I have a

few students that have been labeled as attention-deficit disorder and a couple that I think should be labeled that way. I put them in with kids who would work well with them, kids who are great academically but are shy and really passive. The attention-deficit kids just want to get their hands on things, they want to make and to do, so I thought that would be a good combination. The group that did the hydroelectric power plant had one of the boys with attention-deficit. With this particular boy—it was the most I've seen him do all year. It was probably the only thing I've seen him finish, because, you know, they say these kids don't like to complete anything and that's so true with him. He will never complete a homework assignment; he'll start it, he will never finish. He was in charge of making the display. He was really excited about it. It depressed me that I lost him after that. We went on to other things where we couldn't do this type of thing. I just saw that he got all excited and he worked really hard and then we went on to the next unit and he was, like, "Well, this isn't fun anymore."

We went to the library. They had to show me that they could look in a table of contents or index to find information. It was funny because I had so many who would look at one book and say, "I can't find it anywhere." I just said, "No, no, you keep looking," and I stressed, every day we were up there, "Expect to look through at least 50 books before you find one bit of information." I kept saying it and finally I had the kids saying it to each other: "No, you have to look in 50 books."

We put some of the projects up in the showcase in front of the main office. They liked that. Since they were all very good, I didn't want to leave anyone's out, so I told them they could come in after school. Whoever came in could put theirs up. So of course, nobody likes to come in after school, I got about six people, and that's all that would fit in the showcase anyway. A project like this is not something you can always do in science. I'll probably do it a couple of times a year.

SCIENCE CURRICULUM

Public dissatisfaction with the science achievement of the nation's high school graduates is motivating the rethinking of the school science curriculum. Poor performance of U.S. students on international tests and concern that our youngsters will not be well enough prepared to live productive lives in the society of the future have fueled a series of national reports. These call for changes in emphasis on what is taught in school science as well as changes in how it is taught. The reports acknowledge the value of scientific literacy to society and to the individual. In the 1950s, after Sputnik, science educators focused on training more scientists. In contrast, current reports assert that the primary purpose of school science is to produce scientifically literate citizens who are intellectually prepared to deal effectively with a declining economy and threats to the environment (Champagne, 1989). Science is no longer seen as the province of a select few. The contributions that scientific literacy makes to a fulfilling personal life, productivity in the workplace, and active participation in civic affairs, make science a requirement for all students. Furthermore, women, minorities, and people with disabilities are to be cultivated in science, both as potential scientists and as future voters (Benditt, 1992).

The fundamental question is how best to prepare generations of scientifically literate citizens. The answers are posed in the national reports. However, the recommendations in the reports are not yet "trends" in practice. New approaches to science teaching can be considered trends only when a large number of schools institute the recommendations as a part of daily practice. Classroom teachers like Ms. Carrese are not yet typical.

The recommendations for achieving the valued goals of school science are practical expressions of psychological theories, philosophical perspectives, and intellectual and social values.

A TAXONOMY OF TRENDS

There are as many ways of organizing the trends in science education as there are educators reflecting on the trends. Our framework is organized around three aspects of school science: the content, the learning environment, and the assessment of learning.

The conventional approach to science content has been to organize it around topics such as dinosaurs, plants, animals, or rocks. Facts and vocabulary are presented within these topics (Bybee et al., 1989). The new trends in presenting content are (1) to place more emphasis on conceptual understanding and application than on simply knowing the facts and principles, and (2) to place science in context. Specific trends are to: (1) teach science in the context of contemporary social issues; (2) integrate science with other school subjects; (3) integrate the science disciplines; (4) organize units or courses around themes; and (5) integrate topics from the history, philosophy, and sociology of science into discipline-oriented science courses.

The conventional learning environment in science has emphasized reading and the passive acquisition of facts. Recommended changes focus on getting students to participate actively in doing science and on creating learning environments that reflect science as it is practiced. Specific trends are to (1) engage students in investigations of the natural world that reflect the ways in which scientists inquire; (2) provide students with opportunities to work in small groups; (3) involve students in tasks that reflect the ways in which people use scientific information and inquiry processes to make personal and social decisions; and (4) help students to know that science is for everyone.

The content and learning environment trends overlap considerably as do the rationales supporting these trends. Taken together, these recommended content and learning environments:

- Better reflect the intellectual structure of science and the ways science is practiced
- Are consistent with psychological theories that demonstrate the importance of direct experiences with the natural world in developing conceptual understanding
- Are consistent with social-psychological theories that demonstrate the importance of talking about science to develop conceptual understanding (social construction of knowledge)
- Are based on the assumption that students will be more motivated by tasks that relate to real life
- Are based on the assumption that learning in context produces knowledge that is "active" rather than inert

The recommended changes in assessment practices derive primarily from shifting the emphasis away from factual knowledge and toward conceptual understanding and the ability to apply science. The purpose of assessment has changed from generating test data used only for grading to generating data to guide teaching decisions on a daily basis. Specific assessment trends are to have students keep portfolios of activities over the course of a year so that they can see their progress and to use group projects for both learning and assessment.

THE TRENDS IN CONTEXT

In this section we describe each of the trends, including further discussion of how they play out in the classroom context, examples of science programs and projects that show the trends in action, and rationales for the trends. It should be noted that in the context of real classrooms, issues of content and learning environment are intermingled.

Content Trends

Trend 1: Teach science in the context of contemporary social issues. Science, Technology, and Society (STS) is the best developed example of an approach to school science that places science in context, in this case in the context of contemporary social issues. The basic STS strategy is to have students identify problems of local interest and find information that will help to resolve the problems. Students exposed to STS curricula become aware of their responsibilities as citizens and of the place of science and technology in local issues. They come to see science content as something that is relevant to their own natural curiosity.

For example, some STS projects have engaged students in the study of their local landfill, in interviewing community members about the effects of major storms, or in measuring the amount of water used by each student in a shower and determining the class' weekly consumption of water. These activities are accompanied by studies of the chemistry of water or of wildlife's need for clean water (Yager, 1990).

Ten years of experience with STS has shown that it is effective for motivating students and helping them to apply science to their daily lives. Students ask more questions and use science process skills as tools to find out their own answers. They also see the need for science skills in a wide variety of careers, not just medicine and academic research, thus motivating more students to stay involved with science.

Ms. Carrese's Archeazoan Project is an example of learning science in context. At the town meeting in which the alternative possibilities for energy generation were presented by students, the class had to consider the scientific principles behind the various options, the comparative costs of the options, and the environmental costs. Multifaceted issues involving science knowledge, such as referendum votes on energy production and waste disposal, are typical of those facing voters across the United States.

Contextual approaches find support from not only curriculum theorists but cognitive theorists as well. Resnick (1987) has pointed out that school learning is characterized by knowledge and skills that are not readily applicable to any context other than formal tests. Once the test is over, children frequently forget what they have been taught. As a remedy to this, Collins, Brown, and Newman (1989) propose that learning should be situated in real-world situations. They believe that learners must carry out tasks in a context that reflects the future uses of the information. This will help students understand the purposes for their knowledge and will help them see the different conditions under which their knowledge will apply.

Trend 2: Integrate science with other school subjects. Especially at the elementary school level, teachers are finding the integration of science with other school subjects a relatively painless way to bring science into the elementary school curriculum. Integration of science with art, language arts, and mathematics can be achieved through science projects as simple as observing live animals. Whether a cricket, a guinea pig, or a fish, children follow up on their observations by recording them. Drawing is one important way of recording.

Students can sharpen their observation skills while developing language skills by discussing their observations with their teacher. Consider the following dialogue:

> *Teacher:* Look closely at the bunny, Marian. What do you observe?
> *Marian:* He has long ears and a shiny nose.
> *Teacher:* Yes. Do you suppose a scientist would notice these things too? Pablo, what do you notice?
> *Pablo:* He can hop and he wiggles his nose a lot.
> *Teacher:* Look carefully. Are his front legs and back legs the same length?
> *Pablo:* I think he likes me. He hopped over to me.

Writing is another way of recording observations and reflections on them; in this class, the children went on to write about the bunny. Mathematics also can be integrated with science classes. Measurements of an animal's growth or eating patterns, for example, are quantitative observations that can be entered into a data table. This information also can be displayed in graphic form.

With the departmentalization that occurs in the middle and senior high school, integration of science with other school subjects becomes more difficult. Schools that have adopted interdisciplinary work have shown that with even minimal planning, students benefit when mathematics and science teachers refer to each other's classes. For example, teachers can discuss the close relationships of historical developments in mathematics and science, such as Sir Isaac Newton's development of calculus to mathematically prove his theory of gravitation.

Biographies of scientists (especially minority scientists) can be included on reading lists. Further, history takes on a new depth when viewed through the lens of science. What scientific knowledge and technology were available at a given time? How did this affect people's world view or their daily lives? For example, people living at the time of Copernicus believed that the earth was the center of the universe; students can consider how people's view of the importance of humankind changed when Copernicus demonstrated that the sun rather than the earth is the center of the solar system. Or, students can trace the development of antiseptics. During the Civil War, the best antiseptics available were the crushed leaves of sphagnum moss or yarrow plants, and wounds were covered with leaves and then wrapped with cloth strips. Since yarrow was only partially effective, twice as many soldiers during the Civil War died from infections as from gunshots. By World War I, chemists had figured out how to manufacture better antiseptics, but mercurochrome and iodine sting the wound and are brightly colored. Today, colorless, painless antiseptics can be found in every drugstore.

Integration of science with other subjects is advantageous also because it offers many hooks to grab the students' interest. For example, a child who "doesn't like science" may be intrigued with the story that Alfred Szent Gyorgyi discovered a good way to synthesize Vitamin C because he didn't like green peppers. When his wife served green peppers for dinner, he didn't have the courage to say he didn't want them. Instead he told her they might be useful to test for Vitamin C. He took them to his laboratory rather than eat them. Green peppers turned out to be an excellent source of the vitamin (Moss, 1988).

Returning to Ms. Carrese, she and her fellow teachers have developed units that integrate science with other subjects. They describe it this way: "Now we're into radiation. This is the big interdisciplinary unit with social studies, English, and art. It's based on World War II, the historical developments, the race to develop the atom bomb and to split the nucleus of the atom. Students read some of the great literary works of World War II and they also study some of the works of art that came out of the war."

Trend 3: Integrate the science disciplines. General science has long been a part of the school curriculum. These courses cover topics from earth, life, and physical sciences in the same year. On the surface at least, general science courses appear to integrate the science disciplines, but in fact such courses and texts treat topics in isolation. A serious attempt to integrate the science disciplines is underway under the sponsorship of the National Science Teachers Association. Called the Scope, Sequence, and Coordination Project, it seeks to restructure the school science curriculum radically. In this plan, biology, chemistry, physics, and earth science are all taught every year beginning at grade 7 and throughout high school; integration is achieved via horizontal strands that link the disciplines. For example, in studying the heart, students consider anatomy, fluid mechanics, and the chemistry of blood.

Trend 4: Organize units or courses around themes that cut across the academic disciplines. Themes are concepts that appear in all science disciplines and are used to organize the total science curriculum. Interest in themes as a way of illustrating the relationships of the science disciplines has become a trend via the publication of Science for All Americans (American Association for the Advancement of Science, 1989). Six themes appear in this report:

Systems. Any collection of things that interact is a system. The solar system, a watershed, or a weather system can all be studied in terms of component parts and their interactions.

Models. Models can be equations, drawings, mental images, or computer programs that suggest how things work. Children can compare familiar models with the real thing. Toys can provide an introduction to models. What can we know about the real thing by looking at the model? Conceptual models often are metaphors and analogies, which makes a good tie to the language arts curriculum.

Constancy. In order to understand the meanings of equilibrium, scientists study things that do not change. In many chemical interactions, change in one direction is counterbalanced by change in another. Another kind of constancy is constancy of form. Children change into adults, but they always are shaped like human beings.

Patterns of change. Change is common and easily visible to children. They can study dramatic changes in a short time as well as slow changes that are harder to see.

Evolution. Plants and animals, music, technology, and language are all things that have taken their present form gradually, arising from materials of the past. Children can look at pictures to study this kind of change.

Scale. Scale ranges from the minuscule to the galactic. Children can compare sizes of buildings, cars, and ants to begin to visualize the range of sizes dealt with by scientists. Students should experience huge things and tiny things to understand the concept of scale (AAAS, 1989).

A different set of organizing themes for elementary students has been proposed by the National Center for Improving Science Education (Bybee et al., 1989). These nine concepts are thought to be so fundamental and powerful that they will provide a firm foundation for all future science learning. The themes are: organization, cause and effect, systems, scale, models, change, structure and function, discontinuous and continuous properties (variation), and diversity.

As an example, we can consider the theme of models. A unit or course organized around the idea of a model would provide students the opportunity to understand the similarities and differences among a variety of models and to learn how the scientific disciplines employ models in the development of scientific knowledge. In the elementary school, the development of the idea of model might begin with models in the children's experience.

Models of toy trains, planes, dolls, and even dinosaurs are in the experience of all youngsters. How is the model truck similar to an actual truck? How is it different? How is the small plastic dinosaur similar to the model of a dinosaur in the local museum? What kinds of questions do biologists answer using models of animals such as dinosaurs? In the middle and high school, examples of models become more complex. The physicist's model of an elephant bumping down a rough mountain is either a point mass sliding down a frictionless incline or a collection of abstract mathematical expressions expressing the quantitative relationships among the elephant's mass and the angle of the incline. Chemists' models are different from those of physicists. The orientation of atoms in molecules is represented using balls and sticks that represent the atoms and the bonds that hold them together.

Trend 5: Integrate topics from the history, philosophy, and sociology of science into discipline-oriented science courses. Harvard Project Physics is an example of a high school physics course developed in the 1960s that integrated physics with other disciplines, especially history. In the current round of science curriculum reform, this trend has been later to develop than others; however, many articles advocating this approach have been written and the Biological Sciences Curriculum Study has recently published a framework for the integration of the history and philosophy of biology with biology (BSCS, 1992).

Learning Environment Trends

Trend 1: Engage students in investigations of the natural world that reflect the ways in which scientists inquire. This trend is often expressed as the hands-on approach to developing conceptual understanding. However, it is much more that just having students manipulate physical objects. Instead, it involves all aspects of conducting investigations or inquiry into the natural world, including formulating questions and drawing inferences. This approach is consistent with new ideas about how people learn.

In the past 15 years, cognitive psychologists have been developing greater understanding of how people learn science. The current view is that existing knowledge, theories, and beliefs act as lenses through which people interpret what is experienced. These lenses dictate how students interpret the lectures they hear, the text they read, the demonstrations they observe, and the experiments they conduct. Before students can understand scientific explanations of natural phenomena, they must become aware of what they believe about the phenomena and contrast their own interpretations with the scientific interpretation. Only when personal and scientific interpretations are congruent will students achieve conceptual understanding (Champagne & Bunce, 1991).

This view of the learner has motivated rethinking the nature of laboratory work in the sciences. Following step-by-step directions does not enable students to integrate observations made in the laboratory with their prior knowledge. In contrast, inquiry approaches to science give students the opportunity to design ways to answer questions that grow out of their own experience. Teachers wishing to integrate more inquiry work into laboratories can use the framework suggested by the National Center for the Improving of Science Education.

According to that framework, the teacher begins by *engaging* students through their curious approach to the materials. Next, the teacher and students *explore and discover* what can be known about the materials, and they observe, record, and interpret data. The teacher then helps the students *process for meaning* by discussing the data, clarifying concepts, and applying new knowledge in other contexts. Finally, the students and teacher *evaluate* the experience, by applying and extending the concepts, process, and skills of the activity (National Center for Improving Science Education, 1991).

Ms. Carrese shares an interesting story about how a science trade book generated students' questions and their subsequent inquiry.

> Right now we're just finishing up magnetism. I have a book, *The Compass in Your Nose* (McCutcheon, 1989), which says all humans have traces of iron in their ethmoid bone. When I read this to them they said, "Gee, can we do a lab?," and I said, "Why not? You never know. Studies have shown that some people have more deposits of iron in their ethmoid bone and they can actually orient themselves and navigate better than others." So we designed our ethmoid bone lab. We did our First Annual Ethmoid Bone Iron Deposit Convention. The slogan was, Who will be this year's winner? The kids said, "Oh gosh, if someone has a big deposit, can we call the Guiness Book of World Records?" I said, "I don't think we're going to find anything." We had a magnet suspended from a ring stand. We had them approach real slowly, and a partner would hold their bangs back. They tried to eliminate any exterior or environmental things that would get in the way of their data. The whole lab was run in complete silence. The kids were getting mad, "Stop talking, your sound waves might affect our data." Some kids reported feeling a tingling sensation, and there were two kids who insisted, "I swear, I swear, I swear, I saw a force of attraction." You could see the magnet move toward them. Basically it is a sixth sense, but we have forgotten how to use it because we have

evolved not to need it any more. There are people who don't even have to use the north star; they can orient themselves. They may have more deposits of iron or they just, for some reason, are able to use it better.

In the First Annual Ethmoid Bone Iron Deposit Convention, the students explored an intriguing idea the way a scientist would. They set up an apparatus to collect data, tried to remove extraneous variables, and then tried to make sense of their data.

Trend 2: Provide students with opportunities to work in small groups. The trend to encourage small-group work has its origins in social-psychological theory and the private sector's call for workers who can function effectively in small groups. The cooperative learning movement is an educational response that places emphasis on the definition of roles in the group and on students' learning the social skills to function effectively.

Although social skills are prerequisites for groupwork, the fundamental reason for using small groups in the science classroom is intellectual. Students construct knowledge through discussion, explaining their understanding, and attempting to understand the views of their peers. This social construction of knowledge leads to deeper elaboration and longer-term retention of science concepts.

The importance of social process in the development of conceptual understanding is central to the social-psychological theory of L.S. Vygotsky. His research demonstrates the necessity of social and cultural experiences for knowledge development (Vygotsky, 1978). In groups, learners elaborate on concepts and become more aware of their own learning processes (Johnson & Johnson, 1975). Peers learn from one another because they are in tune with each other's knowledge. As students interact with each other, they are motivated to take ownership of their own knowledge. Researchers in social psychology have demonstrated that cognitive abilities are "(1) socially transmitted, (2) socially constrained, (3) socially nurtured, and (4) socially encouraged" (Day, French, & Hall, 1985, p. 51). For these reasons, the trend in science education is to provide students with more opportunity for discussion in small groups.

Trend 3: Engage students in tasks that reflect the ways in which people make personal and social decisions. Another trend in education that has its origins in the demands of the workplace and in psychological research is to engage students in tasks that reflect real-world challenges (Holdzkom & Lutz, 1989). In most work outside of school, meaningful tasks are worked on by groups of people. Complex tasks help learners understand the uses of their knowledge. By situating learning in a task that has immediate meaning for the learner, educators encourage people to learn actively.

When learners must formulate their own approaches to a problem and find the information necessary to solve the problem, they become invested in the project's outcome. In the library, Ms. Carrese's students were motivated to look in 50 books. Also, defending one's ideas in a group encourages consideration of underlying reasons and varying perspectives (Brown & Palincsar, 1989). These discussions model the kinds of discussions that adults hold when making decisions about political and social issues.

Trend 4: Help students to know that science is for everyone. The science education reform movement is different in one significant respect from the one that occurred in the 1960s. School science is now for all students. Historically, the stereotypical scientist has been a white male. Because of this, teachers and students may still make a subconscious assumption that being a white male is a prerequisite to becoming a scientist. Studies in classrooms have shown that teachers often expect less of girls and minorities in science classes (American Association of University Women, 1992; Sadker & Sadker, 1989).

In reality, however, science is currently being practiced by women, minorities, and individuals with disabilities. Encouraging students in populations underrepresented in the sciences is a trend in science education motivated by the nation's need for scientists as well as by a strong sense of social justice. Consequently, science teachers are being called upon to give all students the opportunity to learn science.

Studies have shown that the reasons that girls and minority students do not continue in math and science involve social pressures and lack of skills. Successful programs address these issues by creating more inclusive social norms in the classroom and by providing extra opportunities to practice skills (Skolnick, Langbort, & Day, 1982). Social approaches may include discussions of the contributions of females, Hispanics, and African Americans to scientific discoveries (Carey, 1993). Skill development results whenever students are encouraged to design and conduct their own experiments.

REDEFINING THE NATURE OF ASSESSMENT

When learning science was defined as passive acquisition of large numbers of facts, multiple choice tests were adequate measures of student achievement. They are, however, not effective when the goal of school science is conceptual understanding and the ability to apply scientific information and reasoning to situations encountered in the workplace and in daily living. Consequently, educators and policy analysts are exploring the potential of many new forms of assessment.

Assessment in a classroom can serve many purposes, and assigning grades is only one of them. Teachers can use assessment to find out what students already know about a topic, to find out what students have learned in order to make decisions about what to teach next, to decide how to group students effectively, to let students know what is expected, and to document what students have learned. Assessment also can be used beyond individual classrooms to document the success of new programs and to help set educational policy. To meet these various goals, tests must assess three areas of science learning: (1) conceptual understanding; (2) science process and reasoning skills; and (3) skills required for the application of science.

New forms of testing are under development to assess reasoning skills and applications to real-life situations (Champagne & Newell, 1992). These testing tools are concerned as much with what students *do know* and *can do* as with finding out what they don't know (Bybee et al., 1989; NCISE, 1991). Portfolios and performance tasks are two methods for assessing the currently valued outcomes of school science.

Portfolios

Portfolios have several advantages. They show student growth over the course of a year. They enhance students' self-image by focusing on accomplishments rather than deficiencies. They allow recognition of differences in learning styles, which makes assessment less biased and less culture dependent. Since students engage actively in selecting what goes into a portfolio, they get practice in self-evaluation. Students end up with a clear picture of their own progress, rather than a mysterious number. Portfolios also can include information about student attitudes toward science. Journal entries and descriptions of how students feel about science can give teachers feedback about success on this important objective (Stenmark, 1989).

A science portfolio might include samples of the following kinds of student work conducted over the course of a school year:

- Descriptions of experiments done by the student
- Pictures or dictated reports (for younger students)
- Date tables and graphs showing use of mathematics skills
- Diagrams of equipment used and directions for use
- Responses to homework problems
- Group reports and photos of finished projects
- Comments about an individual's contribution to the group
- Entries from the student's journal
- Book reports and other library research
- Artwork using techniques of scientific illustration
- Videotapes of individual work or groupwork

Performance Tasks

Ms. Carrese used performance assessment in the context of a unit on static electricity. The task assigned to the students was to understand a topic in static electricity well enough to teach it to the other students.

> With the electricity unit, I assigned each group a topic and they were responsible for teaching it to their classmates. I told the other students that if they didn't understand it they had to go to these kids.
>
> I had them write down a rough draft of what they were going to do. They had to decide whether they were going to do a lecture with a demonstration or a lecture with a lab. These were in groups of four. They had almost a week to plan. I had a format of questions that I asked to help them shape what they would do for those 40 minutes. Once I had approved their rough draft, I had to see the final draft before they gave their presentation. If they needed equipment, they got it all set up for the next day.
>
> They did demonstrations; they ran labs. They wrote the directions. I made copies; they were real excited about having their stuff xeroxed and passing it out to everyone. They handed out the papers and they ran the lab and answered questions. They graded the other students' responses, presented them to me, and I looked over the grades. Then I put them in my book.
>
> While they gave the class, I evaluated it. Each person got an individual grade for participation in the project. I observed them while they were working and then I evaluated them for their presentation. It was fun. Actually, three of the labs, I kept for next year. One team brought in balloons, sugar, and cloths for each group. The kids really liked it; you rubbed your balloon with the cloth and you put it near the sugar and all the sugar made little mountain peaks.

Ms. Carrese communicated clearly to the class about how she would evaluate their performance. She told the students that she would be judging their work in the group, their knowledge of static electricity, and their ability to explain it to others. The presenters were to grade the papers of their fellow students. This gave them immediate feedback about how well they had taught the session. This learning activity involved self-evaluation by the students, and individual and group evaluation by the teacher.

This is a good example of the way in which performance assessment blurs the distinction between instruction and assessment. Students are assessed while they are engaged in the ongoing flow of classroom activity. At the beginning they are told what standards the teacher will be looking for.

This more natural form of assessment allows the teacher to see and honor the full range of student abilities. The teacher can observe the students' abilities to reason soundly, raise questions, observe, infer, formulate hypotheses, use equipment, discuss scientific ideas in groups, design and conduct experiments, and get excited about science. The teacher may use a checklist or a scoring rubric to keep track of what is happening in a busy classroom. This gives the teacher a richer source of information for summative grading.

Group performance tasks are effective when the tasks are too large or too time-consuming for an individual to complete. In one method, known as the jigsaw technique, individuals take pieces of the project to work on. The group then integrates all the work into a finished product (Aronson, 1978).

A second type of group task includes all members of the group in collecting data and drawing conclusions from their data. An example of this is an assessment conducted by seventh graders at Local Suburban Middle School. Students were given a vignette describing disagreements about the effects of acid rain on forests. Each group also was given three radish seedlings grown in acid solutions of three dilutions. Students were asked to choose three characteristics of the plants, collect data on these characteristics, and create a bar graph showing their data. Then they were to use these data to relate their observations to the larger question of the effects of acid rain.

A drawback of alternative assessment is that there is no single way of scoring performances and portfolios of such diversity. The most common solution is the development of scoring rubrics specific to the task. These rubrics are descriptions of the varying degrees of success to be expected in the task. Sometimes the rubrics are prespecified; at other times they are created after reading a series of papers to get a sense of the range of likely responses (Stenmark, 1989). A typical rubric for a written response to a science problem is as follows:

20 EXEMPLARY	Papers in this category will be clear, coherent, unambiguous, and well organized. The science will be correct.
16 VERY GOOD	Papers will be carefully thought out with a clear explanation. They will cover correctly most important elements of the problem.
12 COMPETENT	Papers will be reasonably clear and answer the majority of the question correctly.
8 MINOR FLAWS, BUT SATISFACTORY	Papers will have an adequate answer but may leave out a large part of the question or may have several errors.

4 PROBLEMATIC — Papers may omit significant parts of the question or contain serious errors in thinking. However, attempts to answer are evident.

Alternative assessment is not intended to replace multiple choice and other short answer formats completely. These techniques remain effective for assessing factual knowledge. Rather, the newer formats should extend the repertoire of the teacher, so that it is possible to evaluate a wider range of students' abilities. Alternative assessment is particularly useful in gathering information to help plan instruction. Moreover, since students often respond more positively to alternative forms of testing, they are motivated to continue studying science.

CONCLUSION

The recommendations made for science education by national task forces have resulted in several new trends in the teaching of science. Applying science to daily experiences and technological issues creates a context for thinking about abstract scientific concepts that makes them more accessible. Mingling science and math with reading and writing motivates students who enjoy one of these subjects and dislike the others. Thematic science can help make connections between ideas that students would not make on their own. Following one's own curiosity in inquiry science is more engrossing than book learning for many students.

Most important of all is the emphasis on observation and hands-on activities. Science, with its origins in the natural world, provides a unique opportunity for students to build abstract concepts and formal ways of reasoning on the foundation of direct experience. The effective teaching of science draws on the inherent curiosity children have about the natural world. Educators must design the science curriculum to keep this curiosity alive. It is a profound motivating force for all future studies of science. The current recommendations are designed to create a new generation of scientifically literate citizens who will enjoy science throughout their lives.

REFERENCES

American Association for the Advancement of Science. (1989). *Science for all Americans: Project 2061*. Washington, DC: Author.

American Association of University Women. (1992). *How schools shortchange girls*. Washington, DC: Author.

Aronson, E. (1978). *The jigsaw classroom.* Beverly Hills, CA: Sage.

Benditt, J. (Ed.). (1992). Women in science—Pieces of a puzzle. *Science, 255,* 1356–1376.

Brown, A. L., & Palincsar, A. (1989). Guided cooperative learning and individual acquisition. In L. Resnick (Ed.), *Knowing, learning and instruction: Essays in honor of Robert Glaser* (pp. 393–451). Hillsdale, NJ: Erlbaum.

BSCS. (1992). *Teaching about the history and nature of science and technology: A curriculum framework.* Colorado Springs: Author.

Bybee, R., Buchwald, C., Crissman, S., Heil, D., Kuerbis, P., Matusumoto, C., & McInerny, J. (1989). *Science and technology education for the elementary years: Frameworks for curriculum and instruction.* Andover, MA: National Center for Improving Science Education.

Carey, S. J. (Ed.). (1993). *Science for all cultures: A collection of articles from NSTA's journals.* Arlington, VA: National Science Teachers Association.

Champagne, A. (1989). Scientific literacy, a concept in search of a definition. In A. Champagne, B. Lovitts, & B. Calinger (Eds.), *This year in school science, 1989: Scientific literacy* (pp. 1–14). Washington, DC: American Association for the Advancement of Science.

Champagne, A. B., & Bunce, D. (1991). Learning-theory-based science teaching. In S. M. Glynn, R. J. Yeaney, & B. K. Brittan (Eds.), *The psychology of learning science* (pp. 21–41). Hillsdale, NJ: Erlbaum.

Champagne, A. B., & Newell, S. T. (1992). Directions for research and development: Alternative methods for assessing scientific literacy. *Journal of Research in Science Teaching, 29*(8), 841–860.

Collins, A., Brown, J., & Newman, S. (1989). Cognitive apprenticeship: Teaching the crafts of reading, writing and mathematics. In L. Resnick (Ed.), *Knowing, learning and instruction: Essays in honor of Robert Glaser* (pp. 453–494). Hillsdale, NJ: Erlbaum.

Day, J., French, L., & Hall, L. (1985). Social influences on cognitive development. In D. Forrest-Pressley, G. Mackinnon, & T. Waller (Eds.), *Metacognition, cognition and human performance: Vol. I. Theoretical perspectives* (pp. 35–52). New York: Academic Press.

Holdzkom, D., & Lutz, P. B. (Eds.). (1989). *Research within reach: Science education.* Arlington, VA: National Science Teachers Association.

Johnson, D., & Johnson, R. (1975). *Learning together and alone: Cooperation, competition and individualization.* Englewood Cliffs, NJ: Prentice Hall.

McCutcheon, M. (1989). *The compass in your nose and other astonishing facts about humans.* Los Angeles: Jeremy P. Tarcher.

Moss, R. W. (1988). *Free radical: Albert Szent Gyorgyi and the battle over Vitamin C.* New York: Paragon House.

National Center for Improving Science Education. (1991). *The high stakes of high school science.* Washington, DC: Author.

National Science Teachers Association. (1992). *Scope, sequence, and coordination of secondary school science: Vol. 1. The content core: A guide for curriculum designers.* Washington, DC: Author.

Resnick, L. (1987). *Education and learning to think.* Washington, DC: National Academy Press.
Sadker, M., & Sadker, D. (1989). *Sex equity handbook for schools* (2nd ed.). New York: Longman.
Skolnick, J., Langbort, C., & Day, L. (1982). *How to encourage girls in math and science: Strategies for parents and educators.* Palo Alto, CA: Dale Seymour.
Stenmark, J. K. (1989). *Assessment alternatives in mathematics: An overview of assessment techniques that promote learning.* Berkeley: Lawrence Hall of Science.
Vygotsky, L. (1978). *Mind in society: The development of higher psychological processes.* Cambridge, MA: Harvard University Press.
Yager, R. (1990). STS: Thinking over the years. *The Science Teacher, 57*(3), 52–55.

Response

Current Trends in Science Education: Implications for Special Education

Margo A. Mastropieri and Thomas E. Scruggs

Science has recently returned to the forefront of American educational reform efforts, as evidenced by the number of organizations recommending change in current science education (Aldridge, 1990; California State Department of Education, 1990; National Academy of Sciences, 1990; Rutherford & Ahlgren, 1990; U.S. Department of Education, 1991). Unlike previous reform movements in science education, present thinking emphasizes the importance of inclusion of all segments of society in the promotion of scientific literacy, including individuals with disabilities. It has been suggested that individuals with disabilities may benefit particularly from science education, in that science can develop background knowledge, promote concrete learning experiences, and develop problem-solving and reasoning skills (Esler, Midgett, & Bird, 1977; Patton & Andre, 1989). Further, it has been argued that science may be helpful in improving functioning in specific disability areas. That is, students with physical or sensory disabilities may develop compensatory skills in observing, manipulating, and classifying scientific phenomena (Hofman & Ricker, 1979; Linn & Thier, 1975). Students prone to fantasy or unrealistic thinking may benefit from the study of predictable, cause-and-effect relationships in nature (Hadary & Cohen, 1978; Lamendola, 1976). Students with cognitive or intellectual disabilities may benefit from the development of general background knowledge as well as such "process" skills as observing, predicting, classifying, and inferring (Corrick, 1981; Thresher, 1963).

Without question, then, students with disabilities deserve to be included in the present dialogue about science education. Champagne, Newell, and Goodenough have explicated the themes being promoted in current science education reform efforts. In this response, we briefly summarize characteristics of students with mild disabilities that typically interfere with science

Curriculum Trends, Special Education, and Reform: Refocusing the Conversation. ISBN 0-8077-3562-0 (pbk), ISBN 0-8077-3563-9 (cloth).

learning, and then discuss (a) the interaction of these characteristics with contemporary themes of science reform, and (b) additional considerations for the mainstream science education of students with disabilities.

CHARACTERISTICS OF STUDENTS WITH DISABILITIES

Scruggs and Mastropieri (1993) identified four domains of school functioning in which students with disabilities have been shown to exhibit difficulties. These domains are language and literacy, cognitive/conceptual development, psycho-social functioning, and sensory/physical disabilities. Although all students with disabilities will not have difficulties in all domains, most students with disabilities will have difficulties in at least one domain. However, in considering characteristics of students with disabilities, it is important to emphasize that deviations in functioning do not occur in isolation, but only as they interact with the characteristics of curriculum and instruction. The interaction of the characteristics of mild disabilities and the themes of science reform is discussed in the section that follows.

IMPLICATIONS FOR MAINSTREAMING STUDENTS WITH MILD DISABILITIES

The themes of reform in science education considered in the chapter by Champagne, Newell, and Goodenough include the integration of content areas, the inclusion of hands-on approaches to science learning, the notion of "less is more" in curriculum, technological applications, and the theme of discovery or inquiry-based learning. Each is considered with respect to the characteristics of students with disabilities.

Integration of Science with Other Content Areas

The integration of themes across scientific disciplines, and across content areas such as mathematics, social studies, history, and philosophy, is intended to facilitate students' understanding of the interrelatedness of the world around them. An instructional approach that integrates such themes will facilitate the understanding of the holistic aspects of learning, rather than emphasize discrete content areas in science, math, or social studies. Such an approach may prove especially beneficial for students with mild disabilities, who often exhibit difficulties applying, relating, or generalizing newly acquired information (e.g., Scruggs & Mastropieri, 1984).

Although an integrated approach to science education is likely to be helpful, several potential problems should be noted. First, the specific relationships among the various content areas may need to be explicitly demonstrated, as students may lack the inferential reasoning skills necessary to understand such relationships spontaneously (see Bos & Tierney, 1984). Second, students with mild disabilities may lack one or more of the preskills necessary to apply and integrate other content areas. For example, activities that integrate mathematics and science may require specific problem-solving or computational skills that have not been learned previously (Mastropieri, Scruggs, & Shiah, 1991). Finally, students with mild disabilities may lack relevant prior knowledge necessary to integrate content area information independently (e.g., Pressley, Johnson, & Symons, 1987). For example, an integrated science problem may require students to draw upon specific prior knowledge in social studies, which students with mild disabilities may lack. In such cases, lack of prior knowledge or prerequisite skills in other content areas may inhibit learning of science content.

In spite of these concerns, integrated thematic instruction can potentially benefit students with mild disabilities because this approach may help students generalize information across different content areas. However, teachers may need to assess the skill levels and background knowledge of special education students who are integrated into regular education classrooms, and preteach (or arrange peer mediation of) prerequisite skills, concepts, and content.

Hands-On Activities

All current science reform efforts emphasize incorporation of hands-on activities. These activities involve the active manipulation of concrete phenomena such as rocks and minerals, electrical circuits, and microscopes. Hands-on approaches to science education typically de-emphasize the language and literacy requirements inherent in textbook approaches, and emphasize scientific process skills such as observation, measurement, prediction, estimation, hypothesizing, and experimenting. Many activities-based approaches also recommend using collaborative or cooperative groups during the learning process. Taken together, the use of concrete, meaningful objects, the de-emphasis of language and literacy skills, the active manipulation of real phenomena, and working with mainstream peers are common features of hands-on approaches to science. Such approaches have the potential to be very successful for students with mild disabilities, who may lack appropriate literacy skills and have difficulty dealing with abstractions.

Few direct comparisons of activities-based versus textbook approaches have been conducted with students with mild disabilities (Mastropieri &

Scruggs, 1992b). In one of the few existing studies, Scruggs, Mastropieri, Bakken, and Brigham (1993) taught science content to seventh- and eighth-grade learning disabled students using both an adaptation of the *Full Option Science System* (FOSS, 1990) and a textbook covering the same content. Students learned and correctly applied more information and, in addition, reported enjoying science more under the activities-based instructional condition.

Several areas of concern, however, also arose from the Scruggs and colleagues (1993) investigation. First, many of the students exhibited poor social skills when working in collaborative groups. It may, therefore, be necessary in future investigations to teach collaborative group skills in addition to the science tasks (e.g., Brigham, Bakken, Scruggs, & Mastropieri, 1992). Second, many students exhibited difficulties in manipulating scientific apparatus necessary to construct telegraphs, indicating that specific material adaptations, such as those recommended by Mastropieri and Scruggs (1993), may be needed for specific science activities. Third, neither instructional condition was very effective in facilitating learning of important vocabulary and terminology. Although current thinking in science education supports the de-emphasis of vocabulary learning, a certain core knowledge is necessary for effective reasoning and communication. Even when activities-based approaches are used, it may be necessary to use specialized techniques, such as mnemonic instruction (e.g., Scruggs & Mastropieri, 1992), to facilitate vocabulary learning of students with learning disabilities.

Finally, the use of an activities-oriented curriculum does not obviate the need for effective teaching skills (e.g., Mastropieri & Scruggs, 1994a). Brigham, Scruggs, and Mastropieri (1992) reported that level of teacher enthusiasm made a substantial difference in academic learning and social behavior of students with learning disabilities, even when the same activities-oriented atmospheric science curriculum was employed in both conditions. Clearly, activities-oriented approaches are of great potential utility with students with mild disabilities; however, additional adaptations may be needed to ensure success.

Less Is More

With respect to curriculum coverage, the notion of "less is more" is also widely promoted in science reform efforts (e.g., Champagne et al., this volume; Rutherford & Ahlgren, 1990). Teachers, it is argued, should devote more time to teaching fewer science units, thereby promoting depth of understanding over breadth of content coverage. This conceptualization of science education is in direct contrast to most contemporary science textbooks, which tend to cover, on a superficial level, enormous amounts of content. "Less is more" is especially compatible with the needs of students with mild disabilities, many of whom need additional time and redundancy in content coverage (Mastropieri & Scruggs, 1992b).

Inherent within the idea of "less is more" is the practice of prioritizing science objectives and placing differential emphasis on those objectives thought to be most important. It may be important to prioritize objectives further for students with mild disabilities and provide them with even more emphasis on those prioritized objectives. This may be necessary due to a lack of preskills and prior knowledge as well as the need for more time for learning to take place. For example, many students with disabilities may find themselves having difficulty with the fine motor skills necessary to prepare slides and operate a microscope. Given direct instruction and sufficient practice, these skills often can be acquired. If, however, the observation of certain small things, and not the operation of lab equipment, has the highest priority, alternative means for observing are available that do not require the manipulation of lab equipment (see Scruggs & Mastropieri, 1994a). It also has been noted that students with mild disabilities may benefit from repeated opportunities to complete the same or very similar activities to ensure that understanding has occurred (Mastropieri & Scruggs, 1992a).

In addition to the potential benefits of the "less is more" concept, some potential challenges also appear. First, the emphasis on studying concepts "in depth" in some cases may reach a level of conceptual complexity that is difficult for some special education students to comprehend. Additionally, the emphasis on longer-term science projects may tax the abilities of some students to generalize many skills simultaneously and exhibit persistence of effort toward long-term goals. In both cases, modifications of curriculum demands may be appropriate for some individual learners.

"Less is more" is a concept that is essentially compatible with the instruction of students with disabilities. However, prioritizing, redundancy, and curricular modification beyond that required for most students may be necessary in some cases.

Technological Applications

One commonly mentioned feature of recent trends in science education is the integration of technology in science learning (Aldridge, 1990; Aldridge & Yager, 1991), and several mainstream innovations may prove potentially beneficial for students with disabilities. For example, videodisc technology (e.g., VideoDiscovery, Seattle) allows students to view scientific phenomena in interactive video format, often in place of science textbooks written beyond their reading level. The interactive format allows for cause-and-effect demonstrations, focus, and practice. In some cases, the technology is sufficiently simple to execute that students can be taught to study scientific principles that otherwise could not be shown in the classroom. This advantage may be particularly helpful for students who may have difficulty generalizing the principles learned in classroom simulations (e.g., "pendulums," "whirligigs") to outside settings.

Another potentially helpful use of technology is in computer-assisted science instruction. Some new computer programs allow students to practice applications of newly acquired scientific concepts in ways that would be difficult or impossible in classroom settings. For example, a popular recent program, "Miner's Cave" (MECC software, Minneapolis), allows students to select pulleys, levers, or inclined planes to suit different space constraints and energy requirements, thereby providing opportunities for practice that otherwise would be difficult or impossible in a classroom setting.

A third example of potentially beneficial applications of technology is in the curriculum materials for "Voyage of the Mimi" and "Voyage of the Mimi II" (WINGS for Learning/Sunburst, Scotts Valley, CA). These materials combine video and computer-assisted formats to present integrated science/social studies lessons. The videos are highly motivating to students, as they depict a group of young people investigating whales (I) and Mayan archaeology (II). As the group encounters difficulties, students are called upon to think through solutions. In "Voyage of the Mimi II," one of the characters is an amputee and spends some time discussing the operation, the prosthetic, and her rehabilitation. Both programs include computer software that can be used to practice the concepts covered in the video.

Although there are several potentially valuable uses of technology for students with disabilities, adaptations probably will be necessary, in the form of peer assistance, repeated presentations, and skill development. Other considerations for mainstream classroom use of technology in science learning are described by Mastropieri and Scruggs (1993).

Discovery and Inquiry-Based Emphasis

As Champagne and her colleagues have noted, most science reform efforts emphasize the need to make science activities inquiry-based or discovery-oriented. Such approaches have seemed to be successful with typical learners. It is argued that students who "construct" their own knowledge will comprehend the principles at a deeper level than will those who are simply provided with information, for example, through lecture or reading.

More research is needed to determine whether "constructivist" approaches to science learning are efficacious for students with mild disabilities (Mastropieri & Scruggs, 1992b). In fact, it can be argued that such approaches may interact negatively with the cognitive/conceptual characteristics described earlier. Activities requiring insight or "catching on" may prove difficult for students with low psychometric intelligence (Jensen, 1989) or students with learning disabilities (Ellis, in press). Further, the additional time that typically is required to promote learner insight may be excessive for students with mild disabilities, and the time consequently lost may prevent students from acquiring other valuable skills or knowledge.

In spite of the lack of research in "constructivist" approaches to learning in special education, some supporting arguments can be made. First, it cannot be denied that many students with mild disabilities could stand to benefit from improved reasoning abilities or thinking skills. Since the type of direct instruction often practiced in special education tends not to emphasize thinking skills, some alternative way of achieving such objectives should be considered.

Second, some empirical evidence recently has begun to emerge that the learning *and* thinking skills of students with mild disabilities can be facilitated by the use of highly structured questioning procedures. Scruggs, Mastropieri, Bakken, and Brigham (1993) concluded that students with learning disabilities learned science content better when they answered scientific questions for themselves than when they were directly provided with the same information. Scruggs, Mastropieri, Sullivan, and Hesser (1993) reported that students with learning disabilities and mild mental handicaps learned and remembered more when they were coached to reason actively through natural history content using "elaborative interrogation" procedures, than when they were directly provided the same information. Finally, Scruggs, Mastropieri, and Sullivan (1994) and Sullivan, Mastropieri, and Scruggs (1995) reported that students with mild disabilities who had actively reasoned through life science content learned, remembered, and comprehended more information than students who had been provided with drill and practice on the same content. It is interesting to note that in the latter investigations, students who never were directly provided with information outperformed students who had been directly provided with the information, with total instructional time being held constant.

The results of these investigations suggest that more inquiry-driven instructional models can be beneficial for students with mild disabilities, at least for information that is logically interconnected. However, these results cannot be taken to mean that students with mild disabilities can easily succeed in mainstream classes that employ constructivist teaching methods (Scruggs & Mastropieri, 1994b). Although students with mild disabilities can learn to use and develop their inferential reasoning abilities, without coaching they may fail to draw inferences of the type that nonhandicapped learners automatically execute (Bos & Tierney, 1984). Further, students with mild disabilities, especially those with low psychometric intelligence, may require a level of coaching that would be inappropriate for normally achieving students of the same age. In sum, although guided inquiry may be appropriate, or even optimal, in influencing science learning of students with mild disabilities, the level of coaching provided in mainstream instruction may not be appropriate to their needs. Further investigation should be helpful in resolving these issues.

IMPLEMENTING THE PASS VARIABLES IN SCIENCE TEACHING

In this response, we have argued that the current trends in science education are theoretically compatible with observed characteristics of students with disabilities (see also Scruggs & Mastropieri, 1993); however, implementation of the current reform agenda in itself will be insufficient for inclusion of such students. Current science approaches were not developed for the purpose of accommodating special learning needs; indeed, accommodation of the special needs of students with disabilities is not mentioned in either the influential book disseminated by the American Association for the Advancement of Science, *Science for All Americans* (Rutherford & Ahlgren, 1990) or the *Handbook of Research on Science Teaching and Learning* (Gabel, 1994) endorsed by the National Science Teachers Association. Nevertheless, science teachers can address the needs of students with disabilities in their classes by including what we have referred to as the "PASS" variables (Mastropieri & Scruggs, 1992b, 1993, 1994a). These variables include the following: Prioritize, Adapt, "SCREAM," and Systematically Evaluate, and are shown in Figure 2.1. If all these variables are in place, students with special needs will have the best chance of succeeding in the mainstream science class.

SUMMARY

Many aspects of current trends in science education, including content integration, hands-on approaches, "less is more," technological applications, and inquiry-based learning, are potentially compatible with the characteristics of students with mild disabilities, and may in fact be optimal compared with traditional textbook/lecture-based approaches to science learning (Mastropieri & Scruggs, 1994b). Further, it could be argued that current thinking in science education can benefit from considering diversity in learner needs. Such consideration potentially compels curriculum reformers to think clearly about objectives, methods, principles of learning and characteristics of learners, and appropriate assessment of all science learners.

Nevertheless, specific adjustments must be made to ensure the success

Figure 2.1 Helping Students "PASS" Science

Prioritize Instruction

1. Articulate and arrange objectives in order of importance
2. Devote the most time and resources to the objectives with highest priority
3. Consider eliminating some less important objectives

Adapt Instruction

1. Make changes in methods, materials, and the environment that reflect the characteristics of students with special needs
2. May include material modification, additional time and practice, peer assistance, technological assistance
3. Refer to Corrick (1981), Hadary and Cohen (1978), Hofman and Ricker (1979), or Mastropieri and Scruggs (1993) for specific recommendations

SCREAM

These "effective teaching" variables (Mastropieri & Scruggs, 1993, 1994a) include structure, clarity, redundancy, enthusiasm, appropriate pace, and maximized engagement. These variables are critical components of high-quality instruction and are as important as, if not more important than, curriculum adaptations (e.g., Brigham et al., 1992).

Systematic Evaluation

1. Formative and ongoing
2. Tied to prioritized objectives
3. Used frequently for instructional decision making

of students with mild disabilities in science classes. These modifications most likely will include prioritizing objectives, adapting methods and materials or instruction, implementing "effective teaching" variables, and employing systematic evaluation to monitor progress.

The present reform movement has emphasized the accommodation of diversity in science education. The role of special educators is to help ensure that science teachers acquire the skills and knowledge to enable them to accommodate diverse student populations, including students with disabilities, and to ensure successful learning experiences in science for all Americans.

REFERENCES

Aldridge, B. G. (1990). *NSTA's scope, sequence, and coordination project enters R and D phase: Grants support trials at five sites, coordination, assessment.* Washington, DC: National Science Teachers Association.

Aldridge, B. G., & Yager, R. E. (1991, May). "Basic science" or STS: Which is better for science learning? *NSTA Reports!,* pp. 8–9, 32–33.

Bos, C. S., & Tierney, R. J. (1984). Inferential reading abilities of mildly mentally retarded and nonretarded students. *American Journal of Mental Deficiency, 89,* 75–82.

Brigham, F. J., Bakken, J., Scruggs, T. E., & Mastropieri, M. A. (1992). Cooperative behavior management: Strategies for promoting a positive classroom environment. *Education and Training in Mental Retardation, 27,* 3–12.

Brigham, F. J., Scruggs, T. E., & Mastropieri, M. A. (1992). Teacher enthusiasm in learning disabilities classrooms: Effects on learning and behavior. *Learning Disabilities Research and Practice, 7,* 68–73.

California State Department of Education. (1990). *Science framework for California public schools kindergarten through grade twelve.* Sacramento: Author.

Corrick, M. E. (Ed.). (1981). *Teaching handicapped students science.* Washington, DC: National Education Association.

Ellis, E. S. (in press). Integrative strategy instruction: A potential model for teaching content-area subjects to learning disabled adolescents. *Journal of Learning Disabilities.*

Esler, W. K., Midgett, J., & Bird, R. C. (1977). Elementary science materials and the exceptional child. *Science Education, 61,* 181–184.

Full Option Science System [Curriculum materials]. (1990). Chicago: Encyclopedia Britannica Educational Corp.

Gabel, D. D. (Ed.). (1994). *Handbook of research on science teaching and learning.* New York: Macmillan.

Hadary, D. E., & Cohen, S. H. (1978). *Laboratory science and art for blind, deaf, and emotionally disturbed children: A mainstreaming approach.* Baltimore: University Park Press.

Hofman, H. H., & Ricker, K. S. (1979). *Science education and the physically handicapped.* Washington, DC: National Science Teachers Association.

Jensen, A. R. (1989). The relationship between learning and intelligence. *Learning and Individual Differences, 1,* 37–62.

Lamendola, A. (1976). Science and the emotionally disadvantaged child. *Science and Children, 13,* 17–18.

Linn, M. C., & Thier, H. D. (1975). Adapting science material for the blind (ASMB): Expectation for student outcomes. *Science Education, 59,* 237–246.

Mastropieri, M. A., & Scruggs, T. E. (1992a, November). *Guidelines for mainstreaming in science.* Workshop presented for the Mesa Public Schools, Mesa, AZ.

Mastropieri, M. A., & Scruggs, T. E. (1992b). Science and students with disabilities. *Review of Educational Research, 62,* 377–411.

Mastropieri, M. A., & Scruggs, T. E. (1993). *A practical guide for teaching science to students with special needs in inclusive settings.* Austin, TX: PRO-ED.

Mastropieri, M. A., & Scruggs, T. E. (1994a). *Effective instruction for special education* (2nd ed.). Austin, TX: PRO-ED.

Mastropieri, M. A., & Scruggs, T. E. (1994b). Text-based vs. activities-oriented science curriculum: Implications for students with disabilities. *Remedial and Special Education, 15,* 34–43.

Mastropieri, M. A., Scruggs, T. E., & Shiah, S. (1991). Mathematics instruction for learning disabled students: A review of research. *Learning Disabilities Research and Practice, 6,* 89–98.

National Academy of Sciences. (1990). *National Science Resources Center annual report.* Washington, DC: Author.

Patton, J., & Andre, K. E. (1989). Individualizing for science and social studies. In J. Wood (Ed.), *Mainstreaming: A practical approach for teachers* (pp. 301–351). Columbus, OH: Merrill.

Pressley, M., Johnson, C. J., & Symons, S. (1987). Elaborating to learn and learning to elaborate. *Journal of Learning Disabilities, 20,* 76–91.

Rutherford, F. J., & Ahlgren, A. (1990). *Science for all Americans.* New York: Oxford University Press.

Scruggs, T. E., & Mastropieri, M. A. (1984). Issues in generalization: Implications for special education. *Psychology in the Schools, 21,* 397–403.

Scruggs, T. E., & Mastropieri, M. A. (1992). Classroom applications of mnemonic instruction: Acquisition, maintenance, and generalization. *Exceptional Children, 58,* 219–231.

Scruggs, T. E., & Mastropieri, M. A. (1993). Current approaches to science education: Implications for mainstream instruction of students with disabilities. *Remedial and Special Education, 14*(1), 15–24.

Scruggs, T. E., & Mastropieri, M. A. (1994a). Refocusing microscope activities for special students. *Science Scope, 17,* 74–78.

Scruggs, T. E., & Mastropieri, M. A. (1994b). Successful mainstreaming in elementary science classes: A qualitative investigation of three reputational cases. *American Educational Research Journal, 31,* 785–811.

Scruggs, T. E., Mastropieri, M. A., Bakken, J. P., & Brigham, F. J. (1993). Reading vs. doing: A comparison of textbook-based and inquiry-oriented approaches to science. *Journal of Special Education, 27,* 1–15.

Scruggs, T. E., Mastropieri, M. A., & Sullivan, G. S. (1994). Promoting relational thinking skills: Elaborative interrogation for mildly handicapped students. *Exceptional Children, 60,* 450–457.

Scruggs, T. E., Mastropieri, M. A., Sullivan, G. S., & Hesser, L. S. (1993). Improving reasoning and recall: The relative effects of elaborative interrogation and mnemonic elaboration. *Learning Disability Quarterly, 16,* 233–240.

Sullivan, G. S., Mastropieri, M. A., & Scruggs, T. E. (1995). Reasoning and remembering: Coaching thinking with students with learning disabilities. *Journal of Special Education, 29,* 310–322.

Thresher, J. M. (1963). Science education for mentally retarded children: A rationale. *Mental Retardation, 13,* 152–162.

U.S. Department of Education. (1991). *America 2000: An education strategy.* Washington, DC: Author.

Response

Science Education Trends and Special Education

Charles W. Anderson and Marcia K. Fetters

Like previous science education reform efforts that have spanned over 50 years, the current reforms described by Champagne, Newell, and Goodenough are multifaceted and sometimes working at cross-purposes. Collectively, however, they can lead to a thorough revamping of the school science curriculum, learning environments, and assessment. In contrast with the elitist orientation of reforms that occurred in the 1960s, a primary goal in both policy documents and research and development efforts associated with this current wave of reform is *science for all* (e.g., American Association for the Advancement of Science, 1989; National Research Council, 1996; National Science Teachers Association, 1992). Reformers hope to achieve this goal by trading depth for breadth in the science curriculum—emphasizing deeper understanding of less scientific content—and by changing instruction and the social organization of classrooms to involve all students in more authentic scientific activities.

At the same time, important changes have been occurring in special education. Special education students are spending less time in separate classes, where they often received little or no science instruction to begin with. As they move into mainstream classrooms, special education students are encountering new and challenging environments, both academic and social. Academically, they must deal with science content that the majority of their mainstream classmates find difficult and sometimes unintelligible. Socially, they must deal with the fact that they inevitably will be marked as different from their mainstream classmates as a result of being labeled as special education students, their different and often separate educational backgrounds, and their own cognitive difficulties in learning science.

Meeting this dual challenge of achieving meaningful understanding of science and social acceptance in science classrooms will require both sustained effort by special education students themselves as well as supportive

Curriculum Trends, Special Education, and Reform: Refocusing the Conversation. ISBN 0-8077-3562-0 (pbk), ISBN 0-8077-3563-9 (cloth).

classroom environments. In this response we will try to focus on factors that are likely to affect special education students' responses to the academic and social challenges that they face in mainstream science classes. In trying to understand the nature of these challenges and how special education students are likely to respond, we will draw heavily on a few studies that have focused specifically on science learning by special education students and by other students who are thought to be at risk due to cultural, linguistic, or social class differences. Most of these studies describe cases involving a single classroom (e.g., Burgess & Tomlinson, 1993; Fetters, Templin, & Anderson, 1992; Heath, 1983; Rosebery, Warren, & Conant, 1990; Roth, 1992). Some of the stories in these studies are success stories; others are less so. In general, they suggest that while the kinds of reforms described by Champagne and colleagues have the potential to create more supportive general classroom environments for special education students, many important problems are still to be worked out before this potential is realized.

THE ACADEMIC CHALLENGE: MEANINGFUL UNDERSTANDING FOR ALL

"Meaningful understanding" and "science for all" have been espoused goals of the current science education reform efforts since their inception. In particular, these reform efforts have been driven by evidence that the vast majority of regular education students have not achieved meaningful learning from the traditional science curriculum. Studies of new methods of science teaching often have focused on the needs of mainstream students (e.g., Anderson & Roth, 1989; Lee, Eichinger, Anderson, Berkheimer, & Blackeslee, 1993; Linn & Songer, 1991) and have been successful in increasing the percentage of students understanding key science concepts from the 0–20% range to the 50–90% range. These are clearly significant improvements. However, each study also showed that substantial numbers of students still were not achieving adequate understanding, especially when the student populations studied included large numbers of students who generally were thought of as being at risk for educational failure. The evidence, in other words, seems to indicate that some students are still being left behind even when changes in teaching methods seem to benefit many of their peers. We are concerned that many special education students are included in that number.

Our discussion focuses on two aspects of the reforms described by Champagne and colleagues, reforms that have the potential to make meaningful science learning possible for a wider range of students. The first is the development of Science, Technology, and Society (STS) approaches to science teaching. The second is the development of alternative methods of assessment. In each case, we see substantial difficulties that have yet to be adequately resolved.

STS Approaches to Science Teaching

In advocating STS approaches to science teaching, Champagne and colleagues are suggesting a controversial solution to a widely recognized problem. The current science curriculum recognizes only a few types of achievement, such as mastery of specific details and abstract theoretical analysis. When students fail to demonstrate mastery of these narrowly defined goals, many teachers respond by constraining the curriculum even more, focusing on helping students recall the contents of textbooks or practice narrowly defined "science process skills." Much research on science teaching for students who have difficulty achieving in science focuses on these same narrow outcomes (Mastropieri & Scruggs, 1992).

In contrast, advocates of STS approaches to science teaching recommend accepting—even celebrating—diversity in the contributions that different students make to science classes and in the range of acceptable learning outcomes. Advocates of STS approaches contend that one way to help more students be successful is to recognize many more different kinds of success. Ms. Carrese's student who never finished his homework but became deeply involved in making the model hydroelectric power plant is an example of a student who benefits because in his science class a wider range of activities are accepted as legitimate achievements. Thus, STS classrooms are potentially "multiple ability classrooms," as advocated by Cohen (1986) and her colleagues.

Most scientists and science educators would agree with the above criticisms of the science curriculum. Many science educators also would agree that it is important to recognize the diverse abilities and achievements that students bring with them to science classrooms. Proposals to expand the range of acceptable outcomes beyond the limits of traditional Western science, however, are more controversial.

Critics of STS approaches (e.g., Roth, 1989) wonder whether we have broadened the science curriculum so much that we have "thrown out the baby with the bath water." It may be that Ms. Carrese's student who spends his time building a model power plant is being successful, these critics would say, but is he really learning *science*? Where shall we draw the line between meaningful understanding of *science* and other kinds of learning that—while perhaps useful and important—are not really *science*?

Thus, while most current reform efforts advocate that many different ways of making sense of nature and technology be accepted in science classrooms, there is a wide range of opinions about what kinds of reasoning and communicating should be privileged, or treated as acceptable goals, for student learning. Recently developed national goals for science education (AAAS, 1989, 1993; National Research Council, 1996) generally take a narrower position than that advocated by supporters of STS teaching. While recognizing the importance of relationships among science, technology, and society, they still draw their contents almost entirely from the Western scientific canon.

This position is not as narrow-minded as it may appear. From our perspective, science is worth studying because the community of scientists has developed powerful intellectual tools that we can use to understand the world. Scientists were able to develop these powerful ideas because they rigorously excluded types of evidence and standards of reasoning that did not fit the mold of what they considered acceptable. How can students fully appreciate or benefit from the power and the beauty of scientific ideas without learning to conform to the standards for evidence and logic that are central to the scientific enterprise?

Thus, at the same time that science educators are virtually unanimous in rejecting recall of text and narrowly defined skills as acceptable goals for *any* science students, they also are faced with a dilemma that is as yet unresolved. Relatively loose definitions of scientific literacy like those advocated by STS and multicultural approaches to science teaching recognize the knowledge and the contributions of many different people, but they risk losing the power and elegance that make scientific knowledge worth studying. On the other hand, narrower definitions risk the continuing alienation of students who, like Ms. Carrese's student with attention-deficit disorder, feel little connection with either scientific cultures or scientific reasoning.

Using Alternative Assessment to Develop Rich Descriptions of Student Progress

Questions of content and process are not the only academic challenges in reforming science education. While the trends described by Champagne and colleagues are likely to make science classrooms more complex environments, where a greater range of abilities and outcomes are recognized and substantially different kinds of activities take place, they also must be places in which clear goals, standards, or ways to measure progress exist. In other words, helping special education students achieve meaningful understanding depends not only on the range of abilities that are recognized, but also on the ways that are available to acknowledge and give students credit for progress.

Champagne and colleagues suggest that alternative methods of assessment may provide the information we need to understand students' difficulties and to see progress that remains invisible under traditional assessment methods. Interpreting the results of alternative assessments, however, represents a serious challenge for teachers. We offer two examples of student performance on nontraditional assessments. The first comes from the journal of a special education student in a tenth-grade biology class. Lisa (a pseudonym) responded to similar questions in the following ways at the beginning of the course and then 2 months later:

> Journal question for September 19:
>
> *Name three things animals need to live and explain why they need them.*
>
> Lisa's response:
>
> > food (*sugar*)
> > water
> > air (*oxgin*) (Fetters, Templin, & Anderson, 1992, p. 15)

The words in parentheses in her entry were added after writing the initial entry.

> Journal question for November 19:
>
> *Name two things yeast need to live and explain how you know.*
>
> Lisa's response:
>
> > sugar—this is food for the yeast, they need to breethe and multiply
> > warmth—yeast kept in the refrigerator didn't breath and multiply like the yeast kept near the heeter
> > What else do yeast eat? (*molasis—Is this sugar?*)
> > How much heet to yeast need? (*Too much heet kills yeast—oven*) (Fetters, Templin, & Anderson, 1992, p. 17)

The students in our second example were recent Haitian immigrants enrolled in a bilingual program in an alternative school in Newton, Massachusetts in which instruction was conducted in Haitian Creole. The program involved students in a wide array of activities and investigations associated with the general themes of water purity and water quality (Warren, Rosebery, & Conant, 1989). The interview with Andrew was conducted at the beginning of the school year; the interview with Kenia was conducted near the end. The interview question first describes the water in Boston

Harbor in observational detail (floating garbage, dead fish, bad smells, and so forth) and then continues with, "You are a famous scientist. The Mayor of Boston asks you to find out what is wrong with the water. What would you do?" Here are excerpts from their answers:

> Andrew (Fall interview) began by asserting the garbage made the fish die, leading to this exchange:
>
> I: How would you know that it was garbage that was making the foam and the fish die?
> Andrew: The garbage made the fish die.
> I: How would you make sure?
> Andrew: Because fish don't eat garbage; they eat plants under the water.
>
> Kenia (Spring interview) also suggested that garbage made the fish die.
>
> I: What might make the fish die?
> Kenia: They're allergic to the dirty garbage.
> I: OK; how would you make sure that what you think is true?
> Kenia: I would take a little garbage in the water. I would take a fish, and give it to it to eat to see if it would die.
> I: What if it doesn't die?
> Kenia: If it doesn't die, it's another reason.
> I: Can you think of another reason the fish might die?
> Kenia: If the water had too much fecal in it.
>
> (Kenia goes on to describe how she would test for "fecal," using a method that they had studied during the year.) (Rosebery, Warren, & Conant, 1990, p. 13)

It seems clear that the responses made later in the year had improved, but how exactly might we describe the nature of the progress? The content of the later answers is not all that different. Lisa suggested "correct" answers in both of her journal entries; Andrew and Kenia both correctly noted that garbage made the fish die. Nor did improvement in the later answers depend on the extensive use of technical vocabulary. We see other ways, however, in which the later answers do demonstrate important progress.

One area in which we can see progress concerns the students' mastery of the *discourse of science*. In September Andrew and Lisa treated the questions that they were asked as "school questions" that called for correct answers and nothing more. Lisa answered the question with a list of single words. When the interviewer tried to treat Andrew's response as a hypothesis that might be tested, Andrew responded by essentially restating his answer. In contrast, both of the later responses show the children using linguistic forms that are essential elements of scientific discourse. Lisa came to see journal writing as an occasion for giving reasons and posing questions as well as writing down lists of words. Kenia mastered the "speech genre" (cf. Heath, 1986; Wertsch, 1991) of hypothesis testing, in which possible answers are held tentatively and may be modified if the tests provide new evidence.

A second area of improvement concerns the development of a sense of *personal agency* or *efficacy* on the students' part. Lisa came to see posing questions and providing explanations as part of her role in the science class; these activities were no longer limited to the teacher and the "smart" students. Unlike Andrew (and the other students in the fall interviews as well), Kenia's spring interview showed her taking on the role of "famous scientist" suggested by the interview question. Rather than providing a rote "school answer" in which she was not personally involved, Kenia spoke confidently in the first person, describing how she would act in the situation. Both Lisa and Kenia seemed to be making initial connections between the academic meaning of science and the social role that fosters inclusion in science class.

These examples indicate that alternative forms of assessment provide both new opportunities and great challenges to teachers of special education students and others thought to be at risk. The fundamental nature and purposes of assessment are changed; rather than merely grading or scoring, alternative assessments involve teachers in *interpreting* students' responses, using them as windows into student thinking. Using alternative assessments to investigate students' scientific thinking has been a major focus for science education research during the past decade (e.g., Driver, 1983; Driver, Guesne, & Tiberghien, 1985; Novak, 1987; Osborne & Freyberg, 1985).

While we accept that alternative forms of assessment are essential for recognizing the abilities of students who formerly have not been successful in science, as well as for monitoring student progress toward scientific literacy, we note that there are important barriers to their widespread use in science classrooms. They are usually more time-consuming to develop than traditional forms of assessment, and they demand a careful analysis of student responses that is very different from traditional grading. Most science teachers are poorly prepared to engage in this kind of assessment development and analysis. Changing the nature of teachers' preparation and the assessment materials available to them will be a long and difficult process and may thus affect the progress of inclusionary practices in science classrooms.

THE SOCIAL CHALLENGE: ACHIEVING TRUE INCLUSION

As noted earlier, the challenges that special education students encounter in mainstream science classrooms are social as well as academic. In some important ways, the social experience of special education students in mainstream science classes parallels the experiences of African American students. That is, once students of color had been physically included, there remained other significant social and cultural barriers to successful learning.

The difficulties encountered by African American students have been widely described and analyzed (e.g., Delpit, 1988; Heath, 1983; Ogbu, 1987, 1992; Steele, 1992). In particular, we would like to focus on what Steele describes as "stigma." Like African American students, special education students who are included in mainstream science classrooms inevitably will be stigmatized—literally marked as different from their peers by labels, by differences in educational history, and by differences in physical or cognitive abilities. As the authors cited above and others have noted, students who are stigmatized face a fundamental choice. They can struggle, perhaps unsuccessfully, to reduce the differences between themselves and their classmates. Or they can preserve a sense of self-worth by choosing alienation, adopting what Ogbu describes as an "oppositional social identity," and avoiding effort directed toward goals that seem impossible to achieve. Special education students who spend increasing amounts of time in general education classrooms risk alienation both from scientists and scientific communities and from their mainstream peers. From our perspective, overcoming such alienation constitutes the social challenge of inclusion.

Alienation from Science and Scientists

If special education students are to achieve real inclusion, they must recognize science as personally important and useful, and scientists as people who somehow are like them, rather than as an entirely different class of people who think and use language in mostly incomprehensible ways. This is a tall order, since science classes have a way of making even students who are otherwise smart and successful in school feel inadequate; we often meet competent and successful adults who, on hearing that we are science educators, immediately feel compelled to tell us they never were very good in science.

Special education students in science classes often have these feelings in spades. Nan, for instance, was a special education student in a fifth-grade science class taught by our colleague Kathy Roth. Here is what Nan wrote in her journal early in the school year, when she was asked to draw a picture of a scientist and explain what the scientist is like as a person.

> This scientist is making a lickwind [liquid]. I think this scientist work is important because. I think it is important but I cannot think why. I think not like to be friends with this scientist because I do not like science and I do not like scientist. (Roth, 1992, Fig. 10)

Nan's response makes clear her sense of separation and alienation from science and scientists, and this sense of alienation is in itself a formidable barrier to successful learning. Students who feel alienated in science classes often develop strategies for getting by with as little effort as possible, while devoting most of their energy to the pursuit of other agendas that are more satisfying personally.

It is not inevitable, though, that students like Nan will fall into an oppositional social identity. Here, for example, is the way that Nan responded several weeks later to another writing assignment at the conclusion of a unit on ecology, photosynthesis, and the nature of scientific communities. When asked to describe a time during the unit when she felt like a scientist, Nan responded as follows:

> The time I was scientist the time that we had a talk about what is food for plants we have some ides but not anufe. We tolk about are evidence. Like whot is the evidenc ot the plant that food is. Like food we had to have evidenc to pove that food is some thing you eat I feel like I am a scientis wane I put ? in the book [a book of questions that students asked that was kept by the class]. I feel good a littel but not a lot. I feel like a real scientist. I wiss I was. (Roth, 1992, Fig. 10)

Nan's response is poignant in that it shows both her recognition of a tenuous connection between herself and the scientific community, and a belief (unfortunately, probably correct) that her hopes for a stronger connection may never be realized. Roth's teaching, which created and nurtured this sense of connection, drew on many of the instructional techniques described by Champagne and colleagues, but included other important elements as well, for example:

- A strong personal involvement of the teacher with the students
- Explicit attention to scientists and their work, and to the similarities between the scientists and the students
- The development of a classroom learning community that had many of the elements of a scientific community, including public sharing and revision of ideas, valuing and respecting of others' ideas, and the use of evidence and shared expertise

Others who have written about successful teaching for students who traditionally have been left out, have emphasized these teaching strategies as well as others (see, for example, Delpit, 1988; Heath, 1983; Steele, 1992; Warren, Rosebery, & Conant, 1989). All of these writers emphasize the need to both address students' cognitive difficulties and encourage a sense of personal identity and connection. If reforms in science education do not include both of these elements, then special education students who are physically included in science classes are likely to remain alienated from science and scientists.

Alienation from Peers

As Champagne and colleagues point out, many of the proposed reforms in science education rely on collaborative work by students in small groups. This means that special education students are likely to find themselves working with mainstream peers in situations where the teacher does not always have knowledge of what students are saying to each other. In these circumstances, it is not unusual for other students to act in ways that may reinforce special education students' feelings of isolation and separation. Consider, for example, the following exchanges among a small group of students in a sixth-grade classroom. The students, who were studying states of matter, were supposed to decide whether it would be better to store water on a spaceship as a solid, liquid, or gas. Each student was to bring to the group his or her ideas about the best state of matter and a reason for those ideas. Sally, a student with academic difficulties who had been absent, initially did not have a reason.

Emily: [to Sally] What was your reason for gas?
Brian: Yeah, what was your reason?
Jim: Yeah, what was your reason? [pounding the table]
Brian: Shut up, Jim.
Emily: Don't badger her.
Jake: Badger?
Sally: I don't have a reason yet.

Later:

Emily: What do you think it's going to be?
Brian: Gas. [turning to Sally] Do you have any reason yet?
Jim: She doesn't have a reason because she's dumb.
Jake: OK, OK.
Sally: Because liquid water and solid water take up more space and water vapor stores better. [Everyone begins to write "Stores better"]

Still later, after Brian decided to change his answer from "gas" to "liquid":

> *Emily:* [to Sally] Did you change yours?
> *Brian:* Well, you don't have any reasons. I had all your reasons and then I turned to water and you argued my point so you're arguing that it's water. [pause] OK. It's liquid—Sally—it's liquid, unless you can argue your point real well, it's liquid.

The discussion that took place in this small group was positive in many ways. The students carried on a sustained discussion of the merits of each state of water, eventually reaching a conclusion that was scientifically reasonable and rationalized far better than any of the students' individual conclusions at the beginning of the session. However, Sally did not benefit from the scientific content of the discussion; of 189 statements in the transcript, she contributed three. While Emily generally defended Sally and tried to include her in the discussion, the boys were less kind. Brian treated Sally in a way that was fair by his lights; he expected everyone to "follow the rules" by stating conclusions and defending them forcefully. Jim harassed her whenever he saw an opportunity.

At the high school level, most students are more subtle than Jim, but competitive and exclusionary peer norms are generally accepted by both special education students and their mainstream peers. For example, on an occasion when a pair of academically less successful students (one a special education student) had set up a lab successfully in a high school biology class at a time when the other pair in their small group (both "A" students) had made a mistake, one of the students announced with pride to the class, "See! You guys think we're dumb—but we did it right!"

This moment of triumph notwithstanding, it is unlikely that special education students ultimately will feel included in science classes if their small groups are controlled by the norms of the peer culture, in which small-group work can become a kind of sport where students compete for peer status. Although competition for status also plays an important role in scientific communities (cf. Kelly, Carlsen, & Cunningham, 1993; Traweek, 1988), this is one respect in which we may not want scientific activity in the classroom to be completely authentic.

The alternative, however, is a difficult one. Teachers who use small groups in their teaching must find ways to influence student norms for personal interaction in the small-group work—by explicit statements of alternative norms, by the use of reward systems that emphasize responsibility and tolerance, by careful monitoring of groupwork, and by direct intervention in groups that are not functioning well. The teacher's role as a model is also important. When teachers recognize and acknowledge the contributions of special education students, taking advantage of their abilities while helping them to overcome their disabilities, mainstream students are more likely to follow suit. Teaching with small groups that successfully include special education students is possible, but the process demands hard work, skillful technique, and personal involvement from the teacher. It is a cognitive as well as an affective challenge, for teachers must truly understand their students' abilities and achievements.

Authors such as Cohen (1986), Palincsar, Anderson, and David (1993), and Cobb and his colleagues (Cobb, Wood, Yackel, & McNeal, 1992; Cobb, Yackel, & Wood, 1989) emphasize that students of diverse backgrounds and abilities are most successful working together when teachers consciously shape the implicit social norms that govern relationships among them. Cohen (1986) suggests specific exercises to teach students social norms and patterns of behavior that encourage all members to be included in small-group work. Palincsar, Anderson, and David (1993) explicitly stated and taught social norms favoring inclusion and engagement with scientific ideas. Cobb, Yackel, and Wood (1989) describe how one skilled elementary teacher influenced her students' "emotional acts," helping them to see engagement with mathematical issues, rather than correct answers, as a basis for pride and feelings of accomplishment. Thus, teachers in classrooms where special education students are included in small-group work must learn to nurture norms of tolerance, respect, and mutual understanding among all of their students.

CONCLUSION

When special education students are included in mainstream science classrooms, there are important potential benefits. The new proximity opens the possibility of learning about science from their work both with mainstream classmates and with teachers who are well trained in the subject. Special education students, in turn, make science classrooms more diverse and interesting places. However, they also may encounter challenges and difficulties. These include the academic challenge of meaningful science learning and the social challenge of achieving real inclusion, rather than alienation and isolation.

Science classrooms traditionally have been difficult environments for the majority of students, let alone those with disabilities. The current program of reforms in science education is in part a response to evidence that only a few of the best students really have understood the content of science courses. Thus, while changes in science education described by Champagne and colleagues probably will be beneficial to special education students who are included in mainstream science classes, the changes are not being designed with the specific needs of those students in mind.

Our reading of the available evidence suggests that these reforms will help to make science classrooms more supportive environments for all students than they have been in the past, but that the trends described by Champagne and colleagues will not be sufficient to help special education students achieve the full benefits of inclusion. They are insufficient not so much in the sense that broad new categories of reform are needed, but in the sense that no one has yet figured out in detail how they will work to accommodate the special needs of individual students.

Thus the inclusion of special education students constitutes a challenge to science educators that in many important aspects remains unanswered. Academically, we must work out ways of defining, measuring, and supporting meaningful learning that will make authentic success in science classes accessible to all students, including special education students. Socially, we must develop learning environments where personal relationships and social norms help special education students to overcome the alienation that many feel from scientific communities and from their own peers. While we understand something about the nature of these challenges, most of the work of meeting them still lies ahead.

ACKNOWLEDGMENTS

The authors would like to acknowledge the help of Larry Burgess, Lowell Rudd, Brian Templin, Jeanne Tomlinson, and Randy Yerrick, whose concern and careful attention to the experiences of special education students in science classes have helped us to become aware of, and understand the issues discussed in, this response.

REFERENCES

American Association for the Advancement of Science. (1989). *Science for all Americans: Project 2061*. Washington, DC: Author.

American Association for the Advancement of Science. (1993). *Benchmarks for science literacy.* New York: Oxford University Press.

Anderson, C. W., & Roth, K. J. (1989). Teaching for meaningful and self-regulated learning of science. In J. Brophy (Ed.), *Advances in research on teaching* (Vol. 1, pp. 265–310). Greenwich, CN: JAI Press.

Burgess, L., & Tomlinson, J. (1993, April). *Including special education students in sciences classes.* Paper presented at the annual meeting of the National Science Teachers Association, Kansas City, MO.

Cobb, P., Wood, T., Yackel, E., & McNeal, B. (1992). Characteristics of classroom mathematics traditions: An interactional analysis. *American Educational Research Journal, 29*(3), 573–604.

Cobb, P., Yackel, E., & Wood, T. (1989). Young children's emotional acts while engaged in mathematical problem solving. In D. B. McLeod & V. M. Adams (Eds.), *Affect and mathematical problem solving: A new perspective* (pp. 117–148). New York: Springer-Verlag.

Cohen, E. G. (1986). *Designing groupwork: Strategies for the heterogeneous classroom*. New York: Teachers College Press.

Delpit, L. (1988). The silenced dialogue: Power and pedagogy in educating other people's children. *Harvard Educational Review, 58*(3), 280–296.

Driver, R. (1983). *The pupil as scientist?* Milton Keynes: Open University Press.

Driver, R., Guesne, E., & Tiberghien, A. (1985). *Children's ideas in science*. Philadelphia: Open University Press.

Fetters, M. K., Templin, B. P., & Anderson, C. W. (1992, March). *Addressing the needs of low achieving and special education students in high school biology classes: Implications of a conceptual change model of instruction*. Paper presented at the annual meeting of the National Association for Research in Science Teaching, Cambridge, MA.

Heath, S. B. (1983). *Ways with words: Language, life, and work in communities and classrooms*. New York: Cambridge University Press.

Heath, S. B. (1986). Sociocultural contexts of language development. In *Beyond language: Social and cultural factors in schooling language minority students*. Los Angeles: California State University, Evaluation, Dissemination, and Assessment Center.

Kelly, G. J., Carlsen, W. S., & Cunningham, C. M. (1993). Science education in sociocultural context: Perspectives from the sociology of science. *Science Education, 77*(2), 207–220.

Lee, O., Eichinger, D., Anderson, C. W., Berkheimer, G. D., & Blackeslee, T. D. (1993). Changing middle school students' conceptions of matter and molecules. *Journal of Research in Science Teaching, 30*(3), 249–270.

Lemke, J. L. (1990). *Talking science: Language, learning, and values*. Norwood, NJ: Ablex.

Linn, M. C., & Songer, N. B. (1991). Teaching thermodynamics to middle school students: What are appropriate cognitive demands? *Journal of Research in Science Teaching, 28*(10), 885–918.

Mastropieri, M., & Scruggs, T. (1992). Science for students with disabilities. *Review of Educational Research, 62*(4), 377–411.

National Research Council. (1996). *National science education standards*. Washington, DC: National Academy Press.

National Science Teachers Association. (1992). *Scope, sequence, and coordination of secondary school science: Vol. 1. The content core: A guide for curriculum designers*. Washington, DC: Author.

Novak, J. D. (1987). *Proceedings of the second international seminar on misconceptions and educational strategies in science and mathematics* (3 vols.). Ithaca, NY: Cornell University.

Ogbu, J. U. (1987). Variability in minority school performance: A problem in search of an explanation. *Anthropology and Education Quarterly, 18*, 312–334.

Ogbu, J. U. (1992). Understanding cultural diversity and learning. *Educational Researcher, 21*(8), 5–14.

Osborne, R. J., & Freyberg, P. (1985). *Learning in science: The implications of children's science*. Portsmouth, NH: Heinemann.

Palincsar, A. S., Anderson, C. W., & David, Y. (1993). Pursuing scientific literacy in the middle grades through collaborative problem solving. *Elementary School Journal, 93*, 643–658.

Rosebery, A. S., Warren, B., & Conant, F. R. (1990). *Appropriating scientific discourse: Findings from language minority classrooms.* Newton, MA: Bolt, Beranek, & Newman.

Roth, K. J. (1989). Science education: It's not enough to "do" or "relate." *American Educator, 13*(4), 16–22.

Roth, K. J. (1992). *The role of writing in creating a science learning community* (Elementary Subjects Center Series No. 56). East Lansing: Michigan State University.

Steele, C. M. (1992). Race and the schooling of black Americans. *Atlantic Monthly, 269*(4), 68–78.

Traweek, S. (1988). *Beamtimes and lifetimes: The world of high energy physics.* Cambridge, MA: Harvard University Press.

Warren, B., Rosebery, A. S., & Conant, F. R. (1989). *Cheche Konnen: Science and literacy in language minority classrooms.* Newton, MA: Bolt, Beranek, & Newman.

Wertsch, J. V. (1991). *Voices of the mind: A sociocultural approach to mediated action.* Cambridge, MA: Harvard University Press.

* *CHAPTER 3* *

A New View of the Goals and Means for School Mathematics

Robert B. Davis and Carolyn A. Maher

To understand the current changes occurring in mathematics education one needs to consider three levels of activity: first, the actual direct needs of living and working, or what it takes to get the job done; second, the organizational and bureaucratic requirements and expectations that students face; and third, the research studies and scholarly analyses of experts. We shall examine all of these presently, but first we attempt to summarize what might be called the "new" view of school mathematics, as expressed, say, in the important report *Everybody Counts,* from the National Research Council (Mathematical Sciences Education Board [MSEB], 1989) and the document *Curriculum and Evaluation Standards for School Mathematics,* from the National Council of Teachers of Mathematics (NCTM) (1989; see also MSEB, 1990). Summarizing the message of these influential documents inevitably involves judgments and interpretations that might be disputed, but we would argue in defense of the following interpretations:

- Mathematics is not merely arithmetic, but includes general ways of dealing with quantities, spatial arrangements, interpreting data, and considering implications.
- Mathematics requires thought, and competent mathematical performance cannot be achieved by meaningless rote instruction.
- Fortunately (and contrary to popular expectations) *thinking* is actually easier (and more natural) than *relying on rote memory.*
- What is required of a teacher who wants to empower a child's *thinking* is quite different from what is required for rote memory instruction.
- Similarly, what is required of an evaluation program that focuses on *thinking* is quite different from what is required for evaluation that focuses on rote memory.

Curriculum Trends, Special Education, and Reform: Refocusing the Conversation. ISBN 0-8077-3562-0 (pbk), ISBN 0-8077-3563-9 (cloth).

- The world of the real needs of jobs and living requires mathematical thought far more than it requires rote symbol manipulation.
- As real work is changing in very substantial ways, the world of schools, bureaucracy, and public expectations lags far behind, which confronts teachers and educational planners with some agonizing decisions.

To this list, we would add some further items dealing with resource allocation, and some items of a more political, and therefore a decidedly more controversial, nature. First, regarding resource allocation, standardized examination procedures imposed upon schools by external agencies (such as state departments of education) are not likely to improve the situation, but on the contrary *are* likely to make it more difficult for teachers to meet the real needs of their students. Further, what students actually *do* as they work on mathematical tasks is not well captured by most paper-and-pencil tests, and can be captured better, and analyzed more thoughtfully, by direct observation, especially when what the students do is recorded on videotape. Regarding the political question, the economy and culture of the United States require that schools produce many people who are willing and able to work at minimum-wage service jobs, and who are *not* qualified for any jobs that might be more demanding (see, e.g., Apple, 1992a).

We turn now to the context that gives rise to the preceding conclusions regarding mathematics teaching in schools.

THE WORLD OF WORK

By the words "real work" we mean the world where things get done, where things are made, or transported, or planned and recorded, or bought and sold, and so on. This includes what a carpenter actually does, or a lawyer, or a dentist, or a real estate salesperson, or someone who works behind a counter at a fast-food restaurant.

The changes in the way mathematics is used in the world of real work continue to be momentous. Perhaps most people have not yet recognized the magnitude of this revolution. Yet, anyone who looks carefully at the world outside of schools sees that the role of mathematics has been altered almost beyond recognition, and will move on to even greater changes in the years ahead. In large part this is a consequence of the ubiquity of computers, as components of dishwashers, cash registers, airplanes, supermarket check-out counters, automobiles, television sets, cameras, personal address books, checkbooks, meter-reading apparatus, wristwatches, or even standing by themselves on the desk to help us write letters and make telephone calls and amuse ourselves with electronic games. Computers are also part of laboratory equipment and can be seen in the offices of dentists and doctors.

What does this mean for methods of making a living? You can work in a fast-food restaurant and have the cash register do the arithmetic for you. You can add up your checkbook and have a calculator do the additions and subtractions. You can pilot an airplane and have a computer help you with the mathematical problems associated with flying, and if you are an engineer you almost certainly have a computer help you with your calculations. Mortgage computations are easily done on a spreadsheet, and letters are written more readily with word processing software. In the world of real work, mathematics is now quite different from what it was even as recently as, say, the 1970s, and certainly different from what it was in the 1950s. It used to be that if you wanted to balance your checkbook, or see if you had enough money for some purchase, you had no choice but to write some numbers on a piece of paper and make use of some familiar symbol-manipulation algorithm. Today you have a choice, and most of us choose some other way of proceeding. In the world of real work, the change is unmistakable.

THE WORLD OF SCHOOLS AND EXPECTATIONS

The situation is greatly complicated by the fact that popular expectations, bureaucratic requirements, and schools have not kept pace with these changes. Thus, while we may know on good evidence (see, e.g., Cockcroft, 1982; Howson, Keitel, & Kilpatrick, 1981; MSEB, 1990; Romberg, 1992) that the needs of real work have changed, and that present school algorithms do not serve well the needs of everyday life, school curricula and pedagogy do not reflect these facts. This is true at every level of expertise, from someone preparing a meal at home, or shopping in a supermarket, to the military leaders planning the defense of our nation. Lave's (1988) observations of people preparing meals in their own homes show that ordinary people typically are able to solve any necessary mathematical problems, but probably do not use methods that are taught in school. The same is true for youngsters parking cars in Brazil when they need to make change, and milk deliverers in England when they fill orders (Schliemann, Dos Santos, & Da Costa, 1993). The list is long, and rapidly growing, but schools do not, for the most part, respond. Romberg (1992) comments on this by referring to an educational classic, *The Saber-Tooth Curriculum* (Peddiwell, 1939).

> The world has changed and schools need to change; otherwise we will still be teaching our young to use fire to scare saber-tooth tigers long after . . . [saber-tooth tigers] have become extinct. (p. 433)

For teachers, the failure of schools and expectations to keep pace with reality poses something of a dilemma: If one ignores the inappropriate tests that students will be required to deal with, and focuses instead on what they will really need to know, one may limit the students' futures, because those inappropriate tests are still there and still constitute hurdles that must be dealt with. Yet, if one accepts these inappropriate tests as main targets, one leaves the inappropriate obstacles in place and may fail to help students learn the things they ultimately will need to know in order to survive in the world of real work and real life. We would argue that, if teaching is to be a true profession, this is a matter that teachers cannot afford to ignore. (See also Apple, 1992a, p. 427, and Maier, 1987.)

WHAT IS MATHEMATICS?

The heart of the matter may lie in a new idea of what constitutes "mathematics." In most traditional school curricula, "mathematics" was seen to mean a collection of algorithms for paper-and-pencil symbol manipulation, which were to be learned by rote. One might describe this as conformity to a prespecified orthodoxy; there was one right way to solve each addition (or multiplication, or subtraction, or division) problem, and students were expected to learn this "one right way." If one accepts this as the goal, then there are fairly obvious ways to try to achieve it, and to evaluate both the success of students and the success of instructional programs.

The newly emerging position, embodied in the *Standards* and in *Everybody Counts,* rejects this view. In *Everybody Counts* this collection of traditional rote algorithms is referred to as "the shopkeeper arithmetic of a bygone age" (MSEB, 1989, p. 20); this is not what you will use if you are working in a modern fast-food restaurant, where arithmetic is done by the cash register. It is certainly not the heart of what you will use if you become a civil engineer, or a physician, or a psychologist—or even in your own personal housekeeping.

What is needed today is closer to what the *Standards* refer to as "mathematical power." This is not entirely easy to understand, but we will attempt to define it by giving some examples. One example, which we will present below, shows some second graders in Alabama inventing their own methods for adding and subtracting. This might seem too ambitious for most children, let alone for special education students, but the present evidence suggests that it is *easier* to invent one's own methods than it is to memorize meaningless methods conveyed by other people. A second example deals with fourth graders who are inventing the idea of "mathematical proof." This is an elusive and abstract idea that one almost certainly could never have told to them with any good results. They were, however, able to invent the idea for themselves.

Davis (1992) summarizes the difference between the old and new views of mathematics (see Figure 3.1).

THE CHANGES SCHOOLS NEED TO MAKE

The important NCTM *Standards* present a number of suggestions on changes that need to be made in school mathematics. For example:

> On CONTENT: Clearly, paper-and-pencil computation cannot continue to dominate the curriculum, or there will be insufficient time for children to learn other, more important mathematics. (p. 44)
>
> On PEDAGOGICAL STRATEGY: Strong evidence suggests that conceptual approaches to computation instruction result in good achievement, good retention, and a reduction in the amount of time children need to master computational skills. Furthermore, many of the errors children typically make are less prevalent [when a stronger conceptual foundation is developed in the child's mind]. Helping children develop thinking strategies for learning basic facts enables them to understand relationships and to reason mathematically. (p. 44)
>
> On the EXPERIENCES THAT CHILDREN NEED: Children need more time to explore and to invent alternative strategies for computing mentally. Both mental computation and estimation should be ongoing emphases . . . integrated throughout all computational work. The frequent use of calculators, mental computation, and estimation helps children develop a more realistic view of computation and enables them to be more flexible. . . . Calculators should be used to solve problems that require tedious calculations. (p. 45)
>
> Exploratory experiences in preparation for paper-and-pencil computation give children the opportunity to develop underlying concepts related to partitioning numbers, operating on the parts, and combining the results. (p. 47)
>
> On the ALLOCATION OF TIME: Educators [must] rethink traditional scope-and-sequence decisions. . . . Teachers must reduce the time and the emphasis they devote to computation and focus instead on . . . other mathematical topics. (p. 46)
>
> On TESTING AND EXPECTATIONS: Premature expectations for students' mastery of computational procedures not only cause poor initial learning and poor retention but also require that large amounts of instructional time be spent on teaching and reteaching basic skills. (p. 46)

Figure 3.1 Old and New Views of Mathematics Compared

Previous View	**Newly Emerging View**
"Mathematics" is about *symbols written on paper.*	"Mathematics" is *a way of thinking* that involves *mental representations* of problem situations and of relevant knowledge, that involves dealing with these mental representations, and that involves using *heuristics.* It may make use of written symbols (or even physical representations with manipulatable materials), but the real essence is something that takes place within the student's mind.
Knowledge of mathematics is constructed from words and sentences (usually sentences about what to write on the paper, and where to write it).	These critical mental representations are built up from pieces learned as a result of previous experience. This often means concrete experience, but it does not always mean this. One kind of "piece" often is called an *assimilation paradigm.* The key pieces of mental representations usually are *not* about written notations—they are not about the symbols, but rather about the things denoted by the symbols. The mental representation of a 7-foot-tall man is not primarily about the numeral *7,* or about the three-letter word *man,* but rather about a very tall male human being (maybe a basketball player?). *Words* may be used, primarily to guide the construction of mental representations, but the mental representations themselves are *not* built out of words. (If I say "dog," I may cause you to think of the three-letter word "dog." In my case, I think first of a standard poodle named Eudoxus, who was large, friendly, and black.)
"Teaching mathematics" means getting students to write the right thing in the right place on the paper.	"Teaching mathematics" is a matter of guiding and coaching the student's own development of his/her repertoire of basic building blocks (from which mental representations can be constructed) and helping students to develop skill in building and using mental representations.
The point of learning mathematics is to learn a few facts (such as "3 times 4 = 12"), a few standard algorithms for writing symbols on paper, and a few definitions. The point of advanced mathematics is to memorize a few proofs. In both cases, the goal is conformity to a prescribed orthodoxy—one wants students to write the standard algorithm in the standard way.	The goal of studying mathematics is to learn to think in a very powerful way, as described above.

(Continued)

Figure 3.1 *(continued)*

Previous View	Newly Emerging View
Students would not be able to invent algorithms themselves.	Students often invent their own algorithms, even though they may try to conceal this from the view of adults who would probably disapprove.
"Assessment" means finding how well students conform to the prescribed orthodox rituals. This is easily done by asking them to carry out certain standard calculations. It is often unnecessary to observe the student's actual work, but merely to check that he or she arrives at the correct answer.	"Assessment" or "evaluation" means finding out how a student thinks about some interesting problem. It is usually more instructive to ask the student to solve some novel problem that he/she has not seen before, and to observe carefully how the student deals with it. Frequently students can be asked to try to talk aloud as they work, to tell us (as best they can) what and how they are thinking about the problem.

Source: Reprinted from Davis (1992).

> On WORKING WITH STUDENTS: Success is possible for almost all children when they receive careful instruction. Still, teachers should be sensitive to problems individual children might have and should be prepared to use a variety of methods to teach and assess computational knowledge. (p. 47).

Many of these remarks—especially the last one—may not be news to many experienced special education teachers, but they do stand in opposition to the present trend toward greater reliance on statewide or nationwide testing programs. The desire to make sure that no child is being left out (which is presumably the motivation for statewide testing) is admirable and proper, but in practice these statewide testing programs all too often get transformed into something else: a set of abstract requirements and a timetable that may fail completely to take account of individual personal attributes of students, that ignore specific student needs for sense making, and that substitute performance for understanding, which in the long run is a bad exchange. The changes that the *Standards* ask of teachers and schools may seem simple and straightforward but in fact are not easy at all. Using manipulatable materials in helping students learn mathematics requires special understanding on the part of teachers. So, too, does a shift toward more emphasis on student thought processes. These and other changes recommended by the NCTM can make important improvements, but they demand careful study by teachers who wish to implement them.

Teaching and Learning

For teachers confronted with these new goals, there is genuine good news. Children like to think about mathematics, and they are actually good at it.

We who teach merely need to find ways to take advantage of this proclivity and to help the children acquire ever greater power in thinking about mathematical situations.

The situation is described in *Everybody Counts:*

> All students engage in a great deal of invention as they learn mathematics; they impose their own interpretation on what is presented to create a theory that makes sense to them. Students do not learn simply a subset of what they have been shown. Instead, they use new information to modify their prior beliefs. As a consequence, each student's knowledge is uniquely personal. (MSEB, 1989, p. 59)

To give greater emphasis to this point, a special note is presented:

> MYTH: Students learn by remembering what they are taught.
> REALITY: Students construct meaning as they learn mathematics. They use what they are taught to modify their prior beliefs and behavior, not simply to record and store what they are told. It is students' acts of construction and invention that build their mathematical power and enable them to solve problems they have never seen before. (p. 59)

These are both very brief statements and may therefore be hard to understand, but we would argue that they are right on target! The viewpoint described in these brief accounts often is called "constructivism." (For a more extended discussion, see Davis, Maher, & Noddings, 1990.)

One can see constructivist teaching at work in the videotape *Double-Digit Addition: A Teacher Uses Piaget's Theory* (Kamii, 1989), where second-grade children who have had experience with numbers as a result of playing simple games are asked to *invent* ways to solve some addition problems.

In the videotaped classroom, the teacher poses the problem 87 + 24 = ?, and asks the children to invent some ways to find the answer. One girl says, "Eighty and twenty are a hundred. Six and four is ten, so seven and four are eleven, so the answer is one hundred and eleven." [There is not even a six in the problem! This is really an instance of taking the initiative!]

Despite the title, the videotaped lesson also includes subtraction.

The teacher poses another problem: 26 − 17 = ? One child says, "Twenty minus ten is ten; take away seven . . . leaves three; now add the six, so it's nine." She, in effect, as a second grader, invents negative numbers (although, of course, she lacks the language to deal with them as we would): "Twenty, take away ten, is ten. Six from seven is zero." This is what she *says,* but she has the right idea—she knows that six of the seven have been "canceled out," but she still needs to find one more to "take away." "One from ten is nine," so she "went and got the extra one that she needed." Her tone of voice announces that this "nine" is her final answer, and she is *very* confident about it.

Traditional practice would assume that the only possible way to proceed would be to tell these second graders how to add and how to subtract. The constructivist approach typically avoids this. Instead, the children get extensive experience working with numbers, often in the form of playing games, after which *the children themselves invent ways to add and to subtract.*

Second-grade children inventing ways to add and to subtract, as the videotape shows, is not unusual. Many children regularly do this, but school programs typically ignore this fact—often with the result that "school" methods may be in conflict with methods invented by the children themselves. This conflict can create real problems (see, e.g., Corwin, 1989; McNeill, 1988). In the long run, one has more—not less—success with children when one tries to give them space to think and one tries to work with the child's thought processes. Memorizing meaningless symbol manipulation is *not* a normal or natural or easy human activity; making sense of one's environment is.

We might adopt the format of *Everybody Counts* and write:

> MYTH: Children cannot think for themselves. It is necessary for knowledgeable adults to tell children how to do mathematics.
>
> REALITY: It is usually easier for children to invent appropriate ways of proceeding than it is for them to take in someone else's words, try to make sense of them, try to interpret them as directions, try to carry them out, and try to remember them. However, this kind of learning requires very different behavior from teachers. Primarily, it requires that teachers listen to children and treat the children's thinking with respect.

Of course, children cannot possibly invent "appropriate ways of proceeding" unless they are provided with considerable experience, from which they can build mental representations that can then become "tools to think with." They cannot be expected to invent "the one right way of proceeding," which is really in part a question of historical accident. One can invent "an appropriate" way, but one cannot necessarily invent "the official" way. Fortunately, it usually is not necessary, in the world of real work, to use some special "officially approved" way. What is needed is *any way that works.*

One can argue that there may be good reason, *after* a child has invented his or her own methods, to show them some "official" method, on the grounds that it may be more efficient or that it will be what other people may expect. At this point in the child's learning, there usually will be no great mystery about "ways of proceeding," and it is relatively easy to see that one is faced with nothing more than somebody else's way of dealing with problems of the type in question. If one has worked out the same sort of thing oneself, there is nothing basically mysterious to cause confusion.

The proposed new emphasis on the thought processes of individual students represents a major departure from typical past school practice. The evidence is clear: Students *do* think for themselves, sometimes in very precise and powerful ways, which ought to be made the basis for classwork—but sometimes in very *unsatisfactory* ways, which need to be recognized and modified, lest they cause serious subsequent confusion. (See, for example, Corwin, 1989; MacNeill, 1988.) These are not minor matters: They are significant for students, whose progress is directly involved, and they are demanding on teachers, most of whom have not learned the skill of interacting with the thought processes of individual students.

The Importance of Mental Symbols and Nonverbal Teaching Methods

One aspect of the new approach deserves special emphasis. In earlier views, an addition problem such as $3 + 2 = 5$ often would have been seen as dealing primarily with the written notations "3" and "2" and "+" and "=" and "5." The contemporary view has a different goal. As it sometimes is expressed, "one wishes the students to regard those symbols as *windows,* through which one can look and see real situations and real experience." Thus, for the example $3 + 2 = 5$, one would wish the child to be able to visualize something like three wooden blocks in one pile, and two blocks in another pile. This visualization has a great power that is not present within the written symbols of mathematics. One can, for example, imagine shifting one block from the pile of two, and placing it atop the pile of three. This gives a pile of four, and a pile that consists of only one block, which could be described as $4 + 1 = 5$.

When a child thinks in terms of mental symbols such as the wooden blocks, he or she can call upon a vast experience of playing with blocks (or pebbles, or buttons, or coins, or whatever) and hence has a powerful collection of symbols that are available for mental manipulation or mental "visualization." (See, for example, Davis, 1984.)

Traditional school practice often has attempted to deal with mathematics by "telling" students various things in the usual form of English statements, directions, or explanations. This usually is not effective, because most children are unable to connect the teacher's words to an appropriate set of meaningful mental symbols. Usually, much more can be accomplished by such other devices as working with physical materials or letting several students argue with one another, perhaps with a teacher as moderator.

In a videotaped study of fifth-grade children working on area, a girl named Samantha who is trying to find how many square tiles would fit into a certain region, inadvertently uses tiles that overlap. Traditional practice probably would have told her this, in so many words. In the taped lesson the teacher, believing that such words would not really connect with meaningful symbols in Samantha's mind, chose instead to have several children discuss their methods; in the course of this discussion, it became clear that Samantha's method could give several different answers, depending on how much overlap she allowed. After a while, the teacher proposed that they think in terms of buying carpet and asked Samantha which method she would use to get carpet of the right size. She chose a method proposed by another student (which would in fact give the correct answer). Samantha volunteered the remark that her method would have them buying too much carpet—but, she added, if they did use her method the carpeting would be very deep and very springy. It was clear that she was getting a far clearer idea of what "area" was really all about. The teacher believed that this could not have been achieved, at so deep a level of understanding, had he merely told Samantha what she ought to have been doing.

What Teachers Need to Do

A discussion of teaching in *Everybody Counts* begins as follows:

> In reality, no one can *teach* mathematics. Effective teachers are those who can stimulate students to *learn* mathematics. Educational research offers compelling evidence that students learn mathematics well only when they *construct* their own mathematical understanding. (MSEB, 1989, p. 58)

One of the main tools that a teacher can use in helping students construct their own mathematical understanding is to *listen* to students and to *take seriously the students' thinking.* Probably the most effective ways to acquire this kind of teaching skill are: (1) to study videotapes of teachers who use this approach; (2) to videotape *one's own* students as they work on mathematical tasks; and (3) to have colleagues observe one's own work with students and discuss it with you afterwards. (Be warned: This can be very stressful! Teachers, too, can be confronted with the need for agonizing reappraisals.)

One videotape, entitled *The Development of Fourth-Graders' Ideas About Mathematical Proofs* (Maher, 1992), shows an assessment session where 4 fourth graders present some mathematical proofs. In effect these children have been asked: "Why have human beings found it necessary to invent the idea of 'mathematical proofs'? By the way, what *is* a 'mathematical proof'?

How would you make a mathematical proof? How could you criticize a mathematical proof? If someone found a flaw in your proof, how would you go about the task of repairing it?"

Of course, if the task were presented to fourth graders in precisely this form, nothing good would be likely to result. What the teacher has done, however, does achieve a worthwhile result. She has given the children a large supply of blue cubes and a large supply of red cubes, and has asked them to build "as many towers as you can that are three cubes tall, and are all different." At this point this is perhaps still not really a *mathematical* task. Then the teacher asks: "Please convince the other people at your table that you have not left any out, and that you do not have any duplicates." Now it is a *very* mathematical task—one suddenly needs to prove something about things that are not even present, one needs to prove that any tower that is not in the collection *cannot exist*!

During the course of this session, lasting perhaps 11 minutes, four proofs are presented. Stephanie (a different student in a different class from the previous videotape) says she will make "all the towers that have no blue cubes in them" and does so—there can be only one, consisting entirely of red cubes. Then she says she will make "all the towers that have exactly one blue cube in them." The blue cube must be either at the top, or in the middle, or at the bottom, so there are exactly three of these. Stephanie exhibits them all.

Now she says she will build "all the towers with exactly two blue cubes," and builds two such towers, one with a red at the top and two blue cubes below it, and the other with a red at the bottom, with two blue cubes above it. She then goes on to build "all of the towers with exactly three blue cubes," and does so—but as she is working, Geoffrey is objecting that she has left out one of the towers having exactly two blue cubes. Stephanie says she has not, that she was dealing only with "two blue cubes stuck together," and that she will now go on to deal with "two blue cubes stuck apart," and she builds this. Geoffrey argues that it would be more systematic to deal with *all* of the "exactly two blues" at the same time, and makes an alternative proof based on this. A third student, Milin, says that since the difficulty arises in keeping track of the "exactly two blue cubes," one should deal with this by saying that, since the towers are three cubes tall, if exactly two cubes are blue, then exactly one cube is red, and it is easier to keep track of the single red cube.

Finally, three students, working together, make what might be called a "proof by mathematical induction": They build all possible towers two cubes tall, then point out that from each of these one can build two towers three cubes tall, by putting atop each one either a red cube or else a blue cube. Stephanie then takes this further, concluding that if you were building

Figure 3.2 Teaching Practices Advocated by NCTM Standards

Student Experience

In the lesson recorded on the Kamii videotape, the children were able to invent their own methods for adding and subtracting *because they had had extensive previous experience* playing games that used dice or other materials where counting and combining quantities were an essential part of the activity. This matter of providing a *large amount* of prior experience in meaningful activities is essential for the successful use of the approach in the *Standards.*

The Use of Physical Materials

In nearly all of the examples considered, the actual use of physical materials played an essential role. For most students, only the actual use of tactile materials will enable them to built the kind of robust mental symbols (of blocks, stacks, pebbles, etc.) that can be manipulated within one's mind and that can form a basis for abstractions, such as 3 + 2 = 5, etc.

Discussion Among Students

When students discuss things with other students, they listen in a way that they do not usually listen to teachers. Children often interpret a teacher's words as a set of instructions on what to do, or how to do it. They rarely hear other students' words in this same way and are more likely to think about the words, with a very good chance that they will find themselves disagreeing and subsequently arguing. Few activities lead to a deep understanding of mathematics more quickly than arguing about the subject does.

Taking Students' Thinking Seriously

Past school practice typically has built on an implicit "empty-vessel" theory of knowledge acquisition: Children are "empty vessels," and into this void, a teacher needs to pour knowledge. Hence it seemed entirely reasonable to pay scant heed to the way a child was thinking. (Indeed, when seeing videotapes of children arguing about mathematics, most adults are amazed that children would ever do such a thing.) The modern approach advocated in the *Standards* would change this, and instead pay great attention to the way a child is thinking about the matter at hand. The gradual development of a child's ideas is what mathematics teaching is all about.

towers ten cubes tall, there would be 1,024 of them. These students indicate that they know very well exactly why they are doing this in such systematic ways—"Without a system, it would be harder to convince you!"

To summarize, the *Standards* propose a new view of mathematics and a new view of how to help students learn mathematics. We would mislead readers if we claimed that what is involved could be reduced to a simple list. However, the four matters in Figure 3.2 that play especially important roles in the kind of teaching that the *Standards* advocate, deserve explicit mention.

Assessment

The approach in the *Standards* will be seriously hampered if traditional evaluation measures continue to be used. These consist almost exclusively of asking students to perform some calculation and checking to see whether they use the approved method correctly. The new standards require a shift in emphasis toward *understanding* and assessment needs to reflect this shift (for a complete discussion, see Brewer et al., 1991; California State Department of Education, 1989, 1991; Kamii & Lewis, 1991; Stenmark, 1989).

From this new perspective regarding large-scale testing, it may make sense to create statewide testing programs as a form of quality control, to see that students are being taught the proper skills. What students need to acquire is not so much rote algorithms, but rather what the *Standards* call "mathematical power." This is explained further in *Everybody Counts*:

> Mathematics today is a diverse discipline that deals with data, measurements, and observations from science; with inference, deduction, and proof; and with mathematical models of natural phenomena, of human behavior, and of social systems. . . . As a practical matter, mathematics is a science of pattern and order. Its domain is not molecules or cells, but numbers, chance, form, algorithms, and change. As a science of abstract objects, mathematics relies on logic rather than on observation as its standard of truth, yet employs observation, simulation, and even experimentation as a means of discovering truth. (MSEB, 1989, p. 5)

In summary, if one wants to know the sum of a column of numbers, a hand-held calculator costing three dollars can give the answer. For most practical problems, however, one needs to be able to think.

ADVANTAGES AND DISADVANTAGES

There are two advantages in continuing the "traditional" approach. First, there is considerable safety in doing what one knows how to do best, which for most teachers is to build on the idea of "telling" students what to do and how to do it, "showing" them how, and "drilling" them on these algorithms. It also seems to make good common sense: If you want students to know something, shouldn't you tell them? Second, in the short run, this direct approach to sharply targeted explicit goals usually *seems* to succeed (even though, in the long run, it usually fails).

There are also disadvantages in continuing the traditional approach. First, while students can imitate and recall rote knowledge reasonably well in the short run, few people can assemble these small pieces into meaningful larger wholes that give power to one's thinking in the long run. Second, although the traditional view is that "remembering" should be the easiest way to learn, this in fact seems not to be true. For most students—probably including many special education students—it is easier to make sense of things than it is to remember meaningless rote material. Third, continuing the traditional approach gives students only one available path. If a student has trouble negotiating this path, no alternative is available. "Present educational practice in the United States offers students only one path to understanding—a long, dimly-lit journey through a mountain of meaningless manipulations, with the reward of power and understanding available only to those who complete the journey" (MSEB, 1989, p. 58). Finally, there is little evidence to suggest that rote learning provides a sound foundation for understanding for most students. If all we give students is rote skill in paper-and-pencil algorithms, there are few practical problems that they will be able to solve, or even to understand.

As Apple (1992b) warns, what is best for students may not always determine what is done in schools, where unvoiced implicit political considerations may ultimately become the determining factor. As professionals, we must still give serious consideration to the question of what will be most helpful to those whom we teach, whatever the social agenda of the day may seem to be.

Which of the two competing and opposing views of how to improve school mathematics comes to have the greater influence on U.S. schools, will have important consequences for American education and American society. The impact on special education may be even greater.

REFERENCES

Apple, M. W. (1992a). Do the *Standards* go far enough? Power, policy, and practice in mathematics education. *Journal for Research in Mathematics Education, 23*(5), 412–431.

Apple, M. W. (1992b). Thinking more politically about the challenges before us: A response to Romberg. *Journal for Research in Mathematics Education, 23*(5), 438–440.

Brewer, W. R., et al. (1991). *Looking beyond "the answer": Vermont's Mathematics Portfolio Assessment Program.* Montpelier: Vermont Department of Education.

California State Department of Education. (1989). *A Question of Thinking: A first look at students' performance on open-ended questions in mathematics.* Sacramento: California State Department of Education.

California State Department of Education. (1991). *A sampler of mathematics assessment.* Sacramento: California Department of Education.

Cockcroft, S. W. (1982). *Mathematics counts: Report of the committee of inquiry into the teaching of mathematics in schools.* London: Her Majesty's Stationery Office.

Corwin, R. B. (1989). Multiplication as original sin. *Journal of Mathematical Behavior, 8*(2), 223–225.

Davis, R. B. (1984). *Learning mathematics: The cognitive science approach to mathematics education.* London: Routledge.

Davis, R. B. (1992). Understanding "understanding." *Journal of Mathematical Behavior, 11*(3), 225–241.

Davis, R. B., Maher, C. A., & Noddings, N. (1990). *Constructivist views on the teaching and learning of mathematics* (Monograph No. 4). *Journal for Research in Mathematics Education.* Reston, VA: National Council of Teachers of Mathematics.

Howson, G., Keitel, C., & Kilpatrick, J. (1981). *Curriculum development in mathematics.* Cambridge: Cambridge University Press.

Kamii, C. (1989). *Double-digit addition: A teacher uses Piaget's theory* [Videotape]. New York: Teachers College Press.

Kamii, C., & Lewis, B. A. (1991). Achievement tests in primary mathematics: Perpetuating lower-order thinking. *Arithmetic Teacher, 38*(9), 4–9.

Kozol, J. (1991). *Savage inequalities.* New York: Crown.

Maher, C. A. (1992). *The development of fourth-graders' ideas about mathematical proofs* [Videotape]. Available from Mathematics Projects with Schools, Graduate School of Education, Rutgers University, 10 Seminary Place, New Brunswick, NJ 08903.

Maier, E. A. (1987). Basic mathematical skills or school survival skills? *Arithmetic Teacher, 35*(1), 2.

Mathematical Sciences Education Board (MSEB). (1989). *Everybody counts: A report to the nation on the future of mathematics education.* Washington, DC: National Academy Press.

Mathematical Sciences Education Board (MSEB). (1990). *Reshaping school mathematics: A philosophy and framework for curriculum.* Washington, DC: National Academy Press.

McNeill, R. (1988). A reflection on when I loved math and how I stopped. *Journal of Mathematical Behavior, 7*(1), 45–50.

National Council of Teachers of Mathematics (NCTM). (1989). *Curriculum and evaluation standards for school mathematics.* Reston, VA: Author.

Peddiwell, J. A. (1939). *The saber-tooth curriculum.* New York: McGraw-Hill.

Romberg, T. A. (1992). Further thoughts on the *Standards:* A reaction to Apple. *Journal for Research in Mathematics Education, 23*(5), 432–437.

Schliemann, A. D., Dos Santos, C. M., & Da Costa, S. C. V. (1993). Constructing written algorithms: A case study. *Journal of Mathematical Behavior, 12*(2), 155–172.

Stenmark, J. K. (1989). *Assessment alternatives in mathematics: An overview of assessment techniques that promote learning.* Berkeley: Lawrence Hall of Science.

Response

What Does the "New View" of School Mathematics Mean for Students with Mild Disabilities?

Marjorie Montague

The National Assessment of Educational Progress, which is conducted every 4 years in mathematics, has indicated that the mathematical performance of students is consistently and generally poor (Mullis, Dossey, Owen, & Phillips, 1993). Porter (1989) suggested that poor performance in mathematics can be attributed to curricular idiosyncracies that include teaching large numbers of mathematics topics for exposure with no expectation of student mastery, repeating instruction from grade to grade, emphasizing skill instruction to the detriment of conceptual understanding or application, and being inconsistent with regard to the amount of mathematics instruction students receive. Thus, poor performance for the majority of students in the regular program may translate to a poor curriculum and poor pedagogy. The new standards issued by the National Council of Teachers of Mathematics (NCTM) for learning and teaching mathematics, by focusing on these curricular and instructional concerns, could have a significant impact on mathematics instruction for all students.

The goals associated with the "new view of school mathematics" described by Davis and Maher are based on two national reports on the state and future of mathematics education in the United States: *Everybody Counts* (Mathematical Sciences Education Board [MSEB], 1989) and *Curriculum and Evaluation Standards for School Mathematics* (National Council of Teachers of Mathematics [NCTM, 1989). A third report, *Professional Standards for Teaching Mathematics,* also prepared by the National Council of Teachers of Mathematics (1991), outlined "what teachers need to know to teach toward new goals for mathematics education and how teaching should be evaluated for the purpose of improvement" (p. vii). Although these reports, overall, do not refer specifically to students in special education programs, the *Professional Standards* identify "comprehensive mathe-

Curriculum Trends, Special Education, and Reform: Refocusing the Conversation. ISBN 0-8077-3562-0 (pbk), ISBN 0-8077-3563-9 (cloth).

matics education of every child as its most compelling goal" (p. 4). With this acknowledgment, "what teachers need to know" includes knowledge and skills associated with teaching children with disabilities.

The *Sixteenth Annual Report to Congress on the Implementation of the Individuals with Disabilities Act* (U.S. Department of Education, 1994) indicated that the vast majority of students in special education—approximately 95%—received their education in regular school buildings during the 1991–92 school year. Of this number, 35% were served in regular classes and 36% in resource rooms. Placement in regular programs for all or part of the school day puts students with mild to moderate learning problems at risk for failure in academic subjects. These students, primarily because of differences in ability, achievement, motivation, or behavior, frequently need special curricular and instructional adaptations or accommodations.

Because of the movement toward inclusion, especially for students with mild disabilities, regular and special education teachers and administrators are becoming increasingly concerned about how to address individual differences in regular classrooms. What are the characteristics of students with mild disabilities that may have an adverse effect on their mathematics learning as it relates to this *new* view of the subject areas as described by Davis and Maher?

Students with mild disabilities, including learning disabilities, mild mental retardation, and behavior disorders, typically display a variety of learning characteristics that can adversely affect their mathematics performance:

- Memory and strategic deficits can differentially affect mathematics performance, causing some students to experience difficulty conceptualizing mathematical operations, representing and automatically recalling math facts, conceptualizing and learning algorithms and mathematical formulae, or solving mathematical word problems.
- Language and communication disorders may interfere with students' functioning when they are expected to read, write, and discuss ideas about mathematics.
- Deficiencies in processes and strategies specifically associated with solving mathematical word problems also can interfere with students' conceptual understanding of problem situations and how to address those situations mathematically.
- Low motivation, poor self-esteem, and a history of academic failure can arrest a student's desire to value mathematics and to become confident in his or her ability to become mathematically literate.

Unlike their classmates who may learn despite the system, students with mild disabilities need explicit instruction, systematic guidance, and continuous monitoring to ensure active participation and progress in learning. For example, teachers will need to know how to reinforce conceptual learning for students who have problems understanding and integrating concepts into their knowledge systems. Teachers also will need to know how to engage students with mild disabilities in classroom activities that require problem-solving, reasoning, and verbal abilities. Finally, teachers will need to know how to teach students to represent linguistic and numerical information in mathematical word problems.

Several recent trends in educational practice focus on instructional strategies for effective inclusion of children with mild learning and behavioral disabilities into regular classrooms. The remainder of this response describes emerging practices for mathematics assessment and instruction, and collaborative teaching models to facilitate implementation of these practices in the classroom.

TRENDS IN REGULAR AND SPECIAL EDUCATION

Of the many trends in regular and special education, I have selected three that I believe may directly affect the success of mathematics reform in our schools. These trends seem to correspond well with Davis and Maher's suggestions regarding changes that schools need to make as specified in the NCTM *Standards.* They suggested schools need to change (a) the content of instruction by moving from computation to problem-solving instruction, (b) the pedagogical strategy by emphasizing conceptual approaches to instruction, (c) the experiences of children by providing opportunities to explore and invent new strategies for computing, (d) the amount of time allocated for mathematical learning, (e) the assessment techniques for evaluating children's learning, and (f) the instructional activities to engage students actively in the learning process. The trends in regular and special education that can make mathematics teaching and learning more effective for these students include (a) the use of technology to enhance mathematics learning for students with special needs, (b) cognitively based approaches appropriate for all students, and (c) authentic assessment techniques to measure progress.

Technology for Mathematics Learning

There is ample evidence that computers are natural tools for developing mathematical knowledge and skills in students (Roberts, Carter, Friel, & Miller, 1988). The numerous benefits of computer-assisted instruction (CAI), particularly for low- and underachieving students, have been well documented (Montague, 1987). Moreover, new technologies are available that integrate computers, CD-ROM, hypermedia, and software designed specifically to enhance conceptual thinking and problem solving. These new technologies assist the teacher even more than traditional CAI in providing individualized, quality mathematics instruction to students of varying abilities. To illustrate, the Cognition and Technology Group (1990) at Vanderbilt University has developed several integrated software packages that focus on building confidence, skills, and knowledge that students need to solve problems and become independent thinkers and learners.

Utilizing a concept termed *anchored instruction,* this group studied the effects of situating instruction in videodisc-based, problem-solving environments. These environments permit "sustained exploration by students and teachers and enable them to understand the kinds of problems and opportunities that experts in various areas encounter and the knowledge that these experts use as tools" (p. 3). Their Jasper Series exemplifies an integrated program whose primary focus is on mathematical problem formulation and problem solving. It requires students to work cooperatively as they solve fairly complex mathematical problems that involve the generation of multiple subgoals. In this program, data are embedded throughout so that students first have to generate the problem to be solved and then find the relevant mathematical information that was presented in the video story. The Vanderbilt group has found that both teachers and students are enthusiastic about the program. This technology package appears to foster communication and cooperative problem solving while improving mathematical skills of students.

Not only is technology important for increasing active learning for students, but it also can be used to increase active teaching. Hayden, Gersten, and Carnine (1992) examined the effects of frequent feedback to teachers on student performance during mathematics instruction using a computer networking system to check student understanding of mathematical concepts during math lessons. They conducted their study in general education mathematics classes that included students with mild disabilities. When teachers in the study were coached about how to use the data generated by the system, they increased the amount of time spent on active teaching and providing feedback as well as the number of problems they gave and questions they asked. Teachers also reported that the data shown on the monitor screen enabled them to determine more precisely whether students understood skills presented during the lesson.

In sum, technology can be used to meet goals associated with active mathematics learning and teaching, problem-solving and reasoning ability, cooperative learning, and communication about mathematics. If incorporated appropriately into the learning environment, computers and their companion technologies seem well suited to promoting the "new view of school mathematics."

Cognitively Based Approaches

A second trend that should have a major impact on improving mathematics instruction for students with mild disabilities is the development of cognitively based approaches for teaching mathematics. One program, Cognitively Guided Instruction (CGI), was developed for regular elementary school classrooms (Fennema, Carpenter, & Peterson, 1989). This program provides teachers with knowledge about how children learn mathematical concepts and how they think about mathematics during activity-based learning. The authors stress ongoing assessment of student learning by listening to and observing students as they solve problems in small groups. Teachers develop skills in selecting problems using real-life situations, interacting with students as they go about solving problems, building upon the students' responses, prompting students to apply their knowledge of problem solving, challenging students to test and evaluate their conclusions, and guiding students as they explore new concepts and strategies for solving problems. Students with mild disabilities can participate in these cooperative learning groups, and special and regular education teachers can then share their observations and plan together how they will reinforce learning for these students.

Another program (Montague, 1989, 1992; Montague, Applegate, & Marquard, 1993) also focuses on cognitively based instruction for mathematical problem solving. This program was designed to teach cognitive and metacognitive strategies for solving multistep word problems to middle school students with learning disabilities. To accommodate these students in regular classes, special and regular teachers could easily cooperate in assessing and instructing students. As a team, they first would identify students who need cognitive strategy instruction in mathematical problem solving, using assessment techniques suggested by Montague (1992). Then, the special education teacher would provide intensive strategy instruction for mathematical problem solving to groups of eight to ten students. Most students are able to apply problem-solving strategies effectively and efficiently after 2 or 3 weeks of small-group instruction. When students master the strategies and reach a performance criterion, they should be able to participate in problem-solving activities in the regular classroom. The regular classroom teacher then reinforces strategy application and provides periodic review and practice, which are important for maintaining performance levels (Montague, 1992). As a follow-up to strategy instruction, teachers work together to create interesting and challenging problem-solving situations for students to promote generalization of problem-solving strategies to real-life experiences.

Authentic Assessment

The third trend that may change thinking about mathematics education is authentic assessment. The "new view" of school mathematics has a focus on authentic outcomes related to both academic and real-life experiences. The NCTM *Standards* included suggestions for evaluating mathematics learning with respect to both content and process standards. They recommended that multiple sources of information be used to evaluate student learning in light of real-world problem solving. As Ysseldyke, Thurlow, and Shriner (1992) have pointed out, the NCTM position fits well with special education's emphasis on real-life outcome goals. Student learning can be assessed in a variety of ways, such as written and oral tests or demonstration and formal observation.

Typical testing modifications for students with mild disabilities include using computers for responding, pointing to rather than writing or verbalizing responses, having more time to take tests, taking breaks during testing, and taking tests individually rather than in a group. By using simple accommodations such as these, we often are able to get a better indication of the performance of students with disabilities who may not be able to sustain attention under timed conditions and often may need more time to process information.

Other, less conventional evaluation techniques for documenting learning outcomes of students, could take the form of portfolios of mathematical activities that go beyond typical textbook activities. As an example, the Mathematical Problem-Solving Assessment–Short Form (MPSA–SF) is an interview designed to gain informal information about student perception of mathematical ability, attitude toward mathematics and mathematical problem solving, and knowledge and use of problem-solving strategies (Montague, 1992). The items on the MPSA–SF are both closed- and open-ended. As part of the interview, students solve three mathematical word problems and then respond to approximately 30 questions about mathematical problem solving. The interview yields an individualized "cognitive profile" to help in determining a student's perception of performance and level of strategy knowledge, use, and control. Additionally, error analysis of the word problems provides information on the types of errors students make and their specific strengths and weaknesses in regard to problem-solving knowledge and application.

Portfolio contents also may include other forms of documentation of performance such as audiotapes or videotapes of problem-solving sessions, group-completed problems, self-analyses of progress, error analyses of one's own or a peer's work, interviews with peers about mathematics and problem solving, and self-reports of problem-solving activities at home or in the community. The "new view" of school mathematics requires that we become more innovative in assessing student performance so that instruction reflects an understanding of children's conceptualization of mathematics and is tailored to meet the specific needs of learners.

HOW TO GET THERE FROM HERE

For the "new view" of school mathematics to have a positive influence on mathematics instruction for students with mild disabilities, regular and special educators must cooperate in planning and delivering instruction. Students with disabilities can be integrated effectively into mathematics instruction in regular classrooms if we make maximum use of resources and recognize that cooperation and collaboration are essential. This view fits well with various collaborative models currently practiced in schools. For example, collaborative consultation models support the practice of a special education consulting teacher working directly with the regular classroom teacher in planning and implementing classroom accommodations, instructional adaptations, behavioral management programs, and other educational interventions. In this model, the special education teacher can assist with implementation directly or indirectly by working cooperatively with the classroom teacher. Together, they select specific accommodations and interventions for students from a menu of options, develop strategies for implementing the interventions, monitor the progress of students, and then consult regarding modifications to the student's program.

Various collaborative structures exist to support effective instruction. These structures usually take the form of teams consisting of two or more members who cooperate in identifying and solving classroom problems. The teams could be prereferral teams, cooperative teaching teams, professional sharing teams, interdisciplinary teams, curriculum planning teams, staff development teams, or school-based management teams (Aldinger, Warger, & Eavy, 1991). Regardless of the term used to describe the structure, the underlying purpose and process of such professional collaboration is the same: to identify and solve problems that interfere with student success in the classroom. The process is a multistage, cyclical, cooperative planning process beginning with a procedure for identifying and analyzing a problem, moving on to setting a goal to solve the problem, then planning and implementing the intervention, and, finally, evaluating the short- and long-term outcomes. One team approach that seems to be effective for building relationships between regular and special educators is cooperative teaching. This approach assumes that two or more teachers will work collaboratively in planning and implementing interventions in the regular classroom setting (Warger & Rutherford, 1993).

For a student who is experiencing difficulties in mathematics, teachers, working together, could identify the assessment techniques that will provide the information they need to design an effective individualized instructional plan. To illustrate, teachers may choose to administer a basic-skills test, a mathematical problem-solving test, and an interview to discover how the student approaches mathematics. Assessment could be a shared effort with each teacher administering parts that are conducive to the setting and schedule of the teachers and student. Analysis of the student's strengths and weaknesses and development of the instructional plan would be a cooperative effort as well.

Through cooperative analysis, the teachers may decide that the student is not functioning at an automatic level on math fact retrieval and would benefit from using a calculator for mathematics. Additionally, they may discover that the student does not use problem-representation strategies during problem solving and, therefore, has considerable difficulty solving multistep word problems. The instructional plan may have several dimensions that address strategy acquisition, application, and generalization to the regular classroom setting. The special education teacher could provide explicit instruction in problem-representation strategies in a resource class, while the regular classroom teacher provides a variety of practice opportunities along with peers in the regular classroom.

The team approach to problem identification and solution is advantageous for several reasons. First, teachers share and exchange ideas as they develop and evaluate instructional programs for their students. They bring their own expertise and experiences to the problem-solving process. Second, other students may benefit as a result. That is, aspects of instructional programs designed to solve learning and behavioral problems for one student may be applicable to another student who is having similar problems. Together, teachers adapt and modify effective instructional programs for their students. Third, as a result of evaluating the process and the roles they play in developing and evaluating individualized programs, the team can be a resource for other teachers on ways to make collaboration work.

CONCLUSION

The NCTM *Standards* (1989) created concern among special educators because they did not specifically address students with disabilities. Cawley, Baker-Kroczynski, and Urban (1992) made several recommendations in response to the *Standards* that could serve as goals for implementing the "new view" of school mathematics for students in special education. The instructional practices and collaborative approaches discussed in this response may assist in the attainment of these goals.

The first recommendation is that educators need to recognize students' developmental levels as a basis for curriculum organization and relate these curriculum experiences to life activities across the ages. The second recommendation emphasizes the need to implement schemes of pupil appraisal and progress that employ long-term use of cumulative records, portfolios, and performance assessments in contrived and real-life settings. These two goals relate directly to the move toward authentic assessment, an approach that uses a variety of techniques to assess an individual's performance across situations and settings. This new approach to assessment could provide the information we need to develop, adapt, and tailor the curriculum to individual students. A third recommendation focuses on instructional procedures and methods to develop meanings across curriculum areas and the use of these meanings in settings involving active and collaborative learning. The move toward technology applications and cognitively based instruction directly addresses this goal. By using a multisource approach to assessment to get profiles of individual students, we can provide explicit instruction in mathematics and also tailor instruction to individual learners.

Emphasizing mathematical problem solving and practice with peers in a variety of situations across the curriculum should make mathematical learning more meaningful and relevant for students. In conclusion, use of some of the approaches discussed in this response may enable all students, including those with mild disabilities, to attain the goals associated with the "new view" of mathematics.

REFERENCES

Aldinger, L. E., Warger, C. L., & Eavy, P. W. (1991). *Strategies for teacher collaboration.* Ann Arbor, MI: Exceptional Innovations.

Cawley, J., Baker-Kroczynski, S., & Urban, A. (1992). Seeking excellence in mathematics education for students with mild disabilities. *Teaching Exceptional Children, 24,* 40–43.

Cognition and Technology Group at Vanderbilt. (1990). Anchored instruction and its relationship to situated cognition. *Educational Researcher, 19,* 2–10.

Fennema, E., Carpenter, T., & Peterson, P. (1989). Learning mathematics with understanding: Cognitively guided instruction. In J. Brophy (Ed.), *Advances in research on teaching* (Vol. 1; pp. 195–221). Greenwich, CT: JAI Press.

Hayden, M., Gersten, R., & Carnine, D. (1992). Using computer networking to increase active teaching in general education math classes including students with mild disabilities. *Journal of Special Education Technology, 11,* 167–177.

Mathematical Sciences Education Board (MSEB). (1989). *Everybody counts: A report to the nation on the future of mathematics education.* Washington, DC: National Academy Press.

Montague, M. (1987). Using microcomputers to teach verbal mathematical problem solving to learning disabled students. In D. L. Johnson, C. Maddux, & A. Candler (Eds.), *Computers in the special education classroom* (pp. 121–130). New York: Haworth Press.

Montague, M. (1989). Strategy instruction for mathematical problem solving. *Journal of Reading, Writing and Learning Disabilities, 4,* 275–290.

Montague, M. (1992). The effects of cognitive and metacognitive strategy instruction of mathematical problem solving of middle school students with learning disabilities. *Journal of Learning Disabilities, 25,* 230–248.

Montague, M., Applegate, B., & Marquard, K. (1993). Cognitive strategy instruction and mathematical problem-solving performance of students with learning disabilities. *Learning Disabilities Research and Practice, 8,* 223–232.

Mullis, I., Dossey, J., Owen, E., & Phillips, G. (1993). *NAEP 1992 mathematics report card for the nation and the states.* Princeton, NJ: Educational Testing Service.

National Council of Teachers of Mathematics (NCTM). (1989). *Curriculum and evaluation standards for school mathematics.* Reston, VA: Author.

National Council of Teachers of Mathematics (NCTM). (1991). *Professional standards for teaching mathematics.* Reston, VA: Author.

Porter, A. (1989). A curriculum out of balance: The case of elementary school mathematics. *Educational Researcher, 18,* 9–15.

Roberts, N., Carter, R., Friel, S., & Miller, M. (1988). *Integrating computers into the elementary and middle school.* Englewood Cliffs, NJ: Prentice-Hall.

U.S. Department of Education. (1994). *Sixteenth annual report to Congress on the implementation of the Individuals with Disabilities Act.* Washington, DC: Author.

Warger, C. L., & Rutherford, R. B. (1993). Co-teaching to improve social skills. *Preventing School Failure, 37*(4), 21–27.

Ysseldyke, J., Thurlow, M., & Shriner, J. (1992). Outcomes are for special educators too. *Teaching Exceptional Children, 25*(1), 36–50.

Response

The New School Mathematics and the Age-Old Dilemma of Diversity: Cutting or Untying the Gordian Knot

Edward J. Kameenui, David J. Chard, and Douglas W. Carnine

In an essay about the five hundredth anniversary of Columbus's expedition, Stephen Jay Gould (1992) revealed his ambivalence about celebrating this quincentenary by musing about one of Columbus's small achievements—balancing an egg on its end. When Columbus's dinner guests failed his challenge to balance the egg, he solved the problem by cracking the shell just enough on the bottom to allow it to stand. According to Gould, "Columbus's egg is an emblem for a different kind of ambiguity that we all must face" (p. 8): the ambiguity of accepting or rejecting a clever and innovative solution to a puzzle that requires destroying the puzzle itself.

In another example of puzzle solving, Gould related the story of Alexander the Great and the Gordian knot, "an enormously complex configuration (with a hidden end) that lashed the chariot of Gordius . . . to a pole" (p. 8). According to legend, the person who untied the Gordian knot would conquer all of Asia. When Alexander was shown the famous Gordian knot, he looked at it, drew out his sword, and cut it "clean through" (p. 8). As Gould noted, the stories about Columbus's egg and the Gordian knot are metaphors about "creativity and its meaning" in which "any true creator must wield a mallet against an accepted framework" (p. 8).

The puzzles involving Columbus's egg and the Gordian knot are not unlike some of the puzzles educators currently face, particularly the ones raised by Davis and Maher in their provocative chapter about the competing views of how to improve school mathematics and the consequences for American education and American society. Especially noteworthy is the

Curriculum Trends, Special Education, and Reform: Refocusing the Conversation. ISBN 0-8077-3562-0 (pbk), ISBN 0-8077-3563-9 (cloth).

potential consequence for special education. As the authors note, "the impact on special education may be even greater." The puzzle-solving dilemma facing American educators in general, and mathematics and special educators in particular, is found in the complex set of requirements and expectations embodied, as Davis and Maher note, in the *Curriculum and Evaluation Standards for School Mathematics* (1989), developed and promoted by the National Council of Teachers of Mathematics (NCTM), and in the report *Everybody Counts* by the National Research Council (Mathematical Sciences Education Board [MSEB], 1989). These documents, as Davis and Maher accurately portray, have ushered in a "new" view of school mathematics for teachers who teach children in special education (i.e., children formally identified as those with learning disabilities, emotional disturbance or behavior disorders, or mild mental retardation), as well as children who are potentially at risk because they have, as the NCTM (1989), acknowledges, "different needs and interests" (p. 253).

As it now stands, the NCTM *Standards* and their translation by Davis and Maher into a "new" view of school mathematics ostensibly require teachers to face and solve their own Gordian knot—that of tacitly accepting the *Standards* by teaching the new mathematics to students with diverse learning and curriculum needs. For all practical purposes, these teachers, not unlike Alexander, must decide whether it is possible to untie the Gordian knot thread by thread in order to reveal and address the intricate instructional requirements (Kameenui & Simmons, 1990) *necessary* to teach the newly emerging view of school mathematics to diverse learners—or, as Alexander did, simply cut it off, clean through, that is, expose the curriculum and teaching complexities implied by the NCTM *Standards* and the new view of school mathematics by calling for a moratorium on the *Standards* until substantial evidence is provided that the *Standards* "work" for *all* students.

The choice of either untying the Gordian knot (i.e., teaching diverse learners the new view of school mathematics) or cutting it off is clouded by at least two straightforward considerations. First, contrary to the enthusiastic endorsement of the new view of school mathematics by Davis and Maher, the evidence in support of the effectiveness of this new approach to school mathematics for all students, especially students with diverse learning and curricular needs, simply is not available. Second, when the learning characteristics (e.g., memory capacity, background knowledge) of "students with different needs and interests" (NCTM, 1989, p. 253) are carefully considered, the new view of school mathematics is likely to result in the same problem these learners have faced time and time again in the context of schools—failure.

THE NEWLY EMERGING VIEW OF MATHEMATICS AND WHAT'S NEW ABOUT IT

When the NCTM adopted and published the *Standards* in 1989, it stated three reasons for doing so: (1) "to ensure that the public is protected from shoddy products"; (2) "as a means for expressing expectations about goals"; and (3) "to lead a group toward some new desired goals" (p. 2).

The goals stated in the NCTM *Standards* for *all* students are that they learn to value mathematics, become confident in their ability to do mathematics, become mathematical problem solvers, learn to communicate mathematically, and learn to reason mathematically.

As noted by Davis and Maher, the characteristics of the newly emerging view of school mathematics have prompted the following changes in school mathematics, based primarily on the NCTM *Standards:* (1) less reliance on paper-and-pencil computation, (2) more reliance on conceptual approaches to computation instruction that require "a powerful collection of symbols that are available for mental manipulation or mental 'visualization'" (p. 12); and (3) the use of assessment tools that allow students to "talk aloud as they work, to tell us (as best they can) what and how they are thinking about the problem" (p. 7).

The NCTM *Standards* and goals have been accepted by almost everyone, which is not surprising, because the goals are certainly reasonable: Who could quarrel with building confidence in mathematics, becoming a mathematical problem solver, or reasoning and communicating mathematically? However, the goals are not new (see Rappaport, 1975); what is new is the requirement to integrate thinking and content-area knowledge for *all* students. As Resnick (1989) stated, "Although it is not new to include thinking, problem solving, and reasoning in someone's school curriculum, it is new to include it in everyone's curriculum" (p. 7).

In addition, the research basis for the NCTM *Standards* is open to question. As Bishop (1990) states, "It is a little surprising that there is not much reference to the research literature concerning mathematics learning and teaching. There is no impression of the existence of a substantial body of research on which, for example, the proposals in the *Standards* are based" (p. 366).

THE NCTM STANDARDS AND IMPLICATIONS FOR DIVERSE LEARNERS

One of the primary concerns with the NCTM *Standards* and the report, *Everybody Counts,* is the implications they hold for teaching students with diverse learning and curricular needs, or, as the NCTM *Standards* label them, "those of lesser capabilities and interest" (p. 253). The *Standards* decry the practices of ability grouping and tracking found in special programs for gifted students and students with disabilities. They state:

> We believe that *all* students can benefit from an opportunity to study the core curriculum specified in the *Standards*. This can be accomplished by expanding and enriching the curriculum to meet the needs of each individual student, including the gifted and those of lesser capabilities and interests. We challenge teachers and other educators to develop and experiment with course outlines and grouping patterns to present the mathematics in the *Standards* in a meaningful, productive way. (p. 253)

It is important to note that educators such as Davis and Maher do not recommend a watered-down or second-rate mathematics content for students of "lesser capabilities and interests." Rather, the goal is to devise curriculum and instruction so that these students understand the kind of mathematics that includes higher-order thinking, problem solving, and reasoning. Insisting that all students can benefit from an "opportunity to study the core curriculum" is easy; "expanding and enriching the curriculum" to meet the needs of those with "lesser capabilities and interests" is not easy. The kind of educational tools and actual classroom instruction implied by the NCTM *Standards* are not in place currently, at least not for students who are at risk or have disabilities.

The challenges to meet the *Standards* are enormous and, in some cases, paralyzing. For instance, how should we expand the curriculum for students identified as having learning disabilities and being at risk, whose language and reading deficits contribute indirectly to their difficulties in solving verbal mathematics problems? How do we expand the curriculum for students who are passive victims of what Merton (1968) and more recently Stanovich (1986) term Matthew effects—the sequence of educational effects in which children who are rich in early reading and language experiences get even richer and more advantaged by them. In contrast, children who do not read and do not come from literate homes (i.e., homes that have not given children the requisite 1,000 hours of reading and writing encounters before coming to school) get poorer in cognition, tuition, and motivation, and continue to experience the negative escalating effects set in motion by early reading and language failure (Juel, 1988).

How does one expand and enrich the curriculum for students whose knowledge base is already in serious jeopardy? What knowledge does one expand and enrich? Moreover, the burden of expanding and enriching the core curriculum ultimately will fall to classroom teachers. Curriculum development activities in mathematics are not easy for teachers, as Good and Grouws (1979) pointed out more than a decade ago. In addition, the presence of low-achieving students in the classroom raises questions about teachers' ability to accommodate the learning and curricular needs of these students. For example, in a study of factors that influence change in individual teacher practice, Smylie (1988) noted, "The lower the achievement level of students in the class, the less likely teachers seem to believe that they can affect student learning despite the level of confidence they may have in their knowledge and skills related to teaching" (p. 23).

The NCTM's challenge will not be answered by developing and experimenting with "course outlines and grouping patterns." Instead, the challenge requires, at the very minimum, a two-part strategy. The first part of the answer is given by Stanovich (1986), who argues that instructional questions surrounding students who are in serious educational jeopardy require very specific answers. He states, "The cycle of escalating achievement deficits must be broken in a more specific way to short-circuit the cascade of negative spinoffs" (p. 393). In short, the kind of instruction and curriculum required for *successful* children simply will not do for those who are of "lesser capabilities and interests."

The second part of the answer can be found in the educational tools employed in schools. Most of the teaching that takes place in school is organized around certain tools—commercial textbooks, activity guides, computer programs, films, and so on—which are used in a range of activities, such as lectures, cooperative learning, and independent projects. For the most part, these tools are designed for general education students from middle-class backgrounds and not for students identified by the NCTM *Standards* as those with "lesser capabilities and interests."

In mathematics education, the question is not whether to reform, but where to begin. Responding to the NCTM *Standards* to meet the learning and curricular needs of students with learning problems first will require not "expanding" the curriculum, as called for by the *Standards,* but shrinking the curriculum to *strategically teach less more thoroughly.* We see no other alternative to the curriculum compression facing students who are already too far behind their peers and appear to be victims of Matthew effects. Strategically selecting what critical strategies to teach, teaching less more thoroughly, and anchoring what is taught to big, conceptual ideas and principles is the best way to "enrich the curriculum," as called for by the *Standards.*

KEY PRINCIPLES FOR DESIGNING AND ENRICHING THE CURRICULUM FOR STUDENTS WITH DIFFERENT NEEDS

Interventions designed specifically for students of "lesser capabilities and interests" (e.g., students with learning disabilities and who are at risk) must create a range of successful experiences. Several factors potentially can contribute to these successful experiences:

1. Teaching strategies based on big ideas
2. Using time efficiently
3. Providing clear and explicit instruction
4. Providing appropriate and sufficient practice and review

In this section we offer recommendations for designing and enriching mathematics curriculum material that is sensitive to the characteristics of students with learning problems.

Teaching Big Ideas

Programs designed to develop higher-order cognitive functioning should be organized around *big ideas.* For example, in *Factors and Multiples* from the Middle Grades Mathematics Project, Fitzgerald, Winter, Lappan, and Phillips (1986) write that it "focuses on this fundamental theorem and related ideas such as factor, divisor, multiple, common factor, common multiple, relatively prime, and composite" (p. 2). Broad understanding is facilitated most efficiently by building strategies around "big ideas" that are most central to understanding in a domain (Porter, 1989; Prawat, 1989). Too often mathematics textbooks obscure key relationships. For example, in geometry, students typically are expected to learn seven formulae to calculate the volume of 7 three-dimensional figures (e.g., rectangular prism: $l \cdot w \cdot h = v$; wedge: $\frac{1}{2} \cdot l \cdot w \cdot h = v$; triangular pyramid: $\frac{1}{6} \cdot l \cdot w \cdot h = v$). These equations emphasize rote formulae rather than "root meanings." A "big idea" analysis based on root meanings (as in Figure 3.3) reduces the number of formulae students must learn from seven to slight variations of a single formula—area of the base times the height ($B \cdot h$)—which enhances understanding while simultaneously reducing the quantity of content to be taught (Dixon, Carnine, & Kameenui, 1992). This analysis of root meaning fosters understanding of the key concept or big idea that volume is a function of base times height. As Gelman (1986) stated, "A focus on different algorithmic instantiations of a set of principles helps teach children that procedures that seem very different on the surface can share the same mathematical underpinning and, hence, root meanings" (p. 350).

Using Time Efficiently

This guideline addresses a perennial problem in teaching students with learning disabilities and who are at risk: the problem of teaching such students all they need to know (in both quantitative and qualitative terms),

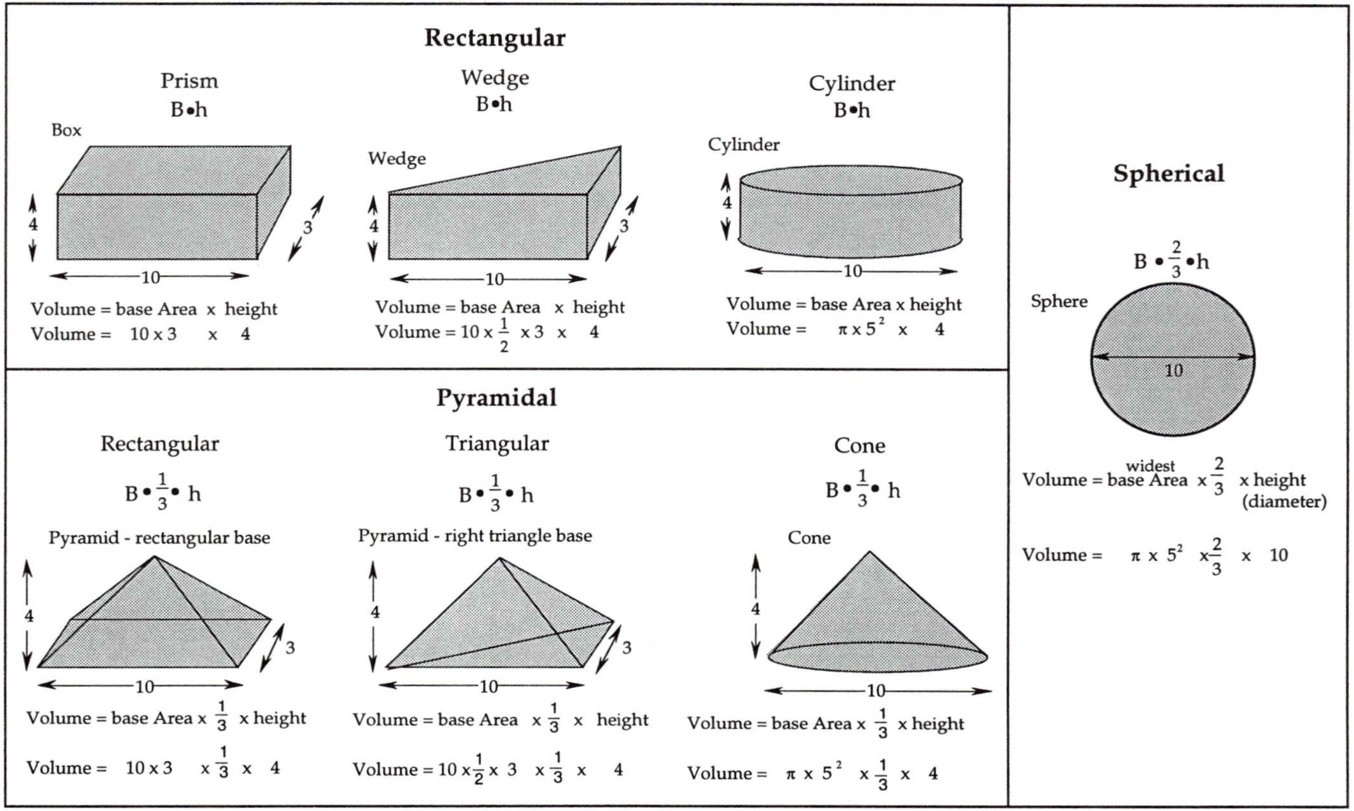

Figure 3.3 Volume as the "Big Idea" of the Base Times a Multiple of the Height

but without "losing" them by trying to teach too much, too quickly. Catching them up with their peers, as efficiently as possible within realistic time constraints, should not involve bombarding students with the kind of teaching activities that exacerbate selective attention and meta-attention problems. Some guidelines are presented below.

Teach fewer objectives more thoroughly. In most cases, basal programs attempt to cover exhaustive lists of learning objectives, with little or no attempt to prioritize those objectives on the basis of their relative contributions to higher cognitive functioning. As we have stated before, not all concepts within a domain are of equal value. If instruction focuses on fewer key concepts, principles, and strategies, then not only is understanding enhanced, but new material can be introduced less frequently and thus be less overwhelming to students.

Ease into complex strategies. The traditional practice of teaching complex strategies in toto within a single instructional encounter introduces too much new material too quickly, which is likely to overwhelm the attention capacities of at-risk students. Instruction of complex strategies comprising many cognitive components can be accommodated in several encounters spread out over a few days time—a method of simplifying the teaching of complex concepts without sacrificing crucial inherent complexities.

Use a strand organization for lessons. Rather than an entire lesson organized around a single topic, as in traditional mathematics basal programs, lessons can be designed around strands with each 5- to 10-minute segment addressing a different topic. There are several reasons for organizing curriculum around strands and utilizing shorter segments on various topics within each lesson.

First, students of lesser capabilities and interests are more easily engaged with a variety of topics. For example, 40 minutes on subtraction renaming, day in and day out, would become quite tedious. In contrast, a lesson consisting of 15 minutes on renaming followed by 10 on estimation and 15 on verbal problems is more likely to keep students engaged.

Second, strands make the sequencing of component concepts and instructional activities more manageable. The many concepts in mathematics curriculum can be arranged in a scope and sequence such that they are taught prior to their integration and are made easier when several of them can appear in one lesson. This advantage of a strand organization was alluded to above in the discussion of "easing into" complex strategies.

Third, lessons organized around strands make cumulative introduction feasible. In cumulative introduction, after a concept is introduced it is systematically reviewed and integrated with other related concepts. Distributed practice is easy to schedule when each lesson is designed to accommodate several segments from several strands.

Communicating Strategies in an Explicit Manner

For many students with learning disabilities or who are at risk, new concepts and strategies should be explained in clear, concise, accurate, and comprehensible language. The following are specific guidelines for facilitating clarity.

Make strategies explicit and clear. Explicit instruction has been shown to be most effective for teaching at-risk students specific concepts, principles, and strategies, probably as a consequence of such students' selective attention and deficits in memory and meta-attention (Egan & Greeno, 1973; Fielding, Kameenui, & Gersten, 1983; Fisher, Berliner, Filby, Marliave, Cahen, & Dishaw, 1981).

Accommodate differences in background knowledge. The phrase "prior knowledge" is used ambiguously in the literature, to mean, for example, prerequisite knowledge, schemata, or background knowledge (see Alba & Hasher, 1983; Sadoski, Paivio, & Goetz, 1991). Background knowledge is potentially important in mathematics principally in conjunction with verbal problem solving. For instance, if students are learning about proportional relationships between the height and volume of various figures, their learning is significantly accelerated if prior instruction on volume and proportion focused on the "big idea" of volume as the area of the base times the height. Not all concepts that come into play in a complex strategy can be strategically linked. In these cases, the components must be established as background knowledge and then combined.

The introduction of any new strategy is likely to require quick and easy cognitive access to one or more categories of prior knowledge. Instruction should accommodate that requirement by testing either (a) to ensure that students possess necessary prerequisites, or (b) to determine what prerequisites need to be taught or retaught before proceeding to the new strategy.

In addition to making initial instruction as explicit and clear as possible, instruction can buttress against meta-attention problems can be reduced by a scaffolded phase of instruction (Tharp & Gallimore, 1988)—that stage of instruction during which control is transferred from the teacher to students. There is a variety of means by which instruction may be scaffolded between initial instruction and self-regulated instruction, including variations of peer coaching or cooperative learning. However, the most central and well-established form of scaffolding occurs through careful teacher monitoring and feedback.

Providing Practice and Review to Facilitate Retention

One goal of a mathematics program is for students to remember and apply what is presented in the program. To develop retention, students must receive carefully planned practice opportunities, spaced over a period of time. Here are several guidelines.

Facilitate automaticity when appropriate. Adequate but judicious practice should be provided to enable students to reach a point of performance that allows them to apply a concept readily as a component of more complex strategies.

Provide integration opportunities. Practice on a newly introduced problem type should be adequate so that students can work the problem with relative ease. After initial instruction, problems of that type should be mixed in with previously introduced problems of a similar nature. This mix provides students with practice not only in applying the steps to solve the problem but in determining when to apply the steps.

Be conservative in assuming that students will be able to generalize to new problem types. Examine similar problems to identify important differences among them. Program developers should not assume that providing instruction on one type of problem will enable students to solve the other types of problems. The best way to determine what type of generalization is reasonable is to try out the program with students.

CONCLUSION

The challenge of expanding and enriching the mathematics curriculum to accommodate students with different needs and interests as called for in the NCTM *Standards* is substantial. Likewise, the curricular and instructional requirements to meet this challenge are substantial, because they involve reconceptualizing and redesigning mathematics curriculum materials and instructional tasks around at least four key principles: (1) teaching strategies that are based on big ideas, (2) using time efficiently, (3) giving clear and explicit instructions, and (4) providing more carefully scheduled practice and review.

As Lajoie (1991) pointed out in the first newsletter of the National Center for Research in Mathematical Sciences Education, "the NCTM *Standards* represent goals for worthwhile or essential mathematics that are designed to make students mathematically powerful" (p. 6). In this response, we have argued that making students with different needs and interests mathematically powerful also will require translating the NCTM *Standards* into concrete teacher practices at the classroom level. The translation of lofty goals into real classroom practice that does not place students of "lesser capabilities and interests" at greater pedagogical risk would represent a significant solution to untying the Gordian knot.

REFERENCES

Alba, J. W., & Hasher, L. (1983). Is memory schematic? *Psychological Bulletin, 93*(2), 203–231.

Bishop, A. J. (1990). Mathematical power to the people. *Harvard Educational Review, 60*(3), 357–369.

Dixon, R., Carnine, D. W., & Kameenui, E. J. (1992). *Curriculum guidelines for diverse learners* (Monograph). Eugene: University of Oregon, National Center to Improve the Tools of Educators.

Egan, D. E., & Greeno, J. R. (1973). Acquiring cognitive structure by discovery and rule learning. *Journal of Educational Psychology, 64,* 85–97.

Fielding, G. D., Kameenui, E., & Gersten, R. (1983). A comparison of an inquiry and a direct instruction approach to teaching legal concepts and applications to secondary school students. *Journal of Educational Research, 76*(5), 287–293.

Fisher, C. W., Berliner, D. C., Filby, N. N., Marliave, R., Cahen, I. S., & Dishaw, M. M. (1981). Teaching behaviors, academic learning time, and student achievement: An overview. *Journal of Classroom Interactions, 17*(1), 2–15.

Fitzgerald, W., Winter, M. J., Lappan, G., & Phillips, E. *Factors and multiples.* Menlo Park, CA: Addison-Wesley.

Gelman, R. (1986). Toward an understanding-based theory of mathematics learning and instruction, or in praise of Lampert on teaching multiplication. *Cognition and Instruction, 3,* 349–355.

Good, T. L., & Grouws, D. A. (1979). The Missouri mathematics effectiveness project. *Journal of Educational Psychology, 71,* 355–362.

Gould, S. J. (1992). Columbus cracks an egg: Was the great voyager also a heavy-handed trickster? *Natural History, 101*(12), 4–10.

Juel, C. (1988, April). *Learning to read and write: A longitudinal study of fifty-four children from first through fourth grade.* Paper presented at the annual meeting of the American Educational Research Association Meeting, New Orleans.

Kameenui, E. J., & Simmons, D. C. (1990). *Designing instructional strategies: The prevention of academic learning problems.* Columbus, OH: Merrill.

Lajoie, S. (1991). A framework for authentic assessment in mathematics. *NCRMSE Research Review: The Teaching and Learning of Mathematics, 1*(1), 6–12.

Mathematical Sciences Education Board (MSEB). (1989). *Everybody counts: A report to the nation on the future of mathematics education.* Washington, DC: National Academy Press.

Merton, R. (1968). The Matthew effect in science. *Science,* pp. 56–63.

National Council of Teachers of Mathematics (NCTM). (1989). *Curriculum and evaluation standards for school mathematics.* Reston, VA: Author.

Porter, A. (1989). A curriculum out of balance: The case of elementary school mathematics. *Educational Researcher, 18,* 9–15.

Prawat, R. S. (1989). Promoting access to knowledge, strategy and disposition in students: A research synthesis. *Review of Educational Research, 59*(1), 141.

Rappaport, D. (1975). The new math and its aftermath. *School Science and Mathematics,* pp. 563–570.

Resnick, L. (1989). Developing mathematical knowledge. *American Psychologist, 44*(2), 162–169.

Sadoski, M., Paivio, A., & Goetz, E. (1991). Commentary: A critique of schema theory in reading and a dual coding alternative. *Reading Research Quarterly, 26*(4), 463–484.

Smylie, M. A. (1988). The enhancement function of staff development: Organizational and psychological antecedents to individual teacher change. *American Educational Research Journal, 255*(1), 1–30.

Stanovich, K. E. (1986). Matthew effects in reading: Some consequences of individual differences in the acquisition of literacy. *Reading Research Quarterly, 21*(4), 360–407.

Tharp, R. G., & Gallimore, R. (1988). *Rousing minds to life: Teaching, learning, and schooling in social context.* New York: Cambridge University Press.

* *CHAPTER 4* *

Issues and Practices in the Social Studies Curriculum

Mark C. Schug and H. Michael Hartoonian

While social studies has long been regarded a central part of the academic curriculum, curriculum leaders and theorists often disagree with one another about the nature, scope, and purpose of social studies in the curriculum. It is contentions about definitions that are at the heart of current debates about the place of social studies in the schools. How definitional problems are resolved has implications for what teachers teach in the name of social studies.

THE CHALLENGE OF DEFINING SOCIAL STUDIES

One way to frame the definitional problem is to consider the relationship between the social studies and the social sciences. Consider, for example, an early definition of social studies, found in the 1916 landmark report entitled *The Social Studies in Secondary Education* (National Education Association [NEA], 1916). It defines the social studies as "those whose subject matter relates directly to the organization and development of human society, and to man as a member of social groups." Note here that social *studies* is defined without any direct reference to social *sciences*. The distinction is important. Social studies leaders often disagree about whether social studies is a loose federation of all the social sciences or whether social studies is better thought of as a fusion of social sciences into something beyond the contribution of each individual component.

The question of definition is an important one—particularly within the context of current efforts at reform. The term *social studies*—which implies a fusion of the social sciences—recently has been abandoned by some. California, for example, refers to its social studies curriculum as the "History–Social Science Framework" (California State Board of Educa-

Curriculum Trends, Special Education, and Reform: Refocusing the Conversation. Copyright © 1996 by Teachers College, Columbia University. All rights reserved. ISBN 0-8077-3562-0 (pbk), ISBN 0-8077-3563-9 (cloth). Prior to photocopying items for classroom use, please contact the Copyright Clearance Center, Customer Service, 222 Rosewood Dr., Danvers, MA 01923, USA, tel. (508) 750-8400.

tion, 1988). The U.S. Department of Education also has abandoned reference to social studies. The Goals 2000: Educate America Act states that citizenship is an important educational goal, but it makes no explicit reference to social studies; only history, civics, economics, and geography are mentioned. While the definition recently offered by the National Council for the Social Studies (NCSS) represents a deliberate effort to resolve the issue in favor of maintaining reference to social studies, the debate continues.

Another way to frame the problem of competing definitions is to consider various interpretations of what is commonly thought of as the goal of social studies education, namely, fostering citizenship. Despite its apparent uniformity, the citizenship goal is itself ambiguous and has been claimed by proponents of at least five different views of the role of the citizen. These views are summarized in Figure 4.1.

These competing rationales lead to very different commitments on the part of teachers regarding what counts as the social studies curriculum, as noted in Figure 4.1. To produce citizens who are patriots, we need to teach and model democratic virtues in social studies. To produce academically oriented citizens, we must teach knowledge, skills, and attitudes derived from scholarship in the social sciences, and this, in turn, will foster good citizenship. To produce citizens as survivors, it is enough for social studies to help students lead satisfying, well-adjusted lives within the context of our democratic system. To produce reformers, we need to encourage active political participation to improve the democratic system. Finally, being a citizen might best mean being a policy maker in one's personal and public life. This ability demands that students be clear thinkers, possess important knowledge, and have the inclination to become involved in civic affairs.

How do these rationales stand up in practice? Leming (1989) observed that social studies theorists have a long tradition of promoting countersocialization, which emphasizes independent thinking and social criticism. He notes that social studies theorists tend to see society in crisis and consequently stress the need for critical analysis and citizen participation aimed at reform. Leming observes, however, that social studies teachers tend to hold a view that envisions a conservative role for social studies, involving the transmission of mainstream interpretations and values. In other words, social studies theorists often are associated with the "citizen as reformer" view of citizenship; conversely, teachers tend to teach the traditional values of our society, stressing the rationales of patriotism and academics.

The case for the existence of an ideological chasm in social studies does not rest upon conjecture and speculation. Leming (1992) reports data from several national surveys, including information regarding political party identification, political ideology, opinions concerning economic opportu-

Figure 4.1 Competing Rationales for Social Studies as Citizenship Education

Rationale	*Outcome*	*Typical Content*
Citizen as patriot	Cherish democratic ideals of United States	Rationale for the U.S. Constitution, individual rights, government limited so that individual freedoms endure
Citizen as academic	Acquisition of knowledge from history, political science, economics, geography, psychology, anthropology, sociology	Traditional subject knowledge, skills in applying evidence to support claims, gathering and using information, applying logic
Citizen as survivor	Knowledge and skills for daily living	Get a job, register to vote, buy a house, file complaint in small claims court, use financial services, and so on
Citizen as reformer	Knowledge and skills to change society through active political participation	Local studies of community problems, organizing action groups, writing letters, registering voters
Citizen as policy maker	Knowledge and skills to develop and implement effective personal and public policies	Identification, development, and evaluation of themes/principles/states toward which persons wish to move; assessing data; developing and implementing policies; mid-course evaluation and corrections

nity, views of religion, current problems, and purposes of social studies education. The case for the existence of an ideological chasm is compelling on each measure but is strongest with regard to political orientation, opinions on economic opportunity, and opinions on current political and social issues. This illustrates that teachers and theorists have failed to resolve issues regarding the purpose of social studies in the school curriculum; in fact, many have opposing views.

COMMON PRACTICES IN SOCIAL STUDIES

Despite these competing definitions and rationales, and while scholars and leaders in the profession argue vociferously about their contending views,

Figure 4.2 Dominant Social Studies Curriculum Organization Pattern

K	Self, School, Community, Home
1	Families
2	Neighborhoods
3	Communities
4	State History, Geographic Regions
5	U.S. History
6	World Cultures, Western Hemisphere
7	World Geography or History
8	American History
9	Civics or World Cultures
10	World History
11	American History
12	American Government

Source: Reprinted by permission from Superka, Hawke, & Morrissett (1980). © National Council for the Social Sciences.

actual classroom practice is remarkably homogeneous and characterized by a clear, familiar pattern. Figure 4.2 summarizes the dominant national pattern of the K–12 social studies curriculum (Superka, Hawke, & Morrissett, 1980).

The pattern for instruction in the elementary grades can be described as an expanding horizons curriculum, with a gradual expansion in the scope of topics from the family to the world. This pattern of study, often criticized for its lack of substance, dates to the 1930s. The secondary curriculum—grades 7–12—is made up of two 3-year cycles, including the study of world history, U.S. history, and government. U.S. history is included at grades 5, 8, and 11. The secondary pattern has roots in the 1916 *Social Studies in Secondary Education* report (NEA, 1916). Schools do, of course, include other, elective courses in the secondary curriculum, but this pattern remains dominant (Morrissett, 1986).

National Science Foundation (NSF) studies in the late 1970s provided us with a clear description of how social studies is taught. The dominant pattern of instruction, like the dominant curricular pattern, looks familiar. Shaver, Davis, and Helburn (1979) summarize many NSF findings:

1. The dominant instructional tool in social studies is the textbook.
2. New materials developed for social studies are not used.

3. The dominant methods of social studies instruction are large-group, teacher-directed recitation and lecture chiefly based on the textbook.
4. Teachers believe in the textbook as a source of knowledge.
5. Social studies teachers believe that perpetuating the values of our society is one of their roles.
6. Inquiry teaching is rare.

The pattern described by Shaver, Davis, and Helburn (1979) is confirmed by additional evidence. For example, Cuban (1991) reviewed seven studies carried out between 1950 and 1986 and he reached similar conclusions about the predominance of textbooks and the persistence of lecture and recitation. Instruction in social studies is marked by stability rather than change.

HOW WELL ARE STUDENTS LEARNING SOCIAL STUDIES?

The results of the common practices for teaching social studies are disappointing. Studies of student learning in history, geography, civics, and economics show American students are not achieving at satisfactory levels. For example, the National Assessment of Educational Progress (NAEP) (1990a) reports that there was little change between 1986 and 1988 in how well students were learning history. Eighth grade students possess some general historical information, but their understanding is largely superficial. For example, over 80% appeared to know how Abraham Lincoln died, but only 25% knew that his goal in the Civil War was to preserve the Union. High school seniors, too, displayed a knowledge of beginning information, but few could see relationships in history. Most seniors could correctly identify famous inventors, but few performed well on questions regarding labor leaders, the union movement, and the growth of big business. Fewer than 5% of students were able to interpret historical information and ideas.

The picture in geography is similar. According to the NAEP (1990b), most high school seniors could correctly answer questions about the locations of major countries but did not perform as well when asked to identify other places, such as cities and physical features, or on the concepts of latitude and longitude. Nearly one-third of students thought the prime meridian was the equator. Students performed relatively well on questions about events and features in the news, with seniors demonstrating an awareness of environmental issues.

Not only are students not learning social studies well, but they also have little enthusiasm for the subject. One review of several studies (Shaughnessy & Haladyna, 1985) concluded that most students in the United States, at all grade levels, find social studies to be one of the least interesting and most irrelevant subjects in the school curriculum.

THE NEED FOR REFORM

Continuing problems of definition, competing rationales for citizenship, and homogeneous and conventional teaching practices have all converged to lead social studies educators to rethink the content and processes of their field. At least three trends can be identified in current calls for reform. They include the return to history and geography, multicultural and global education, and the National Standards Movement.

The Return to History and Geography

Several proponents for reform of the social studies curriculum have argued for programs focused sharply on the teaching of history and geography. Two reports exemplify this view: *Building a History Curriculum: Guidelines for Teaching History in Schools* (Bradley Commission on History in Schools, 1988) and *Charting a Course: Social Studies for the 21st Century* (National Commission on Social Studies in the Schools, 1989).

The Bradley Commission report asserts that history should occupy a large and vital place in the school curriculum. Because Americans are not bound together by a common religion or common ethnicity, the Commission argues, our history is especially important as a means to teach young citizens about common experiences and differences, and in this way to preserve our democratic values. A frequent criticism of the traditional social studies sequence is that it provides superficial coverage of history.

Several of the reforms advocated by the Bradley Commission were approved in 1987 by the California State Department of Education. An examination of the California History–Social Science Framework (Figure 4.3) illustrates several long-standing problems in organizing the social studies curriculum. The California curriculum retains U.S. history at grades 5, 8, and 11, but spreads the content out across these years. Similarly, world history is taught in grades 6, 7, and 11. These changes are intended to bring more depth to the study of U.S. and world history. The role of geography is strengthened by linking its tie to history. The traditional expanding horizons conception at the primary grades, where students study things nearby such as self and family, and gradually expand to the study of community, state, nation, and world, is abandoned in favor of the study of historical concepts and people of the past, with strong emphasis on the use of children's literature.

Figure 4.3 California History–Social Science Framework, Scope, and Sequence

K Learning and Working, Now and Long Ago
Helping children learn their way in their new school role by analyzing problems, considering alternatives, and appreciating democratic values. Readings: *Jack and the Beanstalk, Goldilocks, Aesop's Fables.*

1 A Child's Place in Time and Space
Developing social skills, expanding geographic and economic awareness, building a three-dimensional floor map, neighborhood studies. Readings: *Little Toot, Little Red Lighthouse, Mulligan's Steam Shovel.*

2 People Who Make a Difference
Studying people who supply our needs (farmers and laborers), effect of climate on crops, urban development. Readings: *Johnny Appleseed,* folktales, myths, legends.

3 Continuity and Change
Constructing history of region, California geography, terrain model of locality, Native Americans, classroom timeline. Readings: *White Stallion, Wagon Wheels, The Drinking Gourd.*

4 California: A Changing State
Pre-Columbian times, Spanish Conquest, colonial Mexico, Gold Rush, rapid population growth, new immigrants, physical and cultural geography, modern California urban growth and technology. Topics: the travels of Jedediah Smith, James Beckwourth, John C. Fremont, the Bidwell and Donner parties

5 United States History and Geography: Making a New Nation, to 1850
The land before Columbus, Age of Exploration, settling colonies, settling Trans-Appalachian West, War of Independence, the young Republic, Westward Ho! Readings: *Immigrant Kids, Waiting for Mama.*

6 World History and Geography: Ancient Civilizations
Ancient civilizations to 500 A.D.: Stone Age; Mesopotamia; Egypt; Hebrews and Greeks; early civilizations of India, China, and Rome. Readings: Greek and Roman literature, Bible.

7 World History and Geography: Medieval and Early Modern Times
Medieval times, 500 A.D. to 1789: Fall of Rome, Islam, China, Japan, medieval society, European Reformation and Renaissance, Enlightenment. Readings: *Pillow Book, Song of Roland, Tale of Genji, Koju-ki.*

8 United States History and Geography: Growth and Conflict
Course covers 1783 to 1914: the new nation, Constitution, launching the ship of state, the West, the Northeast, the South, Civil War, industrial age. Readings: *Huckleberry Finn, My Antonia.*

9 Elective Courses in History–Social Science
Semester courses: Our State, Physical Geography, Cultural Geography, Humanities, Anthropology, Psychology, Sociology, Women's History, Ethnic Studies, Area Studies–Culture, Law-Related Education.

10 World History, Culture, and Geography: The Modern World
Unresolved world problems, Enlightenment, Industrial Revolution, imperialism, World War I, World War II, nationalism, Soviet Union, China, Africa, Mexico. Readings: *We, Darkness at Noon, Krystallnacht.*

11 United States History and Geography: Continuity and Change in the 20th Century
Progressive era, Jazz Age, Great Depression, World War II, cold war, postwar American society, recent times. Readings: *Grapes of Wrath.*

12 Principles of American Democracy (one semester) and Economics (one semester)
One semester deals with the Constitution, the Bill of Rights, the court system, federalism, and comparative government. Another semester deals with economic systems, micro- and macroeconomics, and international economics.

The work of the National Commission on the Social Studies in the Schools was another major attempt to reformulate the social studies curriculum. In its report, *Charting a Course,* the Commission attempted to formulate a coherent vision of the role of social studies in general education. The Commission's recommendations were presented as a way to equip young people to be responsible citizens in a society characterized by increasing complexity, diversity, and worldwide dependency. While noting the importance of political science, economics, and the other social sciences, *Charting a Course* clearly stresses history and geography as the primary framework for social studies.

While *Charting a Course* is vague about the primary grades, it moves study of the local community from earlier in the elementary grades to grade 7, where students are developmentally more able to conduct meaningful studies of community life. The most remarkable contribution of this proposed sequence is the integration of U.S. history, world history, and geography called for at grades 9, 10, and 11. The elimination of U.S. history as an independent course is a clear departure from traditional practice. U.S. history is taught only within the context of world history. Note also that *Charting a Course* and the California curriculum both suggest that the traditional course in problems of democracy evolve into a required semester of study of economics and government.

Both of these reports were received as bombshells by social studies theorists deeply concerned about the relatively exclusive focus on history and geography and the reduced importance attached to other social studies areas, such as sociology, psychology, and political science. Sharp criticisms were aimed at the *Charting a Course* report. Nelson (1990), for example, argues that *Charting a Course* "is narrow and conservative, unsupported by theory on research or practice, and essentially anti-intellectual in its lack of concern for contemporary issues and competing ideas" (p. 434). While the debate continues in professional journals and at professional meetings, states, such as California, are trying to implement many of these changes.

The Bradley Commission report and *Charting a Course* pose once again a familiar problem in social studies. Should history and geography, the traditional organizers for the study of human experience in time and space, be the mainstay of the social studies curriculum within which all other knowledge is placed? Or should a clear and significant role be assigned to each of the social sciences where unique perspectives on human behavior, including economic, political, psychological, anthropological, and sociological, can be emphasized?

Multicultural and Global Education

Social studies leaders recently have argued that a lack of multicultural education—education about race, ethnicity, and gender—is a key deficiency in the current social studies curriculum. Demographic trends frequently are cited as providing reasons for this reform, with the percentage of people of color continuing to rise and the 1990 census suggesting that by the turn of the century one out of every three people will be a person of color.

According to Banks (1991), a strong multicultural emphasis would contribute to historical accuracy in social studies programs and better reflect our national commitment to a democratic society. Banks, for example, observes that a study of the American Revolution is included in the social studies curriculum because students must know about it in order to understand the development of the United States. Similarly, content about people of color, women, and persons with disabilities also should be included in the curriculum in order to give students an accurate view of U.S. society and culture. According to this view, schools in a democratic society need to promote the notion of diversity in order to develop commitment to a national ethos of pluralism and equity.

Following the surge in interest regarding multicultural education, the National Council for the Social Studies (NCSS) (1992) updated its multicultural education guidelines. These guidelines present four principles of ethnic and cultural diversity that can be used as standards to help determine appropriate content for the social studies curriculum:

1. Ethnic and cultural diversity should be recognized and respected at the individual, group, and societal levels.
2. Ethnic and cultural diversity provides a basis for societal enrichment, cohesiveness, and survival.
3. Equality of opportunity must be afforded to all members of ethnic and cultural groups.
4. Ethnic and cultural identification for individuals should be optional in a democracy.

A renewed stress on multicultural education is not without problems. One fundamental mission of our schools is to instill shared beliefs and culture, not just separate ethnic identities. While both goals—learning how people are alike as well as how they are different—are vital, priority needs to be given to teaching about the ideals we share. Ravitch (1992) expresses deep concerns that using ethnicity as the organizing principle of social studies is a dangerous development that encourages separatism. She argues that the common culture is an amalgam of the contributions of all the different groups that have joined American society and enriched our common culture. For example, common culture is expressed in teaching about the Constitution and the Bill of Rights, which "majestically delineate the democratic form of government under which we live and the rights that protect us as equal citizens" (p. 10).

The tension between the values of our shared culture and calls for diversity is high among social studies educators. While the NCSS guidelines provide useful standards, many local schools are engaged in divisive debates as they strive to sort these issues out.

Global education is another key dimension of social studies that has received much attention over the past decade. Like multicultural education, global education is concerned with fostering an understanding of diversity, but in a global context. The accelerating growth of global interdependence, challenges to Western dominance, and the globalization of American society are cited as reasons underlying the importance of promoting global education (Anderson, 1990). In addition, global education stresses helping students learn to understand interdependent systems, differing cultural value systems, and emerging global trends.

How will the interest in multicultural education and global education play out? The research base is not altogether encouraging. Research regarding the outcomes of multicultural education, while suggesting positive effects, often is marked by inconsistency (Banks, 1991). Similarly, research regarding global understanding has been described as conceptually weak and methodologically flawed (Massialas, 1991). Moreover, it appears that curriculum development lags far behind the stated goals. Attention often is focused on the development of supplemental materials that are used by relatively few teachers. Textbooks, which depict more diversity than ever, still struggle with the problem of portraying diversity within the traditional context of history. Stronger definitions of these fields, with deliberate attention to common democratic values and widely agreed upon exemplars, would do much to assist the improvement of school practices.

Promises to Keep: The Standards Movement

The National Education Goals Panel (1993) concludes that U.S. students are nowhere near world class in terms of educational achievement. They observe that business leaders express concern about the future of the work force in a highly competitive global economy. University officials find applicants lacking in skills and competencies needed to undertake college study. School graduates, the Panel concludes, are unprepared to participate in their communities and to make educated, well-informed choices.

The advice of the National Education Goals Panel is to establish academic standards. They contend that these goals should be visible, reflected in the curriculum, instructional materials, teacher training, and assessment practices.

Leaders in social studies have devised two categories of standards. First the NCSS has developed *Curriculum Standards for Social Studies* (NCSS, 1994). The goal of the NCSS *Standards* is to provide an umbrella for the integrative potential of the social science disciplines and to build connections to other parts of the curriculum. Second, national organizations in history (National Center for History in the Schools, 1994a, 1994b), geography (Geography Education Standards Project, 1994), civics (Center for Civic Education, 1994), and economics (Saunders & Gilliard, 1995) have undertaken the task of developing separate subject standards. The strength of these standards is the identification of knowledge and skills critical to successful academic inquiry in each subject.

The NCSS *Standards* are an indication that the scholarly community increasingly has been rethinking the lines between disciplines. Perhaps the strongest pressure comes from the large number of scholars who now define themselves by the issues or problems they address rather than the discipline they use. Other pressures on single disciplines derive from:

- Research techniques that make greater use of technology, making cross-disciplinary work more feasible
- The internationalization of the scholarly community, which has tended to erode disciplinary barriers
- The growing specialization among scholars, which has led to more integration of knowledge as students look for ways to use knowledge
- Social issues that are increasingly complex and require more integrated knowledge for understanding

The authors of the NCSS *Standards* recognize that while separate disciplines continue to be important, there is a need to develop a more integrated and coherent framework. It is through this context that the social studies standards were created—paying full attention to the social sciences, humanities, fine arts, as well as to natural science and mathematics.

The NCSS *Standards* include 10 thematic strands in social studies:

1. Culture
2. Time, continuity, and change
3. People, places, and environments
4. Individual development and identity
5. Individuals, groups, and institutions
6. Production, distribution, and consumption

7. Power, authority, and governancy
8. Science, technology, and society
9. Global connections
10. Civic ideals and practices

While the NCSS has stressed the umbrella nature of its standards, the U.S. Department of Education has funded the development of curriculum standards that stress the importance of single subjects. For example:

- The National Center for History in the Schools has developed standards for U.S. and world history.
- The Center for Civic Education has developed standards for civics and government.
- The Geography Education Standards Project has developed standards for geography in cooperation with the American Geographical Society, Association of American Geographers, the National Council for Geographic Education, and the National Geographic Society.

What do these separate subject standards look like? Let's take history as an example. The National Center for History in the Schools stresses that schools require a clear vision of the place and importance of history in the general curriculum. The authors note that while there are many reasons why the study of history is important, none is more important than the recognition that knowledge of history is a precondition of political intelligence. Without history, a society shares no common memory of where it has been, of what its core values are, or what past decisions account for present circumstances. More specifically, the *National Standards for United States History: Exploring the American Experience* (National Center for History in the Schools, 1994a) consists of three components. It includes a list of content standards that define essential content in U.S. history; a description of standards for historical thinking and analysis; and several pages of illustrative teaching activities.

The development of national standards in geography and civics has continued with little controversy. However, widespread criticisms of both the U.S. history and the world history standards threaten the entire standards movement. Ravitch (1994), for example, while crediting the U.S. history standards with identifying key issues, charges the authors with failing to sufficiently stress shared civic values. She cites numerous examples of political and ideological bias, emphasizing that the standards "fail to strike a balance among the nation's ideals, its failures, and its achievements" (p. 40). She further notes that the bulk of these documents limit their usefulness to teachers.

REFLECTIONS ON REFORMING SOCIAL STUDIES

From our perspective, current efforts for change in social studies will strengthen the learning environment to the extent that they require a more intellectually powerful curriculum organized around an agreed upon set of principles that, through widespread application, will lead to greater understanding and more focused instruction. We need a renewed emphasis on developing curriculum that focuses on the barriers and confusions students have as they learn these key social studies principles. Such an approach demands the development of more content-specific instructional approaches.

Over the past few decades, research as well as logic have suggested a new configuration for social studies content. This scholarship, supported by such organizations as the American Historical Association, the National Geographic Society, and the NCSS, suggests that attention should be focused on broad patterns of human development across cultures, on variations in social systems and political economics, and on those people bypassed by the bardic or prescribed versions of the human story. Some scholars (American Historical Association, 1987; Crosby, 1986; Wolf, 1982) seem less concerned with comprehensiveness or with providing a total chronology of human events. Their work leans toward emphasizing thematic conceptualizations that focus on recurring processes like social patterns, conflict technology, and trading networks.

Organizations such as the National Council on Economic Education have developed exemplary curriculum materials that reflect such ideas about teaching recurring patterns with greater depth and application. For example, *Capstone: The Nation's High School Economics Course* (Reinke, Schug, & Wentworth, 1989) and *United States History: Eyes on the Economy* (Schug, Caldwell, Wentworth, Kraig, & Highsmith, 1993) are curriculum programs that focus students on the repeated application of a few simple but powerful principles derived from economics to help them learn to reason about perplexing problems and events. These principles of economic thinking are as follows:

1. People choose.
2. People's choices involve costs.
3. People respond to incentives in predictable ways.
4. People create economic systems with rules that influence incentives and choices.
5. People gain when they trade voluntarily.
6. People's choices have consequences that lie in the future.

These economic principles are not limited to use in economics courses but rather have widespread application to courses in world history, government, and U.S. history. Moreover, research (Clark & Highsmith, 1991) suggests that these curriculum efforts can result in important gains in student knowledge of and attitude toward economics.

Matched by concerns for building a more intellectually powerful curriculum is finding more powerful means of subject-matter instruction. Instructional approaches in social studies have changed little over the past decades. While some new methods, such as the emphasis on whole language learning, cooperative learning, and explicit instruction, may help strengthen students' abilities to understand and apply social studies concepts, there are other fruitful paths to consider. We need to understand the kinds of difficulties students have in learning social studies concepts. Studies in several subjects suggest that how students understand the social world differs from what we teach about the social world. For example, studies of economics education (see, e.g., Berti & Bombi, 1988; Jahoda, 1981; Schug, 1983; Schug & Lephardt, 1992) describe a strange economic world in which elementary school children believe that

- The price of a good depends on its size.
- Money is valuable because of its color, picture, size, or serial number.
- Money is created by running the government printing presses.
- Banks are simply safe places to store money.
- Property is owned by those who are near it or use it.
- The value of a good depends on the resources that go into producing it.
- Demand means wanting something.
- Supply means goods kept in inventory.
- The purpose of trade is to maximize exports and minimize imports.
- A car from Japan could not cost less than a similar U.S. car.

The geographic world may be equally puzzling. It is easy to imagine students sitting through social studies lessons quietly listening to the teacher's explanations of cardinal directions and then persisting in the understanding that north is "up" and south is "down" or failing to see how a person can be a citizen of a city, state, and nation simultaneously.

The point is that social studies may, in part, be failing because our subject has failed to bridge the gap between the misconceptions of students about their social world and the development of a more intellectually powerful curriculum. Teachers need to recognize and correct the confusions that students have about their social world that probably will persist even after textbook definitions have been memorized and test questions answered. Next, we need to develop specific, research-based, and classroom-tested teaching strategies that use as their primary standard the effective teaching of social studies content, skills, and attitudes. We believe that such a strategy, with its clear focus on the nature of subject-area content and of the learner, can more fully address our problems involving poor academic performance and a lack of enthusiasm for social studies.

CONCLUSION

Reforms in social studies may be thought of as a debate over which social studies rationale—citizen as patriot, academic, survivor, reformer, or policy maker—will dominate the curriculum. Multicultural and global education, with the stress on the need for societal change, seeks to reform the society through the curriculum, while the Bradley Commission report seeks a return to academics and traditional values. The National Standards Movement in history, geography, civics, and economics seeks a return to academic excellence but may, due to missteps in the history standards, fail. We suggest yet another approach that draws most heavily on the "citizen as academic" and strives to find new ways to engage students in effectively learning the social sciences. While the rationales for social studies may seem steady, they stress goals that have different outcomes. The content of recent reforms is diverse and reflects these differences in outcomes. While it is uncertain which approach will dominate, curriculum leaders at least can be clear about which goals they are striving to accomplish.

REFERENCES

American Historical Association. (1987). *Essays on global and comparative history.* Washington, DC: American Historical Association.

Anderson, L. F. (1990). A rationale for global education. In K. A. Tye (Ed.), *A rationale for global education in global education: From thought to action* (pp. 13–34). Alexandria, VA: Association for Supervision and Curriculum Development.

Banks, J. A. (1991). Multicultural education: Its effects on students' racial and gender role attitudes. In J. P. Shaver (Ed.), *Handbook of research on social studies teaching and learning* (pp. 459–469). New York: Macmillan.

Berti, A. E., & Bombi, A. S. (1988). *The child's construction of economics.* Cambridge: Cambridge University Press.

Bradley Commission on History in Schools. (1988). *Building a history curriculum: Guidelines for teaching history in schools.* Washington, DC: Bradley Commission.

California State Board of Education. (1988). *History–social science framework.* Sacramento: California State Department of Education.

Center for Civic Education. (1994). *National standards for civics and government.* Calabasas, CA: Center for Civic Education.

Clark, J. E., & Highsmith, R. J. (1991, October). *Does Capstone improve learning in high school economics courses?* Paper presented at the annual meeting of the Joint Council on Economic Education, Louisville, KY.

Crosby, A. W. (1986). *Ecological imperialism: The biological expansion of Europe, 900–1900.* Cambridge: Cambridge University Press.

Cuban, L. (1991). History of teaching in social studies. In J. P. Shaver (Ed.), *Handbook of research on social studies teaching and learning* (pp. 197–209). New York: Macmillan.

Geography Education Standards Project. (1994). *Geography for life: National geography standards.* Washington, DC: National Geographic Research and Exploration.

Jahoda, G. (1981). The development of thinking about economic institutions: The bank. *Cahiers de Psychologie Cognitive, 1,* 55–73.

Leming, J. S. (1989). The two cultures of social studies education. *Social Education, 53,* 404–408.

Leming, J. S. (1992). Ideological perspectives within the social studies profession: An empirical examination of the two cultures thesis. *Theory and Research in Social Education, 20*(3), 293–312.

Massialas, B. G. (1991). Education for international understanding. In J. P. Shaver (Ed.), *Handbook of research on social studies teaching and learning* (pp. 448–458). New York: Macmillan.

Morrissett, I. (1986). Status of social studies: The mid–1980s. *Social Education, 50,* 393–410.

National Assessment of Educational Progress (NAEP). (1990a). *The U.S. history report card.* Washington, DC: U.S. Department of Education.

National Assessment of Educational Progress (NAEP). (1990b). *The geography learning of high school students.* Washington, DC: U.S. Department of Education.

National Center for History in the Schools. (1994a). *National standards for United States history: Exploring the American experience.* Los Angeles: University of California.

National Center for History in the Schools. (1994b). *National standards for world history: Exploring paths to the present.* Los Angeles: University of California.

National Council for the Social Studies (NCSS). (1992). Curriculum guidelines for multicultural education. *Social Education, 56*(5), 274–294.

National Council for the Social Studies (NCSS). (1994). *Curriculum standards for social studies: Expectations of excellence.* Washington, DC: NCSS.

National Commission on Social Studies in the Schools. (1989). *Charting a course: Social studies for the 21st century.* Washington, DC: National Commission on Social Studies in the Schools.

National Education Association (NEA). (1916). *The social studies in secondary education: A report of the committee on social studies on the reorganization of secondary education of the National Education Association* (Bulletin, 1916, No. 28). Washington, DC: NEA.

National Education Goals Panel. (1993). *Promises to keep: Creating high standards for American students.* Washington, DC: U.S. Department of Education.

Nelson, J. (1990). Charting a course backwards: A response to the National Commission's nineteenth century social studies program. *Social Education, 54,* 434–437.

Ravitch, D. (1992). A common culture. *Educational Leadership, 49*(4), 8–11.

Ravitch, D. (1994, December 7). Standards in U.S. history: An assessment. *Education Week,* p. 40.

Reinke, R., Schug, M. C., & Wentworth, D. R. (1989). *Capstone: The nation's high school economics course.* New York: Joint Council on Economic Education.

Saunders, P., & Gilliard, J. V. (Eds.). (1995). *A framework for teaching basic economic concepts with scope and sequence recommendations, K–12.* New York: National Council on Economic Education.

Schug, M. C. (1983). The development of economic thinking in children and adolescents. *Social Education, 47,* 141–145.

Schug, M. C., Caldwell, J., Wentworth, D. R., Kraig, B., & Highsmith, R. J. (1993). *United States history: Eyes on the economy.* New York: National Council on Economic Education.

Schug, M. C., & Lephardt, N. (1992). Development in children's thinking about international trade. *The Social Studies, 83*(5), 207–211.

Shaver, J. P., Davis, O. L., & Helburn, S. W. (1979). The status of social studies education: Impressions from three NSF studies. *Social Education, 43,* 150–153.

Shaughnessy, J. M., & Haladyna, T. M. (1985). Research on student attitude toward social studies. *Social Education, 49,* 692–695.

Superka, D. P., Hawke, S., & Morrissett, I. (1980). The current and future status of social studies. *Social Education, 44,* 362–369.

Wolf, E. R. (1982). *Europe and the people without history.* Berkeley: University of California Press.

Response

Social Studies for Students with Mild Disabilities

Charles K. Curtis

Social studies programs for students with disabilities have been described in numerous curricula for at least the past half century. Curtis (1978) reviewed social studies curricula for special classes, schools, and institutions in the United States and Canada for the period 1950 to 1975, when the Education for All Handicapped Children Act (PL 94–142) was passed, and concluded that the majority of curricula bore little resemblance to social studies programs for students in regular schools during the same period. While the content of most courses in social studies curricula for students in regular classes consisted of traditional history, geography, and civics topics, content in curricula for special students ranged from simplistic modifications of regular social studies courses to instruction in topics not usually considered as social studies, such as personal cleanliness and providing for wild birds during the winter season. Many social studies curricula for the latter group of students placed heavy emphasis on job preparation and on the encouragement of law-abiding, nondisruptive behavior. These patterns continued even during the period following the Woods Hole Conference in 1959, when social studies educators and curriculum developers responded to Jerome Bruner's suggestion that school curricula be based on the academic disciplines. Content based on concepts selected from history, geography, and the social sciences, with inquiry as the primary teaching strategy, generally was ignored in the writings of special educators and in the social studies curricula they developed.

The Education for All Handicapped Children Act established mainstreaming as public policy in the United States, and similar policies are in place in most provinces of Canada. As a consequence, most students with mild disabilities presently are integrated into regular social studies classes, at least at the elementary and junior high levels. Integration raises a number of significant questions about appropriate social studies for these students,

Curriculum Trends, Special Education, and Reform: Refocusing the Conversation. ISBN 0-8077-3562-0 (pbk), ISBN 0-8077-3563-9 (cloth).

many of whom prior to the passage of PL 94–142 would have received their education either in special classes or in separate schools.

Several of the issues raised by Schug and Hartoonian concern social studies teachers, both of integrated classes and, where they still are maintained, of separate classes. For the most part, however, these issues have not been addressed in the literature. Rather than dealing with specific issues, authors of journal articles, publications of education associations, and college methods textbooks, whether writing in social studies or in special education, have tended to focus on general strategies for managing classrooms (Shaver & Curtis, 1996). The purpose of this response, then, is to consider several of the problems discussed by Schug and Hartoonian that have particular relevance for teachers of students with mild disabilities enrolled in their social studies classes. Additionally, suggestions for teaching strategies and for organizing social studies activities to accommodate students with mild disabilities will be offered.

DEFINING SOCIAL STUDIES FOR STUDENTS WITH MILD DISABILITIES

As Schug and Hartoonian noted, a long-standing issue in the literature pertains to the nature of social studies. Rationales for the various definitions of social studies tend to be founded in competing notions of citizenship. Such debates over concepts of citizenship for students with mild disabilities are rare in the special education literature. Reviews of social studies curricula for students most frequently described as slow learners or students with mild mental retardation (Bailey, 1968; Curtis, 1977; Gozali & Gonwa, 1973; Stevens, 1958; Stroud, 1976; Uphoff, 1967) have revealed a narrow conception of citizenship. With few exceptions, there seemed to be a consensus among special educators that good citizenship consisted of being gainfully employed; respecting and obeying the law; maintaining the family home and furnishings in good repair; respecting a neighbor's property; treating neighbors in a courteous manner; helping to keep the neighborhood clean, quiet, and orderly; and returning borrowed articles. While there can be no question that these are worthy attributes for all citizens, during the period that these curricula were taught to special education students, a major focus of social studies for regular students was preparation for responsible citizenship, characterized as effective participation in the democratic process (Curtis, 1978). Good citizenship for graduates of regular programs consisted of being aware of community problems and being committed to their resolution, believing in the quality of individuals and manifesting a concern for the constitutional rights of all citizens; being open-minded; and possessing the decision-making skills requisite for effective participation. Most social studies programs for these students would have been classified by Barr, Barth, and Shermis (1978) as either social sciences or reflective inquiry. Had those authors examined the social studies curricula reviewed by Bailey and the other authors mentioned above, they likely would have concluded that most fit within the category they described as citizenship transmission.

With integration, separate social studies programs for students with disabilities are no longer likely to be an issue for most teachers. This might be inferred from an examination, conducted for this response, of 28 social studies methods textbooks published since 1975, which revealed that when integration was referred to, comments generally consisted of strategies for accommodating students with particular disabilities, rather than descriptions of modified or different content. A similar pattern was found in several special education textbooks in which the authors described programs for students with cognitive disabilities that closely resembled regular social studies curricula (see, e.g., Luftig, 1987; Miller & Davis, 1982; Polloway, Payne, Patton, & Payne, 1985).

In their chapter, Schug and Hartoonian referred to recently published standards or guidelines for developing curricula in social studies and for selecting content from the specific disciplines (e.g., history, geography, economics, and civics) that constitute the social studies. In addition to the themes Schug and Hartoonian identified, the NCSS *Standards* include rationales for making social studies teaching and learning "meaningful, integrative, value-based, challenging, and active" (Task Force of the NCSS, 1994, p. 162). Furthermore, the *Standards* list "skills" that are "essential" (pp. 148–149) outcomes of the social studies program. The extent to which the *Standards* are intended for students with disabilities is unclear from the Task Force document. Support for integration is implied in the argument that "all students need exposure to a diverse range of peers and opportunities to address social problems in group settings" (p. 162). For "special education students" in segregated settings, the document simply states that curriculum planners should give "full attention to social studies as well as other subjects" (p. 162).

The impact of these standards, developed by national organizations for specific subjects, on state or local social studies curricula remains to be seen. Moreover, whether curriculum developers using these standards will modify them to accommodate perceived differences in student capabilities due to mental or physical disabilities also is unknown. However, if the standards provide principles for "powerful teaching and learning," as the Task Force report suggests (p. 159), they should be modified only when it can be clearly shown that not to do so would inhibit students' learning.

For most teachers, the question here is not one of definition or even of curriculum standards. How social studies is defined or its subject content is organized in a particular integrated classroom is not likely to vary for nondisabled students and students with disabilities. What may vary, however, are teachers' expectations for their students. Whether students with disabilities in regular classrooms should be held to the same standards of achievement as their nonhandicapped peers is the question that concerns many teachers.

Questions relating to standards for students with disabilities who are integrated into social studies classes are complex. For example, in conversations with teachers the author frequently is asked, among others, questions such as: Should teachers lower their standards to accommodate students with disabilities? Should such students be expected to write the same examinations and complete the same assignments as other students? Should criteria such as personal growth, effort, or behavior be used to assess the progress of students with disabilities?

Shaver and Curtis (1996) considered these and related questions and suggested that unless there are sound pedagogical reasons for accepting different standards of achievement as satisfactory for students with disabilities, these students should be held to a common achievement criterion. They argued that to hold lower expectations for these students, except in those cases where it is wholly unreasonable not to do so, may lead to or reinforce attitudes that devalue persons with disabilities. Such attitudes are discriminatory and degrading, and they have negative consequences for both students with disabilities and their nondisabled peers. For students with disabilities, they may result in lowered feelings of self-worth that inhibit personal, social, and educational development. For nondisabled students, they may result in a lack of caring for persons seen to be different and, in particular, less able. Negative attitudes toward any group threaten a democratic society's commitment to equality, human worth, and dignity.

WHICH SOCIAL STUDIES FOR STUDENTS WITH MILD DISABILITIES?

In the past, the practice of simplifying regular curricula or developing curricula specifically for students with disabilities enrolled in special classes or schools often resulted in social studies programs that, for the most part, lacked substance and validity. Many of them were of questionable value as preparation for citizenship, including the limited concept of citizenship implied in the special education literature.

Preparation for Citizenship

If students with mild disabilities are to be prepared for effective citizenship roles in their communities and nation, then social studies has a significant role to play in this preparation. However, previous concepts of citizenship were based on assumptions both of student differences in cognitive and affective functioning and of the roles people of different abilities play in community affairs. In a society committed to egalitarian principles, these assumptions must be questioned. We need to be reminded that citizens in a democratic society, including those identified while in school as having disabilities, have the right to vote in elections, join political parties and pressure groups, run for public office, and take part in any legitimate political activity. It follows, then, that a major goal of social studies should be the development of rational participating citizens grounded in an understanding of democratic ideals and in a commitment to human dignity.

Schug and Hartoonian espouse a curriculum closely aligned with the "citizen as academic" rationale. Topics for their curriculum would be selected from themes identified as significant by historians, geographers, and economics educators. If their position that such a social studies curriculum is appropriate for regular students is accepted, then it should hold that it is also appropriate for students with mild disabilities. It is this author's opinion, however, that while it may be argued that the themes and principles mentioned in the Schug and Hartoonian chapter are important for the general education of students, they need to be supplemented with content more closely tied to a commitment to participatory democracy. That is, the social studies program should involve students, both those with disabilities and those without, in studies that examine real problems and issues that are of concern to people in the community. Therefore, to the "citizen as academic" rationale, a second rationale, the "citizen as reformer," should be added. Typical content for social studies programs based on this rationale would include, according to Schug and Hartoonian, "local studies of community problems, organizing action groups, writing letters, [and] registering voters."

In his Presidential Address to the NCSS, in which he discussed the future of social studies, Shirley Engle (1971) suggested that contemporary problems were appropriate content for involving students in the social realities of their communities and for preparing them for active participation in the political process. Support for Engle's statement can be found in the writings of a number of prominent social studies educators, among them Newmann (1970), Ocoha (Engle & Ochoa, 1988), Oliver (1957), and Shaver (1992). In *Building Rationales for Citizenship Education,* Curtis (1977) argued that contemporary problems should be included in social studies programs for learners with disabilities. If upon leaving school, persons with disabilities are to be expected to participate in the affairs of their communities, then it seems reasonable to propose that at least part of the social studies program should be given over to learning experiences that most directly prepare them for this role. Moreover, such investigations of contemporary community problems provide an excellent context for problem-solving, decision-making, and critical thinking exercises—which generally have been ignored in social studies programs for special students. Including contemporary community problems as content in social studies programs fits with the pedagogical model provided in the special education literature. This model embraces content selected from the contemporary scene, with a "here and now" quality, which provides direct contact with reality and, at least during the initial stages, relates to the everyday experiences of the students (Curtis, 1977). Support for contemporary problems as content in social studies programs can be found in special education methods textbooks by Luftig (1987), Price, Ness, & Stitt (1982), and Polloway, Payne, Patton, and Payne (1985).

There is some research that suggests that students with mild disabilities, at least those in high school social studies classes, can engage in such studies. Miller and Weston (1947) conducted such a study with slow-learning students as part of the Detroit Citizenship Education Study. A primary objective of this study was the development of critical thinking skills as students used inquiry activities to examine the problems created by diminishing water resources. Curtis (1978) and Curtis and Shaver (1980) reported a study in which slow-learning students in high school special classes utilized an inquiry approach to investigate the problem of how to provide adequate low-income housing in their communities. Among the materials used as sources were newspapers, magazine articles, government publications, brochures from private interest groups, and tapes of radio hot-line broadcasts. Teaching strategies were designed to increase knowledge of and interest in community problems, open-mindedness, critical thinking, self-esteem, and reading comprehension. Slow-learning high school students also were included among the subjects in the Humanities Curriculum Project conducted in British secondary schools during the period 1968 to 1972 (Hamingson, 1973). Problems for the study were selected from areas such as family responsibilities, employment, relationships between the sexes, and poverty. Two dissertations (Sauers, 1974; Schubert, 1973) completed at Carnegie–Mellon University reported studies in which slow-learning students were taught historical and sociological concepts, which were then used to examine contemporary problems within the context of a particular city.

Instructional Approaches

In their chapter, Schug and Hartoonian refer to the findings of several studies (Cuban, 1991; National Assessment of Educational Progress, 1990; Shaver, Davis, & Helburn, 1979) that a lecture and discussion approach based on the textbook was the predominant approach used by social studies teachers in regular programs. The pedagogical value of such an approach is questionable, especially when students with disabilities are integrated into regular social studies classes. In fact, it runs counter to suggestions in the special education literature that suitable pedagogy in social studies classes should utilize a wide variety of materials and activities and encourage active student participation through role-playing and dramatics, field studies, and community resource persons (Curtis, 1978). Furthermore, since many social studies textbooks have readability levels well beyond grade level (Bradley, Ames, & Mitchell, 1980), many students with mild disabilities might experience difficulty with their use. Where teachers feel bound to use the textbook as their primary resource, they should utilize strategies that will assist poor and marginal readers to read and to comprehend the material. Among the methods that have been reported to have shown significant results are guided reading strategies in which students concentrate on chapter titles and subtitles, vocabulary lists, graphs, charts, maps, and chapter questions (Bean & Pardi, 1979), or complete worksheets on which they record main ideas and important details (Wong, Wong, Perry, & Sawatsky, 1986). Audiotapes of selections from the textbook also have been used with some success (Mosby, 1979; Tyo, 1980), as have supplemental visual materials (Darch & Carnine, 1986).

The chapter entitled, "Social Studies for Students At-Risk and with Disabilities," in the *Handbook of Research on Social Studies Teaching and Learning* (Curtis, 1991) described studies in which procedures for organizing instruction in integrated social studies classes were examined. The majority of these studies, conducted by D. W. and R. T. Johnson and their associates at the University of Minnesota, compared the cooperative learning approach with competitive or individual approaches. Other studies reported the effects of peer-tutoring programs and individualized instruction on the achievement of students with mild disabilities in integrated social studies classes.

Cooperative learning as a means for organizing instruction in integrated social studies classes appears to have a number of beneficial effects. Cooperative learning tends to promote positive interactions between students with disabilities and their nondisabled peers, including friendships outside the classroom (see, e.g., Johnson & Johnson, 1983). Although not entirely clear from the studies reviewed, it is likely that these interactions enhance the self-esteem of students with disabilities. In several studies in which achievement was a factor, students with mild disabilities in cooperative learning classrooms tended to score higher on social studies tests than comparable students in classes where individual or competitive approaches were used (see, e.g., Yager, Johnson, Johnson, & Snider, 1985). Beyond these effects, Curtis (1991) suggested that "cooperative learning may be conceived of as citizenship training [for students with disabilities] by providing a model for developing the skills necessary for functioning effectively in democratic groups" (p. 171).

Studies employing peer-tutoring or individualized instruction have yielded positive gains in achievement for special education students in social studies classes, although such studies have been too few in number to draw any conclusion concerning their effectiveness. However, it seems reasonable to suggest that providing students with disabilities with additional and specific teaching from their nondisabled peers and preparing materials for individualizing instruction are appropriate pedagogical practices.

CONCLUSION

Schug and Hartoonian raised a number of issues associated with the teaching of social studies. Problems relating to definitions of social studies, content base and selection of topics, current practices, and student achievement were identified and discussed. Several of these became the basis for this response.

Based on the author's experiences, it was suggested that definitions concerning the nature of social studies and the organization of curricular content for students with mild disabilities are not likely to be issues for many teachers of integrated classes. Instead, a concern was expressed that teachers acting on presumptions of student differences may set lower standards for some students. Such a practice, except in cases where it is clearly reasonable to do so, is discriminatory. Not only may it fail to encourage integrated students to work to their potential, but it also may serve to reinforce negative feelings of self-worth.

There is much we have to learn about teaching social studies to students with mild disabilities in integrated classes. Identifying effective methods for teaching content and skills to these students in integrated settings should be an important concern of researchers. Integration has been policy for 2 decades; nevertheless, reports of such studies have been few. The findings of studies in areas such as cooperative learning, peer tutoring, and individualized instruction need to be replicated at various grade levels and with a variety of content before generalizations concerning their effectiveness with integrated students can be developed.

The Task Force of the NCSS (1994, p. 152) identified a number of "beliefs and values" that form the tenets of a democratic society. How best to develop commitment to these in students who may have difficulty with abstract concepts, as many students with mild disabilities experience, is an important question for social studies educators. Similarly, how best to encourage acceptance and respect for students with disabilities enrolled in integrated classes is a question for which at present there is no clear answer.

Traditional social studies curricula for students with disabilities were based on a limited concept of citizenship. With integration, perhaps the concept of citizenship for students with disabilities will resemble more closely the concept for nondisabled students. Without doubt, social studies has an important role to play in the preparation of all students for active citizenship roles.

REFERENCES

Bailey, J. D. (1968). *A study and analysis of the content of selected social studies curricula for secondary educable mentally retarded students.* Unpublished master's thesis, University of Kansas, Lawrence.

Barr, R., Barth, J. L., & Shermis, S. (1978). *The nature of social studies.* Palm Springs, CA: ETC Publications.

Bean, W., & Pardi, R. (1979). A field test of a guided reading strategy. *Journal of Reading, 23,* 144–147.

Bradley, J., Ames, W., & Mitchell, J. (1980). Intrabook reliability: Variations within history textbooks. *Social Education, 44,* 524–528.

Cuban, L. (1991). History of teaching in social studies. In J. P. Shaver (Ed.), *Handbook of research on social studies teaching and learning* (pp. 197–209). New York: Macmillan.

Curtis, C. K. (1977). Citizenship education and the slow learner. In J. P. Shaver (Ed.), *Building rationales for citizenship education* (pp. 74–95). Washington, DC: National Council for the Social Studies.

Curtis, C. K. (1978). *Contemporary community problems in citizenship education for slow-learning secondary students.* Unpublished doctoral dissertation, Utah State University, Logan.

Curtis, C. K. (1991). Social studies for students at-risk and with disabilities. In J. P. Shaver (Ed.), *Handbook of research on social studies teaching and learning* (pp. 157–174). New York: Macmillan.

Curtis, C. K., & Shaver, J. P. (1980). Slow learners and the study of contemporary problems. *Social Education, 44,* 302–309.

Darch, C., & Carnine, D. (1986). Teaching content area material to learning disabled students. *Exceptional Children, 55,* 240–246.

Engle, S. (1971). Exploring the meaning of social studies. *Social Education, 35,* 280–288.

Engle, S. H., & Ochoa, A. S. (1988). *Education for democratic citizenship: Decision making in the social studies.* New York: Teachers College Press.

Gozali, J., & Gonwa, J. (1973). Citizenship training for the EMR: A case of educational neglect. *Mental Retardation, 11*(1), 49–50.

Hamingson, D. (Ed.). (1973). *Towards judgment.* East Anglia, England: University of East Anglia, Centre for Applied Research in Education.

Johnson, R. T., & Johnson, D. W. (1983). Effects of cooperative, competitive, and individualistic learning experiences on social development. *Exceptional Children, 49,* 323–328.

Luftig, R. L. (1987). *Teaching the mentally retarded student.* Boston: Allyn & Bacon.

Miller, J., & Weston, G. (1947). Slow learners improve in critical thinking. *Social Education, 13,* 315–318.

Miller, T. L., & Davis, E. E. (Eds.). (1982). *The mildly handicapped student.* New York: Grune & Stratton.

Mosby, R. (1979). A bypass program of supported instruction for secondary students with learning disabilities. *Journal of Learning Disabilities, 12*(3), 187–190.

National Assessment of Educational Progress. (1990). *The U.S. history report card.* Washington, DC: U.S. Department of Education.

Newmann, F. M. (1970). *Clarifying public controversy: An approach to teaching social studies.* Boston: Little, Brown.

Oliver, D. W. (1957). The selection of content in the social studies. *Harvard Educational Review, 27,* 271–300.

Polloway, E., Payne, J., Patton, J., & Payne, R. (1985). *Strategies for teaching retarded and special needs learners.* Columbus, OH: Merrill.

Price, M., Ness, J., & Stitt, M. (1982). Beyond the three R's: Science and social studies instruction for the mildly handicapped. In T. L. Miller & E. E. Davis (Eds.), *The mildly handicapped student* (pp. 363–385). New York: Grune & Stratton.

Sauers, B. J. (1974). *Living in an urban world—Mexico City: A history unit for tenth-grade slow learners.* Unpublished doctoral dissertation, Carnegie–Mellon University, Pittsburgh.

Schubert, J. G. (1973). *Living in an urban world—Ibadan: A history unit for tenth-grade slow learners.* Unpublished doctoral dissertation, Carnegie–Mellon University, Pittsburgh.

Shaver, J. P. (1992). Rationales for issues-centered social studies education. *The Social Studies, 83,* 95–99.

Shaver, J. P., & Curtis, C. K. (1996). Social studies and students with disabilities. In R. Allen & B. Massialas (Eds.), *Crucial issues in social studies, K–12.* Belmont, CA: Wadsworth.

Shaver, J. P., Davis, O. L., & Helburn, S. W. (1979). The status of social studies education: Impressions from three NSF studies. *Social Education, 43,* 150–153.

Stevens, G. D. (1958). An analysis of objectives for the education of children with retarded mental development. *American Journal of Mental Deficiency, 63,* 225–235.

Stroud, M. B. (1976). *The achievement of social studies objectives of a persisting life problems curriculum by educable mentally retarded pupils in four mainstreaming settings in Ohio.* Unpublished doctoral dissertation, Kent State University, Kent, OH.

Task Force of the NCSS. (1994). *Curriculum standards for social studies* (NCSS Bulletin 89). Washington, DC: National Council for the Social Studies.

Tyo, J. (1980). An alternative for poor readers in social science. *Social Education, 44,* 309–310.

Uphoff, J. K. (1967). *Senior high school social studies programs for low achievers.* Unpublished doctoral dissertation, University of Nebraska, Lincoln.

Wong, B., Wong, R., Perry, N., & Sawatsky, D. (1986). The efficacy of a self-questioning summarization strategy for use by underachievers and learning disabled adolescents in social studies. *Learning Disabilities Focus, 2*(2), 20–35.

Yager, S., Johnson, R. T., Johnson, D. W., & Snider, B. (1985). The impact of group processing on achievement in cooperative learning groups. *The Journal of Social Psychology, 126,* 389–397.

Response

The Impact of Issues and Trends in the Social Studies Curriculum on Students with Mild Disabilities

Thomas C. Lovitt

The field of social studies is in a state of flux. While the other major subject areas have come to some consensus regarding standards and trends, social studies educators are still wrestling with the what's and how's and rationales of the trends that are shaping and leading reform in their field. Schug and Hartoonian present a comprehensive overview of one approach to conceptualizing the social studies field. I begin this response by expanding on their view of social studies, drawing on Walter Parker's (1991) work to provide both comparison and contrast. My response continues with a look at key issues facing special educators and how those issues affect students' success in learning social studies, and concludes with some general comments on the convergence of school restructuring and the press for inclusion of students with disabilities.

A LOOK AT TRENDS: ISSUES MOTIVATING SOCIAL STUDIES REFORM

According to Schug and Hartoonian, there are three issues in social studies curriculum that have converged and have led educators to rethink the content and processes of the field. They have to do with the definition of social studies, competing rationales for citizenship, and homogeneous and conventional teaching practices. With respect to definition, the authors note that there are several interpretations of social studies and therefore an ongoing tension is present. The question of definition is crucial, particularly within the context of current efforts toward curricular reform. As for the second issue, competing rationales for citizenship, Schug and Hartoonian remind us that these "competing rationales lead to very different commitments on the part of teachers regarding what counts as the social studies

Curriculum Trends, Special Education, and Reform: Refocusing the Conversation. ISBN 0-8077-3562-0 (pbk), ISBN 0-8077-3563-9 (cloth).

curriculum." Pertaining to the third issue, conventional teaching practices, they note that "despite these competing definitions and rationales, and while scholars and leaders in the profession argue vociferously about their contending views, actual classroom practice is remarkably homogeneous and characterized by a clear, familiar pattern." It is a pattern well known to students, they note, and one that students tend to judge poorly in relationship to many other subjects.

Parker (1991) focuses on three specific curricular and instructional issues that he sees at the heart of the movement toward social studies education reform. He frames them as questions.

- Should the content of social studies in the primary grades be expanded?
- How much social studies should be required in the secondary grades?
- Can students' attitudes toward social studies be improved?

At the primary level, Parker contends that it is important to reduce the gap between the written and taught curricula, and to "secure a place for social studies in the elementary school" (p. 79). With reference to the second issue, involving the secondary grades, Parker welcomes the trend to correct the content-poor social studies curricula that we now have and to "replace electives with requirements in nearly all of the secondary social studies curriculums" (p. 79). These issues dovetail with concerns raised by Schug and Hartoonian regarding definition and its impact on the curriculum. As for the third issue—achieving a more positive student attitude toward social studies—Parker maintains that in order to succeed, social studies classes must be made more relevant, more exciting, and more engaging. This remains one of the goals of curriculum reform trends across subject areas.

Schug and Hartoonian begin by identifying matters of definition, rationales of citizenship, and instruction as issues; Parker (1991) emphasizes instruction itself at the elementary and secondary levels and the interest of students in social studies as an instructional issue. Although their points of departure differ, taken together the two viewpoints provide those concerned with offering proper social studies education to children and youth with disabilities a broader, more complete exposure to the future.

Trends in Social Studies Curriculum

Regarding current trends in social studies curriculum, Schug and Hartoonian identify three: a return to history and geography, multicultural and global education, and the standards movement. For the first trend, they point out that there are influential groups and commissions that promote the separation of the social studies subjects, whereas others advocate the integration of the subjects. With respect to the trend toward multicultural education, they point out that although there is common agreement that there should be more coverage on ethnic and cultural diversity (albeit considerable debate on how to carry it out), a renewed emphasis on that theme is not without problems, one of which is that this accent may encourage separatism.

The emergence of the standards movement is a means both to clarify individual areas within social studies and to link content across disciplines. The standards also are meant to point the way to much stronger patterns of instruction.

Parker (1991) identified five trends that support in large measure the points made by Schug and Hartoonian: back to curriculum, strengthening content, globalizing the curriculum, every day every grade, and more on less. As for the first trend, Parker contends that "social studies educators are asking anew: What social studies knowledge is most important, and how can opportunities to learn it sensibly be sequenced across the grades, K–12?" (p. 82). The second trend, related to the first, is "the increasing demand for history, geography, and civics in all grades" (p. 82). With reference to globalization, the third trend, he maintains that there is a need to build accurate understandings that are neither narrow nor ethnocentric but that take international and cross-cultural variations into account. There is a related "need to assemble a genuinely global habit of mind that inclines learners to *seek* global comparisons and to *want* the facts about the whole planet, not just their little piece of it" (p. 84). As for the next trend, Parker sees and advocates a move toward providing daily instruction in social studies in grades K–12, stating that "educators who specialize in teaching reading and writing skills are realizing that students can't read and write about nothing, and the logical subjects are social studies, science, and the arts and humanities" (p. 84). The fifth tendency, he observes, is a "trend to spend precious instructional time on a limited number of important topics" (p. 84).

So, whereas the two sets of authors differ somewhat in emphasis regarding what constitutes the issues they believe will be important in the future of social studies education, they are in close agreement with respect to current trends in social studies education. This is likely because the everyday teaching practices and the problems and concerns of schools with respect to social studies are remarkably similar from one part of the country to another (the two sets of authors live in different parts of the country). Taken together, then, the notions these different authors offer regarding trends offer a broad base for those concerned about the education of children and youth with disabilities.

ISSUES IN SPECIAL EDUCATION

Keeping in mind this convergence of issues and trends, I will identify and discuss several issues that relate to teaching children and youth with disabilities in the area of social studies.

What Do Children and Youth with Disabilities Need to Learn?

It is extremely difficult to decide what any type of student should *really* know when it comes to social studies. However, it is an even more vexing matter when trying to decide for youth with disabilities, knowing, first of all, that there is tremendous heterogeneity among them. Some have academic difficulties, some have behavior problems, others have physical and sensory problems, and yet others have a combination of problems. To compound all of this, some students are in families or situations that offer them a significant amount of support, whereas others are in circumstances where they are virtually neglected.

To the extent that students with disabilities are able to achieve them, I heartily agree with the five essential areas of learning in social studies: democratic ideal, cultural diversity, economic development, global perspective, and participatory citizenship (Parker, 1991). To the extent possible, students with disabilities should know about each essential area of social studies learning, but I do not see them as being *as* essential as the one regarding citizenship. It is on this last goal that I believe we should concentrate most for children and youth with disabilities.

To participate effectively in a democracy, students with mild disabilities need to know about laws, voting, and governmental and private agencies, bureaus, and divisions, particularly the ones they probably will interact with. They need to know about city and county facilities, parks, post offices, pools, and hospitals. They need to be informed of their rights as individuals with disabilities and how to see to it that those rights are upheld.

As for geography, students with disabilities should know about their neighborhoods, the community transportation system, major streets, and highways. It may be essential for them to know that the geography of their particular area has changed over time and that it undoubtedly will change in the future.

History is also important. Students should know about their families, where their parents, grandparents, aunts, and uncles came from. They need to know about their past. They should know that things are different now than they were 5, 10, 50 years ago, and that things will be different in the future. They need to know that not all of the changes that have taken place are for the best, and that therein lie several debates.

Although this description of what students with disabilities should know, simplifies curriculum goals in social studies, let me reiterate that the heterogeneity among students with disabilities means that, first and foremost, teachers will need to make judgments about what students can and cannot do based on their knowledge of the students, rather than on the disability label that may be in use.

What Do General Education Teachers Need to Know About Students with Disabilities?

General education teachers can benefit from having specific knowledge about children and youth with disabilities who are likely to come into their classes. This knowledge should enhance their capacity to plan instruction accordingly.

Specifically, social studies teachers should realize that many students with disabilities, as well as many who do not have disabilities, work best when they are actively involved with a topic. Because many students with disabilities may read and process information less well than their general education peers, they do best when instruction requires interaction. It has become apparent through my own research in six high schools and interviews with about 100 youths with mild disabilities that, like their counterparts who do not have disabilities, they do not see social studies as an important subject or set of subjects and social studies classes are not their favorites. On the average and across the six schools, students in the study put social studies in fifth place with respect to both importance and being a favorite, generally below the other core subjects: math, science, and language arts (Lovitt, 1995). Keeping students involved with important and relevant activities, then, is one way to increase their interest and is an important goal for improving the teaching of social studies across the board.

Teachers also should be aware that many students with disabilities, like other students at risk, may not have had as many life experiences as have other students. Not as many of them may have been to the nation's Capitol, to Disneyland, or to the Grand Canyon. Not as many of them may come from homes where their parents read to them and discuss current and past events. Consequently, when students with disabilities are asked to learn about various aspects of U.S. government, geography, or history, they may not have the "schema" upon which to draw and to attach new learnings. Knowing this, it is necessary for teachers of children and youth with disabilities to have large repertoires of instructional tactics and strategies on hand. Fortunately, numbers of data-based techniques are available for social studies teachers and others who are called on to "include" students with disabilities in their classes.

How Will Social Studies Teachers Teach Students with Disabilities?

Social studies teachers, in particular, and in fact all teachers, if they are to serve students with disabilities adequately—as well as other students who may deviate from the norm—must have a vast arsenal of instructional techniques at their disposal. They should be able to set up cooperative learning groups (Slavin, 1990), utilize reciprocal teaching (Lovitt, 1994), and peer-tutoring situations (Cooke, Heron, & Heward, 1983). Those arrangements not only would enable teachers to provide instruction on the important lessons of social studies, but would enable youth to experience firsthand the diversity of students in their midst and also learn to work with their peers (see, for example, the work of Maheady, Harper, & Sacca, 1988, on peer-mediated instruction). Teachers also should know about various learning strategies, be able to communicate them to students, and instruct students on how to employ the proper strategies at the proper time. Teachers need to know about strategies for taking notes, for writing essays and reports, and for general organization (see Deshler & Schumaker, 1986; Lovitt, 1991), which are particularly important for social studies. They should know about various strategies for comprehending textual material (see, e.g., Pressley, Johnson, Symons, McGoldrick, & Kurita, 1989). Furthermore, social studies teachers must learn about techniques for modifying textbooks and other materials and about making other instructional accommodations for students with disabilities (see Lovitt & Horton, 1991, for a review of adaptation approaches). Two articles in the July 1994 issue of *Remedial and Special Education* reported on the extent to which elementary and secondary social studies teachers adapted textbooks and other related materials for children and youth with disabilities in their classes (Bean, Zigmond, & Hartman, 1994; Passe & Beattie, 1994).

When instructing teachers on how to use all of these new approaches so that students with disabilities are included, we must keep in mind that these techniques are definitely the means toward the end; the end is the social studies (or any) curriculum, the content that is taught. According to Parker (1991), "the best teaching methods cannot possibly overcome a weak curriculum; good instruction on unimportant content is not victory" (p. 93).

Teachers must be aware that not only should their instruction be related to desired outcomes, but their instruction should be evaluated as it relates to the content of the curriculum. Teachers must be apprised regularly as to the extent to which their pupils are attaining the anticipated goals. Just as abundant instructional techniques are available to support overarching curriculum goals, several appropriate and contemporary ways in which to evaluate progress are at hand.

ASSESSING PERFORMANCE IN SOCIAL STUDIES

Like their counterparts in all other areas of teaching, social studies teachers need first and foremost to drop the commonplace practice of using standardized tests. Alternative assessments should be chosen only after considering the types of students taught and the kinds of information, skills, and concepts being measured. Three of the more frequently mentioned alternatives include curriculum-based assessment, outcomes-based assessment, and portfolio assessment.

Curriculum-based assessment is used extensively in special education practice (e.g., Howell & Morehead, 1987). In this approach, assessment is tied directly to what is taught: If *A* is taught, then *A* would be measured. This approach takes care of a common criticism of evaluation regarding the need for directness. Being direct says nothing about the curriculum, however. If the curriculum is irrelevant, then the assessment is simply a direct way of measuring the extent to which something irrelevant was learned.

A second currently acclaimed approach is referred to as outcome-based assessment and education. In this method, which is not all that different from the one just described, students are assessed on the extent to which they attain the goals of the curriculum. If they come up shy on the tested attributes, they are sent through the process again and retested, and that activity perhaps is repeated a few more times until students reach the criterion.

A third type of alternative assessment is the use of portfolios. When this form of assessment is employed, teachers literally (or sometimes metaphorically) keep a portfolio of a student's work. This might include writing samples, sample worksheets, tests, and pictures. The idea is to present documentation of the child's work in several areas over a period of time. The use of representative work over a continuum of time responds to a second common criticism of evaluation, namely, the frequency of assessment.

Consistent with evolving assessment philosophies, Parker (1991) recommended that assessment of social studies objectives be as "authentic" as possible. In his discussion of the attributes of authentic benchmark assessments, he identifies several that are consistent with these contemporary, alternative assessment techniques and philosophies. For example, consistent with the goal of curriculum-based assessment, he states that assessment tasks need to "go to the heart of essential learnings" (p. 88). He further observes that tasks should be "standard setting" and point students toward higher levels of knowledge, and that all students should attempt all tasks. These attributes of assessment converge nicely with the outcomes-based model. Finally, in relationship to portfolio assessment, Parker believes that assessment tasks ought to resemble real-life challenges rather than busywork; that teachers need to require exhibitions of understanding that are important; and that fewer, but more representative, assessment tasks are appropriate. Equally important, he reminds us that if assessment tasks seem worthwhile and meaningful to the teachers themselves, teachers may see them as being worth expending the effort required to engage in teaching.

Clearly, these new assessment demands are directly related to how the curriculum itself is conceptualized. To overcome the documented displeasure students seem to associate with social studies, not only is a change in the curriculum required, but also a fundamental change is required in how we ask students to display the knowledge they have acquired. Hopefully they will acquire it in a far more motivating and meaningful way than has been the case in the past.

CONCLUSION

Curriculum reform in social studies—as well as in the other content areas—is taking place as part of a major convergence of two movements: school restructuring and the inclusion of students with disabilities into general education classes. It is not enough to participate in only one or the other of these movements; teachers of all types, administrators, students, and their parents need to work together and speak their minds regarding both restructuring and inclusion, and how the two are related.

Special educators should be centrally involved in the general restructuring movement (McLaughlin & Warren, 1992), and general educators need to be involved in learning what inclusion means. Most important, once all the arguments are laid out, all the passionate pleas made, all the data presented in support of or in refute of whatever positions are taken (and that won't take long), school districts need to move toward setting up schools and developing curriculum that will best serve *all* students.

Related to this, and very important, professors in higher education and school people need to work collaboratively as these decisions are made. It makes absolutely no sense to perpetuate the gulf between the two. Housed in schools, university faculty will be in better positions to understand the problems of schools. Together we will then be able to design policies and interventions to deal directly with those concerns, put them into effect in schools while being there to observe the effects, and make adjustments based on the joint efforts.

REFERENCES

Bean, R. M., Zigmond, N., & Hartman, D. K. (1994). Adapted use of social studies textbooks in elementary classrooms. *Remedial and Special Education, 15*(4), 216–226.

Cooke, N. L., Heron, T. E., & Heward, W. L. (1983). *Peer tutoring: Implementing classwide programs in the primary grades.* Columbus, OH: Special Press.

Deshler, D. D., & Schumaker, J. B. (1986). Learning strategies: An instructional alternative for low achieving adolescents. *Exceptional Children, 52,* 583–590.

Howell, K. W., & Morehead, M. K. (1987). *Curriculum-based evaluation for special and remedial education.* Columbus, OH: Merrill.

Lovitt T. C. (1991). *Preventing school dropouts: Tactics for at-risk, remedial, and mildly handicapped adolescents.* Austin, TX: PRO-ED.

Lovitt, T. C. (1994). *Tactics for teaching* (2nd ed.). Columbus, OH: Merrill/Prentice-Hall.

Lovitt, T. C. (1995). Curricular options and services for youth with disabilities. *Journal of Behavioral Education, 5* (2), 211–233.

Lovitt, T. C., & Horton, S. V. (1991). Adapting textbooks for mildly handicapped adolescents. In G. Stoner, M. R. Shinn, & H. M. Walker (Eds.), *Interventions for achievement and behavior problems* (pp. 439–471). Silver Spring, MD: National Association of School Psychologists.

Maheady, L., Harper, G. F., & Sacca, M. J. (1988). Peer mediated instruction: A promising alternative for secondary learning disabled students. *Learning Disability Quarterly, 11,* 108–114.

McLaughlin, M. J., & Warren, S. H. (1992). *Issues & options in restructuring schools and special education programs.* College Park, MD: University of Maryland & Westat.

Parker, W. C. (1991). *Renewing the social studies curriculum.* Alexandria, VA: Association for Supervision and Curriculum Development.

Passe, J., & Beattie, J. (1994). Social studies instruction for students with mild disabilities. *Remedial and Special Education, 15*(4), 227–233.

Pressley, M., Johnson, C. J., Symons, S., McGoldrick, J. A., & Kurita, J. A. (1989). Strategies that improve children's memory and comprehension of text. *The Elementary School Journal, 90*(1), 3–32.

Slavin, R. E. (1990). *Cooperative learning: Theory, research, and practice.* Englewood Cliffs, NJ: Prentice-Hall.

* *CHAPTER 5* *

Toward a Responsible Pedagogy for Teaching and Learning Literacy

Lisa E. Monda-Amaya and P. David Pearson

Our goal in this chapter is to create a vision of a responsible pedagogy for literacy education in the twenty-first century—one that honors the progress that we have made in the past decade as we have moved toward integrated views of literacy at the same time that it builds on the traditions of previous decades of effective instruction, especially for children who are typically not well served by our schools.

We try to build a prototype of instruction as it might be presented by what appears to be an emerging consensus about how reading and writing should be learned and taught. Then we share a set of instructional dilemmas—questions and tensions that arise from the current landscape of literacy learning. Finally, we examine the teacher's role in the literacy curriculum of the future.

A MODEL OF MODERN LITERACY INSTRUCTION

In the next several pages we will propose a modern model of literacy instruction. This consensus model of literacy relies heavily on whole language and cognitive apprenticeship models (see Collins, Brown, & Newman, 1989), but borrows key features from explicit instruction (see Pearson & Dole, 1987; Pearson & Gallagher, 1983) and even direct instruction. This is more than the model that we *perceive* to be emerging from trends of the present and the future; for the most part, it is, we admit, the model that we would like to see implemented in the schools of the twenty-first century.

Features of the Model

Literacy learning is grounded in authentic texts and tasks. The tasks in which students engage are motivated by genuine, personally important

Curriculum Trends, Special Education, and Reform: Refocusing the Conversation. ISBN 0-8077-3562-0 (pbk), ISBN 0-8077-3563-9 (cloth).

communication purposes (learning, informing, enjoyment, insight). The texts children read, the texts they write, and the activities (including assessment tasks) that accompany them extend beyond the world of the school into students' everyday lives.

The texts they read are written not as instructional contrivances; instead they are written by real authors to communicate, inform, entertain, and enlighten. Thus our reading instruction is based on the kind of children's literature that we can find on a library shelf rather than the adapted and abridged sort we traditionally have found in basal anthologies. In opting for literature instead of readers with strict vocabulary control, we can still find ways to scaffold the learning environment for students. With readers that exhibited strict vocabulary control, we assumed that if we introduced the most frequently used words in the language first, it would "scaffold" the learning environment for students by providing them with something familiar to hang onto, something that they could use to "predict" what was in the text. Literature-based reading programs simply substitute one type of scaffolding for another. For example, texts that use rhyme and alliteration provide a kind of "phonemic" scaffolding by making the text memorable and, therefore, predictable. Texts that rely on the use of repetitive patterns (e.g., "The house that Jack built") provide another type of scaffolding and predictability, and the use of natural language patterns represents yet another.

The texts that students write have real audiences, people who want to read what they have written. Students who interact daily with print, read what others have written, and write to others regularly, develop conceptual understandings about the value of literacy. They come to value reading and writing as tools for learning, enjoyment, and personal insight—as ways of both gaining new knowledge and rethinking current knowledge.

When skills and strategies are taught, they are taught to help the learner achieve personal goals, such as understanding a story, figuring out the pronunciation of a word, getting the conventional spelling of a difficult word, or crafting the sentence in a particular grammatical structure to achieve a certain audience effect. The amount of decontextualized instruction offered should be limited, only used for highlighting key features of a skill or strategy, and immediately recontextualized.

Literacy learning is inherently social. We often think of reading and writing as solitary acts, but nothing could be further from the truth. Literacy and literacy learning are inherently social in several senses. First, both reading and writing are social acts of communication, often with an unseen partner (the author or the reader). We write for an imagined audience, even in the most contrived of situations in which, for example, the only audience is our classroom teacher or an anonymous reader who grades our papers. When we read, it is hard not to imagine an author who one day decided to set pen to paper.

Second, literacy acts are more overtly social because we live with a group of peers occupying a common classroom interpretive community, and we occasionally interact with them in response to print. We don't just read texts, we discuss them; and when we do, we sometimes revise the model of meaning we have built. We don't just write texts, we share them; and when we do, we get responses from our peers that encourage us to make our meanings and intentions clearer.

Third, teachers make literacy learning social. The assistance teachers provide in the form of scaffolding is inherently social and quite purposeful for students. With analogies, explicit cues, redirecting, metaphors, elaborations, and modeling, teachers can create a form of assistance that allows students to complete a task before they cognitively understand how to do it and when to apply it. This is the tradition of the cognitive apprenticeship, in which mentors assist apprentices in developing their own expertise and control over the processes.

Fourth, literacy acts are even more overtly social when we move from school to everyday contexts, when we encounter literacy in the community and in our homes. The social perspective of everyday literacy, in a very interesting and direct way, will promote a high degree of authenticity in our teaching and learning: When we understand that every linguistic act is inherently social, we soon will discover that every linguistic act is also inherently *political.* When we communicate, we have motives. We usually want something from the other person. That intention makes communication inherently political (see Edelsky, 1992, for a full elaboration of the political argument). The sooner we admit this fact, and the sooner we are willing to share it with students, the sooner we will be able to *situate* our school-based literacy activities in real-world, everyday purposes. Simply put, when students learn that language and literacy help them get their way, they will be much more disposed to engage in these processes and, hopefully, the instruction that supports them. For example, we would begin at a very early age engaging students in discussions of the ways in which we use language for political purposes.

- The 5-year-old who says, "Gee the cake looks pretty," when what he is really asking is, "Can I have a piece?" has learned a tacit lesson about the role of indirectness in language and how we can get our way by saying one thing while we mean another. That child has taken the first step to understanding how figurative language works.
- The 10-year-old who, when prompted by the teacher, realizes that she

> changes her discourse patterns when she talks to her friends, her classmates, her gender-difference peers, her teacher, her parents, and strangers has taken the first step toward understanding the role of context in language use as well as the political functions and consequences of dialect.

Ultimately it is the social nature of literacy that allows us as teachers to find a way to encourage students to embrace conventions. For example, it is because public writing is read that certain, often instructionally problematic, contentions of language and print (grammar, capitalization, punctuation, spelling) can be understood as instructional enterprises. If we want students to understand why they need to attend to these conventions when they write, we can have them attempt to read and create meanings for texts in which writers have violated these conventions. From a reader's perspective, laborious effort, ambiguity, misunderstanding, and even utter incomprehensibility are the likely results.

Our modern literacy curriculum requires us to admit the social nature of oral language, written language, and learning; it also commits us to the premise that constructing meaning, whether it is a part of reading, writing, listening, or speaking, is an inherently social act (either we do it *with* someone or do it *for* or *to* someone). When we accept these assumptions, we are likely to provide students with well-grounded instruction and learning opportunities.

Literacy learning is community-based. Bringing the world of work and the world of the community into the classroom is surely a goal worthy of our aspirations. We have learned much over the past few years about using parents and community members as resources to help students understand how literacy is used beyond school (e.g., Moll, Vélez-Ibánez, Greenberg, Whitmore, Saavedra, Dworkin, & Andrade, 1990). In an ideal world those programs would be expanded so that students would have an opportunity to observe and talk to role models—adults whom they admire—about how literacy helps them live richer lives and achieve greater job satisfaction.

Schools also can move out into the community. One of our favorite examples comes from Berrien Springs, Michigan, where the elementary principal, Jerry Jennings (1984), for years has encouraged school–community connections. The school's foremost strategy is to publish a school literary magazine and to make sure that it gets into all of the "places where people wait" (and consequently may pick up something to read)—dental offices, doctor's offices, optical offices, restaurants, hospital lounges, executive offices, automobile service waiting rooms. Second, once a year the school publishes, with the financial assistance of local service clubs, a literary supplement to the local newspaper, consisting entirely of pieces composed by students in the elementary school. Third, every notice that goes home to parents, either from a teacher or from the school office, has every square inch of extra white space covered with student work. In short, the school shares and celebrates its literacy with the entire community. The community also is invited into the school for semiannual read-ins. Parents bring sleeping bags, pillows, and comforters to school to join the students and the teachers in the gym or on the playfield, depending on the weather or time of year, for extended, leisurely sessions of pleasure reading.

Literacy researchers have managed to engage in activities that bring school literacy into the community. Shirley Brice Heath, in *Ways with Words* (1983), describes a program in which students and teachers completed community ethnographies about literacy, to learn about the ways in which a host of community members used literacy in their lives. Luis Moll and colleagues (Moll et al., 1990; Moll, Amanti, Neff, & Gonzalez, 1992) at the University of Arizona developed a community-based program in which both students and teachers attend after-school sessions at a community center at which, among other enterprises, students and teachers listen to community members talk about the uses of literacy in their work and daily lives. Teachers gain a side benefit from this experience; they get an opportunity to see their students in another light. For many students, the community context provides an opportunity to demonstrate success rather than failure, competence rather than incompetence, and linguistic prowess rather than silence.

Connecting instruction to work can elicit the same effect. We should listen carefully to the rhetoric of the business community, to their plea for employees who bring higher literacies rather than basic skills to the workplace. Business leaders tell us that through their own training programs, they can handle the basics; what they need are good problem solvers. If we look within education, within our educational institutions, and within our traditions, we may not find the motivation for problem-based curriculum, but if we look beyond education to everyday life and work, we will see the absolute necessity of it (Resnick, 1990). Surely we can bring the spirit of everyday problem solving, with its emphasis on using language processes in integrated ways, into the classroom. Sally Hampton (1992), the language arts coordinator for the Fort Worth, Texas, public schools, tells of the astounding language arts work that was accomplished in a local fifth-grade classroom when she contracted with the students to run the district's annual young authors' conference, an activity that she normally ran out of her office. The planning, negotiation, correspondence, budgeting, program, preparation of a brochure, scheduling—all of these activities demanded that the students use reading and writing (not to mention speaking, listening, and mathematics) as tools for accomplishing personal and collective goals.

The point of all of these examples is that school literacy is rendered more functional, more comprehensible, and more rational when it is connected to literacy in the community and the workplace. Teachers no longer have to invent distant (this will help you when you grow up—or get to high school) or arbitrary (do it because it's the assignment, that's why) motives to entice students into literacy activities. It is exactly this community-based philosophy that undergirds attempts on the part of many teachers to build literate communities in their own classrooms (Hansen, 1987). In these communities, students read and write to, for, and with one another. In other words, authenticity, our first principle of modern literacy instruction, is enhanced by conceptualizing teaching and learning as community-based, and not exclusively school-based, activities.

The Instructional Context of the Model

Literacy instruction, especially reading and writing instruction, do not exist as isolated entities. They are part of the broader school curriculum. We no longer can think of reading and writing as separate subjects. In order for the modern literacy curriculum to be true to its basic features (authentic, inherently social, and community-based), it must exist as an integrated curriculum. In this section, we address the issues involved in realizing an integrated literacy curriculum.

Forces against integration. The tradition of separate, specialized subjects is so strong in American education that the idea of integrating any elements of the curriculum can be viewed, from a cynical perspective, as rhetorical hypocrisy. The whole progression of education, beginning with first grade and continuing right on through graduate school, is a process of requiring students to learn more and more about less and less.

The tension pervades curriculum debates and decision making from preschool through graduate school. In the elementary school, teachers worry that if they integrate reading and writing, something might get shortchanged: "If we try to teach spelling through our reading program or through the children's everyday writing, how can we be certain that they will learn to spell the words that they will need for middle school or, for that matter, for a real job?" At the high school level, when we talk about integrating science and mathematics or history and English, the fundamental question is who is going to concede the first curricular objective? The tension arises at the university level when we begin to think of the idea of interdisciplinary studies, particularly in general education (see Petrie, 1992).

In teacher education, the same tension exists. The trend toward whole language, literature-based reading, and integrated language arts programs in the schools creates increasing pressure for those of us who run teacher education programs to work toward a similar integration of our methods courses (Short & Burke, 1989). Well, imagine the meeting in which the professors who teach the currently separate courses in reading, language arts, and children's literature get together to discuss integration of their methods courses. Who will be the first to concede a topic, a time slot, or an idea to the others? Who is going to say, "Great, you cover that in language arts, so I don't need to worry about it in reading"?

Perhaps the trick is not so much to achieve integration for the sake of integration, but to strike a balance between the competing needs that both societies and individuals have for knowledge specialization and knowledge integration. Maybe we need to start talking about the *integrity of curriculum integration.*

Why integrate the language arts? First, integrated approaches are likely to be more interconnected and thus less intimidating to students. Students in integrated programs should realize that what they are learning in one domain, subject matter, or activity can transfer readily to another domain, subject matter, or activity. Thus, they should be able to avoid the sinking feeling of "starting all over again from scratch." To the contrary, they should be more likely to make discoveries of transfer, such as:

- "Now I see. What you want me to put at the beginning of this paragraph is like that main idea stuff we do in reading class."
- "If you want to see a good example of how to handle flashbacks, look at that Raymond Chandler story we read last week."
- "So when I try to answer questions about character motives, it's okay for me to think about what reason I might have had in that situation."

Second, all things being equal, integrated approaches are more likely to be relevant to life outside of school, and thus they are potentially more motivating to students. Problems in life do not come packaged as reading problems or writing problems or math problems or science problems. As we indicated in describing the community basis of literacy, real problems come in integrated packages, and they invite us to traverse the entire language and literacy landscape—indeed the entire school curriculum landscape—not just a single dimension of either.

Third, and this is the reason at the top of many lists favoring integration, integrated approaches are potentially more efficient. Because of the current duplication in the reading, language arts, and spelling curricula, integration ought to offer savings in instructional time. We purposely placed this reason last rather than first out of fear that it would, as is so often the case in our efficiency-oriented society, dominate the rationalization of integration.

What do we mean by integration? When we say we want to integrate the language arts, what do we mean? Integrate them with one another? With other curricular areas? With everyday life? We think that we mean all of these things. We have already discussed three reasons for integrating the language arts with one another—interconnectedness, relevance, and efficiency. Surely we want to promote such integration so that students will realize that what they are learning in one of these critical language processes helps the development of the others.

Intercurricular integration has been one of the most active curriculum movements at the college, and to a lesser degree at the high school, level, under the guise of the writing across the curriculum movement (Fulwiler & Young, 1982). The intent is to convince subject-matter specialists that learning in their content areas is enhanced when writing becomes a primary vehicle for learning, responding, and assessment. Within the reading field, the content-area reading movement (see Alvermann & Moore, 1991) has had a similar intent and influence. In both movements, the driving force has been to make reading and writing functional tools rather than curricular entities to be studied or mastered in their own right. Indeed, the phrase *reading and writing as tools for learning* (McGinley & Tierney, 1989) is central to both movements. To use the language that is popular in discussions of these movements, reading and writing must be *contextualized,* or *situated,* in authentic learning tasks.

At the elementary level the thematic unit approach has been the most popular vehicle for achieving intercurricular integration. Dating back at least to Dewey (1938, 1943) and the progressive education movement, thematic units have been a mainstay of the more child-centered theorists in language arts, social studies, and general curriculum theory (see Goodman, 1989, for a historical account of much of the early work on integration). As Rand (1994) suggests, thematic instruction is still alive and well in the language arts curriculum. We see it as a key element in future literacy instruction.

We have already discussed many examples of integrating literacy learning into the broader community and the world of work. Such integration renders schoolwork more relevant, interesting, and authentic; as such, it is hard to argue against.

The bottom line is that true integration of the literacy curriculum requires us to consider integration at every level of analysis. The integration among the language arts is a start, but it takes us only part of the way toward real integration. We must situate our literacy teaching and learning in other curricular areas and in the worlds of work and community in order to achieve full integration.

Reprise

So there is our model of modern literacy instruction. The model claims that the teaching and learning of literacy must:

- Ground student work in authentic texts and tasks
- Take advantage of the inherently social nature of language and literacy
- Build a symbiotic relationship with the worlds of work and everyday community life
- Foster integration among the language arts, between literacy and other curricula, and between the literacy of school and the literacy of everyday life

We hope that its roots in its historical predecessors—whole language, explicit instruction, and cognitive apprenticeships—are transparent. We believe that it is a powerful model, one that will help students understand the personal power that literacy can bring to them.

INSTRUCTIONAL DILEMMAS AND QUESTIONS

As much as we are committed to our model of modern literacy instruction, it, like most positive forces, comes shrouded with concerns, dilemmas, and questions. Problematic features of literacy instruction are addressed below.

How Can We Make Complex Processes Manageable for Students?

One of the most prominent sources of controversy in the area of literacy instruction focuses on how teachers help students cope with the inherent complexity of the reading and writing process. In our analysis of various instructional approaches, we have found four approaches to coping with complexity: skill decomposition, skill decontextualization, scaffolding, and authenticity.

Controversy associated with skill decomposition also underlies many of our current curricular tensions, notably the tension in early literacy between emergent literacy and traditional reading readiness, and whether phonics, comprehension strategies, and grammar need to be taught directly. In a sense, the controversy is captured in the question, "Must we teach what must be learned?" On the one side are those who argue that children may not learn what they are not taught directly, explicitly, and intentionally (Gersten & Carnine, 1986; Rosenshine & Stevens, 1984). On the other side of the argument are those who suggest that while it is appropriate, perhaps essential, that students acquire specific skills, those skills are best acquired incidentally while students are engaged in the process of reading and writing (Stephens, 1991). The danger of decomposition is that the breakdown of the curriculum often does not foster knowledge of literacy as a *process* (*whole*), but encourages the view of literacy as a set of specific actions, within which the acquisition of some may be completely dependent on mastery of others.

The notion of decontextualization further complicates the issue. In order to strip away potentially confusing and irrelevant features of the instructional context, specific subskill instruction often is provided out of the context of real reading, writing, and thinking situations. The logic behind decontextualization is similar to the logic underlying decomposition: In both cases, the motivation is to make a complex phenomenon appear simpler. The dark side of decontextualization is its potential to obscure the relationship between the skill as it is taught in school and the skill as it is used in everyday literacy events.

As we suggested in our discussions of explicit instruction and cognitive apprenticeships, scaffolding provides an alternative to decomposition and decontextualization as a way of coping with complexity. The scaffolding metaphor, introduced to us by Wood, Bruner, and Ross (1976) and endemic to socially based views of literacy (e.g., Moll et al., 1990; Vygotsky, 1978), is appealing for those who want to carve out a helpful, but not necessarily a controlling, role for teachers. Just like the scaffolding used in building, instructional scaffolds provide *support* and are both *temporary* and *adjustable.* So, instead of breaking a process like reading down into subcomponents, a teacher can provide the social and instructional support needed to allow a student to engage in a complex task that she might not otherwise be able to manage on her own.

A vivid demonstration of scaffolding (and probably of the cognitive apprenticeship model) is Reading Recovery™ as it has been implemented in the United States. Reading Recovery is the early intervention program for at-risk first graders that was imported from New Zealand in the mid-1980s. It contains many other components besides its cognitive apprenticeship relationship between tutor and student: (a) the consistent use of real texts from the very earliest stages of instruction; (b) a highly contextualized and functional approach to teaching phonics ("phonics on the fly"), which relies mostly on attention to invented spellings as a means of forcing students to confront sound–symbol correspondences; (c) a dogged insistence that children constantly monitor the output of their reading to determine whether it makes sense; and (d) an attempt to ensure that students develop a "full toolbox" of strategies (syntactic, semantic, visual, and phonic analysis tools) to assist them in rendering text meaningful. In each half-hour tutoring session (sessions often continue about 12–15 weeks), children engage in reading connected text under the watchful eye of a tutor for about 25 of those 30 minutes. While the student is reading, the tutor scaffolds the reading (which is, of course, a real rather than a contrived reading task) by modeling, hinting, cuing, and cajoling the student into a successful reading venture.

Scaffolding allows teachers to have students work in what Vygotsky (1978) labeled the "zone of proximal development," that instructional region just beyond their grasp. Scaffolding allows students to use a strategy before they fully understand it, but while they gradually gain control of it. With analogies, explicit cues, metaphors, elaborations, and modeling, teachers can create a form of assistance that allows students to complete a task before they cognitively understand how to do it and when to apply it. Scaffolding promotes learning and self-control as long as it is gradually removed as students gain control of and assume responsibility for the task or process.

For lack of a better alternative, we have appropriated the term *authenticity* to capture that feature of whole language instruction that might be used to explain how teachers can cope with the inherent complexity of literacy learning. The argument is identical to the one put forward earlier to distinguish between two views of decomposition. That is, some suggest that while it is appropriate, perhaps essential, that students acquire specific skills, those skills are best acquired incidentally while students are engaged in the process of reading and writing. In other words, if we just let students engage in genuine acts of communication—in real contexts, for real purposes, with real people—complexity will take care of itself because students will cope as best they can to achieve the communicative competence they desire.

If forced to adopt one of these strategies, we would likely embrace scaffolding as the preferred alternative, but we also would prefer to implement it in authentic learning tasks and contexts. We might even be willing to decompose or decontextualize a task for a fleeting moment in order to highlight some feature of the instructional task or context. Our operative principle, from Pearson (1994) would be this:

> Instruction for skills and strategies should begin and end in authentic learning contexts—contexts in which the skill or strategy helps the reader achieve per-

> sonal goals, such as understanding the story at hand or figuring out the pronunciation of the word she is currently puzzling over. Decontextualized instruction, if offered at all, should be limited to instances in which the teacher wishes to temporarily highlight some important feature of the skill or strategy and should be followed immediately by a recontextualized application. (p. 16)

Who Controls the Literacy Curriculum?

A second dilemma centers on curriculum control, and the central question is, "Who has the right to decide the particular curriculum that a child, a class, a school, or a district will receive?" A related question is, "At what level—nation, state, district, school, teacher, or student—are curricular decisions best made?" Each week, and especially during the past 4 years, we have new calls for high and rigorous national standards (Gursky, 1991; Resnick & Resnick, 1991) so that we might better compete with our international economic rivals or so that we can guarantee a world-class education for all of our students rather than just the wealthy elite. Just how national standards will affect state and local curricula concerns many educators, especially those who have worked hard to carve out consensus in their own states or districts. At the other end of the decision-making continuum are colleagues who argue that the only ethically defensible site for curriculum decision making is the classroom and that the only defensible curricular interaction is between a teacher and an individual student (Harste, 1985). This position is best expressed, we believe, in the concept that Jerry Harste writes about so eloquently when he discusses the idea of the "learner as curriculum informant." Somewhere in between, especially in the past few years, are those who, in the name of site-based management, argue that the school is the most legitimate locus of curricular decisions (Bimber, 1994; Kerchner & Koppich, 1993).

Our own view on the matter of curriculum control, especially as it relates to standards and assessments (both of which can exert considerable curricular control), is that we ought to maintain a healthy tension between a national vision of literacy teaching and learning and local instantiations of that vision. The metaphor of variations on a theme seems apt here. We agree with Pearson (1994).

> We want to be in a position to honor both local knowledge and national values. And we do not want the tension to disappear because, if and when it does, we may find ourselves on the verge of either a national orthodoxy or a large set of local orthodoxies. If standards can perform this function, they can be a catalyst for local curriculum reform. Sizer and Rogers (1993) express the sentiment that we are searching for quite concisely in discussing ways to achieve a balance between civic virtue and individual liberty.

How Do We Know Whether Students Are Making Progress?

A third dilemma concerns the forms of assessment appropriate for evaluating school programs and student progress. While it is really a variation of the curriculum control controversy, it deserves special mention because it breeds so much tension in the field. One group (e.g., Popham, Cruse, Rankin, Sandifer, & Williams, 1985) argues that the standardized tests that have served us for so many decades, if used properly and sensibly, can continue to help us make decisions about how well our literacy programs are doing and about whether individual students should be directed into special programs, schools, or, in the case of college placement tests, universities. Another group (Shepard, 1989; Smith, 1990; Valencia & Pearson, 1987) argue that because the high-stakes game of accountability reporting has driven even the most well-meaning of us to teaching to the test, standardized tests can no longer serve as our primary means of reporting progress to the public. To ask standardized tests to serve as curricular blueprints is to assign to them a role they were never designed to serve; it is also a surefire formula for narrowing the school curriculum. A third group (e.g., O'Neil, 1993) argues that it is just fine for assessment to drive instruction as long as the assessments are capable of driving it in a positive way. The key, they suggest, is developing a system of performance and portfolio assessments that will encourage a thoughtful, challenging curriculum to which all students can and should aspire and be held accountable.

We prefer to embrace the view that assessment should support the curriculum that a community of teachers, students, and citizens have worked hard to craft for their schools. Given our view of the general direction that a curriculum should take, we certainly side with the type of assessments—performance assessments and portfolios—that scholars like Simmons and Resnick advocate. However, we hesitate to accept the position that assessment can, or ever should, be a catalyst for reform. The history of assessment mania is too vivid and too fresh in our minds to believe that any assessment, no matter how virtuous in design and intent, can be worth teaching to (Haladyna, Nolen, & Haas, 1991). What we need, more than reform, is the conviction to place all of our assessments in perspective. We must no longer ask them to perform functions for which they were never designed, functions that are beyond their constitutional capacity.

How Can We Adapt the Curriculum So That All Students Can Benefit from Literacy Instruction?

Populations of students in today's classrooms have become increasingly more diverse, with teachers developing instructional programs that must accommodate both typical learners and students with special needs (those at risk for school failure, those from culturally and linguistically diverse backgrounds, and those identified for special education services). Literacy programs in the future must be responsive to the needs of these diverse populations. Good instruction, after all, should be inclusive and must be extended to all learners (Pearson, Roehler, Dole, & Duffy, 1992).

There is a variety of instructional programs (e.g., Reading Recovery™) and strategies (e.g., Reciprocal Teaching) that have been found to be effective in working with students at varying ability levels. García and Pearson (1991) point to principles shared by successful programs for at-risk learners: (1) teacher modeling through reflective demonstrations, (2) authenticity of the content, (3) a reduction in complexity through scaffolding, (4) shared responsibility for curricular decisions, and (5) a literacy community that guarantees a genuine communicative context. These principles, further described below, should be incorporated into the literacy curriculum to ensure the participation and success of all students.

Teacher modeling has long been promoted as an effective instructional strategy. For students with special needs, this strategy is particularly effective when teachers use reflective demonstration. Through reflective demonstration, the teacher talks the student through a task, within the context of a "real" reading situation, while at the same time providing foundational strategies for completing the task independently in the future.

The second principle pertains to the issue of *authenticity.* While general aspects of authenticity have been described in previous sections, two additional considerations are needed when adapting the literacy curriculum for students with special needs. First, authentic materials and tasks ought to help students with problems in the maintenance, generalization, and application of skills within the curriculum. Often, students with special needs have difficulty maintaining skills at a desired level of skill fluency, generalizing skills across tasks and settings, and applying skills to real-life situations. For these students, incorporating authentic, real-world tasks into the curriculum, with the goal of providing increased opportunities for higher-order thinking, should become the foundation of literacy instruction. Second, authenticity should be defined specific to the individual needs of the learner. A task that is authentic for one might not be authentic for another. Teachers should evaluate carefully the curricular demands, the difficulty level of the materials, and the likely interest of the content and the task to ensure that the curriculum is authentic to the needs of the individual learner.

The third principle promoted by Pearson and his colleagues focuses on questions of how teachers can reduce the complexity of the task of learning new skills, strategies, or content. Students with special needs require support in coping with the complexity of reading and writing processes; this need is especially critical in early stages of skill acquisition. As our earlier discussion of complexity suggests, we are committed to *scaffolding* and *task authenticity* as primary strategies for coping with complexity, but we also acknowledge the possibility that some students will benefit from a step-by-step approach to learning a complex routine.

The fourth principle addresses *the student's participation in the curriculum.* We believe that students with special needs must feel vested in the literacy curriculum. This can be accomplished by allowing them to take part in instructional decisions. From the earliest stages of the school literacy curriculum, students of all achievement levels should be involved in planning reading and writing activities and in evaluating their own performance. Ultimately, as students learn to engage in self-evaluation, they begin to understand the process of taking responsibility for their own learning.

Active participation in the literacy community within the classroom is the fifth principle for working with students with special needs. Often literacy instruction for these students takes the form of decontextualized skills offered out of the context of real-world situations. Opportunities for reading and writing may be limited to a pull-out setting in which there is little opportunity for social interaction. Since reading and writing are inherently social activities, these students should be integrated into a community that guarantees a genuine communicative context. We propose that they should become active participants in a literacy community in which all students work together, learn to appreciate diversity, and see reading and writing within natural contexts as tools for learning, enjoyment, and personal insight.

With all of the press toward accountability at the district, school, classroom, and student level, there is tremendous pressure to exclude some learners from accountability to high and rigorous standards (and the performance assessments used to measure their attainment). The cost of excluding these students from accountability is that they are likely to be excluded from instruction that is supposed to guarantee mastery over those high and rigorous standards. Consequently, the students receive a second-class curriculum, the effects of which they can overcome only at great personal effort and sacrifice.

What Role Should the Teacher Play in the Literacy Curriculum of the Future?

Reading and writing are best learned not as a set of isolated skills, picked up one-by-one along an "assembly line" offered by the teacher and/or the reading program. Instead there is a single central goal, building meaning, that recurs from one situation to the next and fosters independence in individual learners. What changes over time is the level of sophistication of the students' expertise, the sophistication of the texts that they read and write, and the amount of conceptual and contextual support teachers need to provide. Considering this view of literacy education, it is important to examine the teacher's role in the development and delivery of the literacy curriculum in the future.

First, teachers will have to *possess knowledge* of how students develop literacy skills. The basis for understanding literacy development is to understand the relationships among listening, speaking, reading, and writing. At birth, children begin the process of becoming literate. As they grow, they develop critical foundational skills through language, social interaction, storybook reading, and experimentation with writing. Children also learn to break the code as they begin to understand that printed words contain a message, that words are composed of letters, and that letters correspond to sounds in the spoken word (Beck & Juel, 1992). When children come to school, they have certain literacy skills, but for some, those skills are quite limited. As teachers begin formal instruction in literacy, they must not view their function in the classroom as *custodians of wisdom,* whose role it is to disclose the truth to open, empty, and waiting minds; rather, teachers should begin to see themselves as *mentors* working with knowledgeable and purposeful apprentices. Once teachers possess knowledge, the trick is to resist the temptation to implant it in their students. Instead, they must ask how they can support students in their quest to acquire the same sort of knowledge.

Given our commitment to a literacy curriculum that extends beyond the boundaries of the school, it should not be surprising to learn that our second important role for teachers is to *establish and maintain strong home/school partnership.* Ollila and Mayfield (1992) note that one characteristic of a successful reading program is the involvement of parents. They state that home/school partnerships established as part of literacy programs "help parents foster their children's literacy development in partnership with the school" (p. 27).

A third important role for teachers will be to *assume responsibility for curriculum selection.* Teachers cannot leave curricular decisions to committees and boards that do not know their students. Those parties can have a voice in setting broad constraints or guidelines for the curriculum; just as there can be a national vision of literacy, so there can be local visions. The local visions must never be so well developed, however, that there is no room for the signature of individual teachers and their students.

A fourth role for the teacher in designing a literacy curriculum is to develop *assessment devices* that are carefully structured around the curriculum. Good assessment supports, extends, and encourages instruction that is relevant, thoughtful, and integrative in character. Assessments that promote the isolation of skills and skill instruction, that neglect the basic understanding that all literacy activities support, extend, and improve one another, do little to help students learn how to do real reading and writing. Instead, they stall students at a stage where all they can do is school literacy or, even worse, test literacy. On the other hand, assessments that admit, even celebrate, the synergistic nature of reading, writing, speaking, and listening are more likely to help students do real literacy, the kind that helps them solve problems that are real—personally and socially relevant—to them.

Fifth, teachers must *adapt curriculum* to the needs of all students. Teachers begin instruction with some intentions, usually curricular goals—understanding about what reading and writing are and how they work—that they want students to achieve. The moment instruction begins, however, teachers must realize that they have to adapt their goals and their strategies based on their students' and their own emerging and dynamic understanding of the instructional situation. In the schools of the future, with greater emphasis on cooperative learning among students and collaboration among professionals, adaptations will become social negotiations. Just as we ask students to work together to socially construct and revise meanings for texts, we will have to learn to work with one another to socially construct "readings" of students. This sort of collaboration and social negotiation among professionals will be necessary to create positive instructional adaptations for students and ultimately to achieve the goal of making instruction appropriate for all students.

Sixth, teachers should facilitate learning by *providing the strategies* students need for real independence. As we have suggested, scaffolding is the key in strategy instruction. Teachers must develop their own toolbox of helping devices—explicit cues, analogies, redirections, metaphors, elaborations, and modeling—to create a form of assistance that enables students to work through a task before they actually understand how to do it.

Finally, teachers should *establish a classroom community* that nurtures student learning and continually portrays the usefulness and value of reading and writing. Pearson, Roehler, Dole, and Duffy (1992) note that good instruction is rendered even better in an environment where students constantly see how reading and writing help them negotiate daily life in classroom communities. Students who interact daily with print, read what others have written, and write to others regularly, develop conceptual understandings about the value of literacy. They come to value reading and writing as tools for communication, learning, enjoyment, and personal insight—as ways of both gaining new knowledge and rethinking current knowledge. They learn why communication is the heart and soul of any community—especially a community of readers, writers, and learners.

FINAL REPRISE

The present and, we believe, the future of literacy instruction are as filled with tension and challenges as they are with excitement and opportunity. The tensions come from a disposition of public suspicion, scrutiny, and accountability that makes us feel as though we have to "produce" results and students who can "produce" a healthy economy. The challenges, too, come from the public scrutiny; this is the first time that we can remember when the public concern about education has advocated increased emphasis on problem solving and critical thinking rather than a return to "the basics." Another challenge of public scrutiny is whether we can have standards without standardization: Standards seem almost inevitable; the question is whether the standards we develop can and will honor local knowledge and initiative. The excitement comes from the richness of ideas and practices that have evolved in the context of our charge to develop a more challenging and thoughtful literacy curriculum. Literature-based literacy, classroom literacy communities—the list of innovations seems endless; neither of us can remember a time when the ideas and practices were as rich and varied as they are today. The opportunity is to re-energize our profession—to take control of the professional conversation about all of these tensions, challenges, and innovations and build better and more nurturing communities of learning and learners within our nation's schools.

ACKNOWLEDGMENT

Portions of the present chapter were adapted from an earlier piece, entitled "Integrated Language Arts: Sources of Controversy and Seeds of Consensus," appearing in L. M. Morrow, J. K. Smith, and L. C. Wilkinson (Eds.), 1994, *Integrated Language Arts: Controversy to Consensus,* published by Allyn & Bacon.

REFERENCES

Alvermann, D. E., & Moore, D. W. (1991). Secondary school reading. In R. Barr, M. L. Kamil, P. Mosenthal, & P. D. Pearson (Eds.), *Handbook of reading research* (Vol. 2, pp. 951–983). White Plains, NY: Longman.

Beck, I. L., & Juel, C. (1992). The role of decoding in learning to read. In S. J. Samuels & A. E. Farstrup (Eds.), *What research has to say about reading instruction* (2nd ed.; pp. 101–123). Newark, DE: International Reading Association.

Bimber, B. (1994). *The decentralization mirage: Comparing decision-making arrangements in four high schools.* Santa Monica, CA: Rand.

Collins, A., Brown, J. S., & Newman, S. E. (1989). Cognitive apprenticeship: Teaching the craft of reading, writing, and mathematics. In L. B. Resnick (Ed.), *Knowing, learning, and instruction: Essays in honor of Robert Glaser* (pp. 453–494). Hillsdale, NJ: Erlbaum.

Dewey, J. (1938). *Experience and education.* New York: Macmillan.

Dewey, J. (1943). *The child and the curriculum and the school and the society.* Chicago: University of Chicago Press.

Edelsky, C. (1992). A talk with Carole Edelsky about politics and literacy. *Language Arts, 69*(5), 324–329.

Fulwiler, T., & Young, A. (Eds.). (1982). *Language connections: Writing and reading across the curriculum.* Urbana, IL: National Council of Teachers of English.

García, G. E., & Pearson, P. D. (1991). The role of assessment in a diverse society. In E. H. Hiebert (Ed.), *Literacy for a diverse society: Perspectives, practices, and policies* (pp. 253–278). New York: Teachers College Press.

Gersten, R., & Carnine, D. (1986). Direct instruction in reading comprehension. *Educational Leadership, 43*(7), 70–78.

Goodman, Y. M. (1989). Roots of the whole language movement. *Elementary School Journal, 90*(2), 112–128.

Gursky, D. (1991). Ambitious measures. *Teacher, 2*(7), 49–57.

Haladyna, T. M., Nolen, S. B., & Haas, N. S. (1991). Raising achievement test scores and the origins of test score pollution. *Educational Researcher, 20*(5), 2–7.

Hampton, S. (1992). *Action research for teachers and students.* Paper presented at the midwinter conference of the National Conference on Research in English, Chicago.

Hansen, J. (1987). *When writers read.* Portsmouth, NH: Heinemann.

Harste, J. (1985). Portrait of a new paradigm: Reading comprehension research. In W. Crismore (Ed.), *Landscapes: A state-of-the-art assessment of reading comprehension research, 1974–1984* (pp. 12–32). Bloomington, IN: Center for Reading and Language Studies.

Heath, S. B. (1983). *Ways with words: Language, life, and work in communities and classrooms.* Cambridge: Cambridge University Press.

Jennings, J. (1984, July). *Implementing a community-based reading program.* Paper presented at the Ginn Leadership Conference, Asimolar, CA.

Kerchner, C., & Koppich, J. (1993). *A union of professionals: Labor relations and educational reform.* New York: Teachers College Press.

McGinley, W., & Tierney, R. J. (1989). Traversing the topical landscape: Reading and writing as ways of knowing. *Written Communication, 6,* 243–269.

Moll, L. C., Amanti, C., Neff, D., & Gonzalez, N. (1992). Funds of knowledge for teaching: A qualitative approach to connecting homes and classrooms. *Theory Into Practice, 31*(1), 132–141.

Moll, L. C., Vélez-Ibánez, C., Greenberg, J., Whitmore, K., Saavedra, E., Dworkin,

J., & Andrade, R. (1990). *Community knowledge and classroom practice: Combining resources for literacy instruction* (OBEMLA Contract No. 300–87–0131). Tucson: University of Arizona, College of Education & Bureau of Applied Research in Anthropology.

Ollila, L. O., & Mayfield, M. I. (1992). Home and school together: Helping beginning readers succeed. In S. J. Samuels & A. E. Farstrup (Eds.), *What research has to say about reading instruction* (2nd ed.; pp. 17–45). Newark, DE: International Reading Association.

O'Neil, J. (1993). On the new standards project: A conversation with Lauren Resnick and Warren Simmons. *Educational Leadership, 50*(5), 17–21.

Pearson, P. D. (1994). Integrated language arts: Sources of controversy and seeds of consensus. In L. M. Morrow, J. K. Smith, & L. C. Wilkinson (Eds.), *Integrated language arts: Controversy to consensus* (pp. 11–31). Boston: Allyn & Bacon.

Pearson, P. D., & Dole, J. A. (1987). Explicit comprehension instruction: A review of research and a new conceptualization of instruction. *Elementary School Journal, 88*(2), 151–165.

Pearson, P. D., & Gallagher, M. C. (1983). The instruction of reading comprehension. *Contemporary Educational Psychology, 8,* 317–344.

Pearson, P. D., Roehler, L., Dole, J., & Duffy, G. (1992). Developing expertise in reading comprehension. In S. J. Samuels & A. E. Farstrup (Eds.), *What research has to say about reading instruction* (2nd ed.; pp. 145–199). Newark, DE: International Reading Association.

Petrie, H. (1992). Interdisciplinary education: Are we faced with insurmountable opportunities? In G. Grant (Ed.), *Review of research in education* (Vol. 18, pp. 299–333). Washington, DC: American Educational Research Association.

Popham, W. J., Cruse, K. L., Rankin, S. C., Sandifer, P. D., & Williams, P. L. (1985). Measurement-driven instruction: It's on the road. *Phi Delta Kappan, 66,* 628–634.

Rand, M. K. (1994). Using thematic instruction to organize an integrated language arts classroom. In L. M. Morrow, J. K. Smith, & L. C. Wilkinson (Eds.), *Integrated language arts: Controversy to consensus* (pp. 177–192). Boston: Allyn & Bacon.

Resnick, L. B. (1990). Literacy in school and out. *Daedalus, 19*(2), 169–185.

Resnick, L. B., & Resnick, D. P. (1991). Assessing the thinking curriculum: New tools for educational reform. In B. R. Gifford & M. C. O'Connor (Eds.), *Changing assessments: Alternative views of aptitude, achievement and instruction* (pp. 37–75). Boston: Kluwer.

Rosenshine, B., & Stevens, R. (1984). Classroom instruction in reading. In P. D. Pearson, R. Barr, M. L. Kamil, & P. Mosenthal (Eds.), *Handbook of reading research* (Vol. 1, pp. 745–789). White Plains, NY: Longman.

Shepard, L. A. (1989). Why we need better assessments. *Educational Leadership, 46*(7), 4–9.

Short, K. G., & Burke, C. L. (1989). New potentials for teacher education: Teaching and learning as inquiry. *Elementary School Journal, 90*(2), 193–206.

Sizer, T. R., & Rogers, B. (1993). Designing standards: Achieving the delicate balance. *Educational Leadership 50*(5), 24–26.

Smith, M. L. (1990). Put to the test. The effects of external testing on teachers. *Educational Researcher, 20*(5), 8–11.

Stephens, D. (1991). *Research on whole language.* Katonah, NY: Richard C. Owens.

Valencia, S., & Pearson, P. D. (1987). Reading assessment: Time for a change. *Reading Teacher, 40,* 726–732.

Vygotsky, L. S. (1978). *Mind in society: The development of higher psychological processes* (M. Cole, V. John-Steiner, S. Scribner, & E. Souberman, Eds. & Trans.). Cambridge, MA: Harvard University Press.

Wood, D., Bruner, J. S., & Ross, G. (1976). The role of tutoring in problem solving. *Journal of Child Psychology and Psychiatry, 17,* 89–100.

Response

Unpacking Scaffolding: Supporting Students with Disabilities in Literacy Development

Catherine Cobb Morocco and Judith M. Zorfass

Evidence is accumulating that students with learning disabilities not only need but thrive in the kind of authentic learning environment that Monda-Amaya and Pearson envision. Students with learning disabilities, often with a history of failure, can be motivated by communication tasks valued in their community and school (Campione, 1993; Morocco, Riley, Gordon, Howard, & Longo, 1993). They recall information learned in a meaningful context (Riley, Morocco, Gordon, & Howard, 1993) and are more likely to transfer skills learned within the contexts in which they are useful (Bransford, Hasselbring, Barron, Kulewixz, Littlefield, & Goin, 1988).

If authentic learning tasks are inherently motivating, they also are inevitably complex. The kinds of learning Monda-Amaya and Pearson refer to depend on the interplay of knowledge, processes, and social relationships. Students need to be able to move—independently and in collaboration with others—between reading, writing, conversation, and listening activities that require the simultaneous application of multiple subprocesses. While this is what makes the learning task richer, it also creates the complexity in the proposed model.

Monda-Amaya and Pearson argue for the critical role of teacher scaffolding in helping students cope with tasks that are too complex to manage entirely on their own. Scaffolding provides just the right amount of "temporary and adjustable" support to enable a student to carry out a task that otherwise would be too complex. The theoretical underpinnings of scaffolding are well established in a quarter of a century of cognitive and classroom research on, for example, reciprocal teaching (Palincsar & Brown, 1984), collaborative writing (Daiute & Dalton, 1993), cooperative learning (Tateyama-Sniezek, 1990), and supported inquiry science (Morocco, Dalton, Tivnan, & Rawson, 1992). We believe that to make meaning-

Curriculum Trends, Special Education, and Reform: Refocusing the Conversation. ISBN 0-8077-3562-0 (pbk), ISBN 0-8077-3563-9 (cloth).

making processes manageable for students with special needs in the regular classroom, teachers will need to view scaffolding as a core part of their expertise.

ASPECTS OF SCAFFOLDING IN INTEGRATED LITERACY PROGRAMS

This response unpacks the concept of scaffolding so that it can be a more active ingredient in teachers' practice. We have done this by describing four aspects of scaffolding that we observed in our work with experienced and highly inventive teachers in academically diverse classrooms. All classrooms described include students with mild to moderate learning disabilities and other special needs.

- *Scaffolding is multilevel,* aimed at the curriculum, the classroom, and the individual learner. Curriculum-level structures create the overall supportive context whereby a community of diverse learners can fully engage in authentic tasks. Within this "big picture" teachers provide deeper levels of individualized scaffolding to promote meaning making that depends on understanding student needs.
- *Scaffolding is inclusive,* helping individual students to learn in appropriate ways. The art of individualized scaffolding consists of keeping the individual linked with the overall task and having "co-construction of meaning" take place in the classroom.
- *Scaffolding is aimed at promoting higher-level thinking.* The goal is to support meaning making by supporting students. As needed, teachers judiciously use reading, writing, listening, and speaking to support linguistic and cognitive processing.
- *Scaffolding is dynamic and evolving.* Scaffolding is continually under revision as teachers respond to students' emerging needs, assess student performance, and revise teaching approaches.

The cases that follow illustrate how scaffolding can move the entire class forward, ensuring that individual students with disabilities fully participate, contribute, and learn.

ELEMENTARY SCHOOL CASE: A UNIT ON MAKING HARD CHOICES

"Writing is the biggest challenge for our students—and a hard area for us too." With that common ground, teachers from four urban and suburban schools worked over a two-and-a-half-year period with a research team on a project called Teacher as Composer. The project focused on how to include all of their students in challenging "problem-centered" reading and writing units. The units were based around themes with high personal relevance for the students and high-quality literature. The teachers included 7 third- and fourth-grade classroom teachers and the specialists who worked in some of the schools and classrooms.

This case draws mainly on the experiences of two of these teachers, but also integrates examples from some of the other classrooms. In a unit on the theme of "Making Hard Choices," the teachers read aloud a historical novel, *Sign of the Beaver,* by Elizabeth George Speare (1983), on the early settling of New England. They engaged students in thinking, reading, writing, and talking about the dilemmas faced by the main character, a young boy named Matt. In the story Matt has been alone in a cabin in the deep woods in northern New England for several months, waiting for his father to return with the rest of their family. At one point, he has to decide whether to let a bearded and presumably hungry stranger into the cabin; later, after months of waiting, he has to decide whether to remain in the cabin longer or go with his new Native American friend, Attean, to live with his family in his village.

The teachers, together during a workshop, planned the general structure of the unit and some key lessons around those hard choices. They decided that, given the variation in reading levels, *reading aloud* would scaffold the "reading" to include all students. They also decided that focusing on some of the key decision points for Matt would enable students to work together on understanding Matt's alternatives and why his choices were so difficult. They refined those plans with their specialists back in their own schools before carrying out the unit over several weeks. In two additional workshops during the unit, the teachers discussed the specific ways they were elaborating the common plan they had sketched out together in their first workshop; they looked closely at writing samples from selected students with substantial reading and writing difficulties; they practiced some new strategies for facilitating or assessing students' learning that the research staff introduced; and they talked about successful experiences in facilitating individual students' learning.

The students in the project classrooms were successful in this unit in that all were actively engaged in thinking and writing, and all wrote both expository and narrative pieces that showed they had constructed individual understandings of the unit.

Mark's Classroom

First hard choice. The first "chapter book" and book without pictures that Mark read aloud to his third-grade class was *Sign of the Beaver.* As a result, he, the reading specialists, and the speech and language teacher (who worked in his classroom during much of this unit) worked together a good deal thinking about how to begin. His students had some background knowledge about Native American culture at the time of early American settlement because of a prior social studies unit. To have the students begin to think about hard choices, Mark engaged them the previous week in talking about difficult choices they had faced; he also posed some hypothetical dilemmas for discussion.

He scaffolded students' initial listening by telling them how long he would be reading aloud (about 10 minutes) and giving them a brief but provocative summary of the situation: "The story is about a boy whose father is leaving him alone in their cabin in the wilderness and the story begins just as the father has left." He read *Sign of the Beaver* aloud for the promised 10 minutes, up to the point where Matt has to decide whether to let the stranger in. He did not interrupt his own reading but did use his voice for dramatic effect and emphasis. Although two of the students with disabilities were not looking at Mark as he read, both appeared to be listening and neither looked up when someone came in the room. When they came to Matt's decision about whether to admit the stranger, the specialist asked them to "think about where Matt is, think about the things that happened in the story, and write what you think he will do." When one girl who tends to begin work impulsively then quickly run out of ideas lifted her pencil at once, Mark suggested to the class that they "think a moment about what might happen if he lets the stranger in, and what might happen if he doesn't; there's no right or wrong answers."

The students then stood and sat in small groups to talk about the reasons they had written to support their predictions. The teachers circulated among the groups, providing whatever kind of brief scaffolding each group needed in order to carry out a complex discussion of choices and consequences. The reading specialist helped one group get started by asking provocative questions, then leaving the direction of the discussion to the students. When one child said the stranger must be bad because he had a beard, Mark asked, "Does it necessarily mean he's bad?" When a group settled on one interpretation when several were possible, he asked, "Well, what else could happen?"

During this small-group conversation, one of the specialists put her arm around one of the students with disabilities and gently turned him toward the conversation. She mentioned to an observer that she "can pull them back sometimes just with eye contact." Such warm interactions provided emotional and attentional scaffolding for a student who otherwise might not benefit from the "thinking scaffolding" provided by the prediction and the small-group talk.

After an extended conversation about Matt's choices and possible consequences, students "voted" again on what Matt would decide. The 24 students in the class were fairly evenly divided in the predictions (11—"let him in"/14—"keep him out"), and the teachers were surprised that five from each group changed their minds as a result of their close participation in the discussion. One student who said Matt would just have to let the stranger go hungry because it was too dangerous to let him in expanded his argument after the discussion to include the possibility that Matt could "put some soup on the plate and give it to him outside" and thus feed him without putting himself in danger.

Second hard choice. Mark read aloud the part of *Sign of the Beaver* where Attean says, "White father not come. . . . You go with us?"

In a class discussion, Mark elicited reasons that Matt should go or not go with Attean and abandon forever the possibility of reuniting with his family. The teachers wrote the children's arguments for and against going with Attean on big chart paper, so that everyone could benefit from the complete set of arguments. This group writing strategy acknowledged all of the contributions to the discussion while also providing memory scaffolding for particular students. Individually, students predicted which choice Matt would make and began planning a story about what Matt's life might be like after such a decision.

Although most of the students decided quite easily whether Matt would go or stay, and could write a paragraph about their reasons, teachers noted that they found it much harder to shift to writing a story about what the subsequent days in the cabin or the village would be like. Conferring on the spot, the teachers decided that the students needed to expand their knowledge of Native American village life to better remember and visualize it. Even with extensive talk about the challenges he would face if he stayed in the cabin (finding food, snow and ice, sickness, and chores) and ones he would face in Attean's village (language, knowing what is man's and woman's work, learning to hunt, knowing the "sign of the beaver," learning new customs), several students still had difficulty starting their narratives.

The reading specialist wondered if the discussion had too many possibilities, but Mark conjectured that some students were stuck not so much because they lacked ideas or had too many, but because they could not, on their own, call up their "tacit knowledge" of personal narrative structure. Testing his idea, he sat down at an empty desk and "thought aloud" as he began writing a narrative about "Mark's" previous day. Students gathered around him listening. "Mark got up and had the best breakfast he'd had in a long time. He . . . ." He reminded them that they were like the author of the novel and would be writing about Matt's day. He re-read paragraphs from the book where the author described events in the character's day. Several children caught on immediately as a result of this scaffolding, and most began writing in the next few minutes. Mark thought later that giving them the model and examples was the "spark that got them over the transition" from writing argument-style exposition to writing narrative.

Even with Mark's inventive use of modeling, one of his students, Kevin, still could not begin writing. Kevin generally had great difficulty translating ideas into writing and yet had many imaginative ideas ready to begin his story. Mark suggested that Kevin dictate the story to him. Acting as scribe, he left all the decisions about the content to the boy. More than once as Kevin was narrating his story, Mark asked, "What should I write in *your* story?" Mark felt that the boy considered himself the "true" author, because when Kevin later read his story aloud to the class, "his eyes just gleamed."

All of the students read their stories aloud as the culminating point of the unit. The teachers tightly scaffolded the class response to each story by having one or two students make a positive observation after each story. The teachers wanted to make certain their students were aware of how successful they had been. The writing exceeded Mark's and the specialists' expectations, not just in the amount of writing produced by students with disabilities, but in the evidence that students had constructed rich understandings of the alternative perspectives, the choices, and the consequences involved in making hard decisions.

MIDDLE SCHOOL CASE: A "WE-SEARCH" UNIT ON WATER ECOLOGY

This case describes an 8-week, "We-Search" unit carried out by an interdisciplinary team of teachers (language arts, social studies, mathematics, science, Spanish, and resource room). The "we-ness" comes from regular and special education students working in cooperative groups to carry out inquiry-based learning. Based on the work of Macrorie (1988), a We-Search unit is organized into four phases to provide curriculum-level scaffolding.

In Phase I, students become immersed in the unit's theme (water ecology in the case below), which is a real and meaningful theme that touches students' lives, and the overarching concepts of the unit (causes and effects of water pollution, water conservation). They engage in a variety of authentic activities to discover what they already know about the unit's theme and to build background knowledge. Each cooperative group poses an overall We-Search question and a set of related I-Search questions to guide their inquiry. In Phase II, students develop a search plan that details how they will gather information by reading books, magazines, newspapers, or reference materials; watching videos or filmstrips; interviewing people or conducting surveys; or carrying out experiments, doing simulations, or going on field trips. In Phase III, students gather and integrate information following their search plans. In Phase IV, students draft, revise, edit, and publish a We-Search Report with the following sections: Our Search Questions, Our Search Process, What We Learned, What This Means to Us, and References. While the case below is drawn mostly from one middle school in Indianapolis participating in a research study, it also integrates scaffolding strategies used by other schools around the country in implementing this approach.

Levels of Scaffolding Across the Phases of the We-Search Unit

Phase I. Clutching test tubes filled with water from Indianapolis' White River, the seventh-grade team of more than 100 students and their teachers hiked a mile back to school. To launch their We-Search unit on water ecology, they had collected water samples to test for pollution. In cooperative groups back at school, students discovered to their surprise that the water was clean.

Over the next 2 weeks, the tight coordination across classrooms ensured that students would meaningfully construct knowledge over time and across disciplines. The varied activities linking reading and writing took into account different learning styles. For example, water testing continued in science as students next wanted to know if the school's water was polluted. To understand the causes and impact of polluted rivers, students viewed a video on the Rhine River in language arts. With interest aroused about the social, economic, and political implications of water pollution, in social studies students used the computer simulation, *Decisions, Decisions: The Environment.* The students prepared questions prior to another field trip to the city's nearby water treatment plant. When a speaker from the water commission came to school to address the team, students found answers to specific questions. In Spanish, a comic book series about waterborne diseases expanded students' vocabularies in English and Spanish.

Throughout Phase I, teachers ensured that students posed search questions relating to the unit's theme and reflecting a personal investment in the topic. For example, as the social studies teacher explained to her class, "Doing an activity is not enough; you need to think about what you are learning and what it means." To help students process information, after each activity teachers distributed a worksheet to scaffold discussions within the cooperative groups. As students expressed and recorded emerging ideas and issues within their cooperative groups, teachers asked clarifying questions to probe deeper and to model conversations that built understanding. As cooperative groups reported out what they were learning and thinking, teachers kept a running record of "What we are learning" and "What more we want to know," on large chart paper for all to see and review periodically. Students filed their "processing" worksheets in the group's three-ring binder notebook, used as a portfolio. During team meetings, teachers would review the portfolios together to develop a shared understanding of students' growth and needs and, based on this, to formulate supportive strategies.

Each teacher took responsibility for five or six cooperative groups, designating these as their "coaching groups" to make sure that no student (with or without disabilities) would "fall through the cracks." Phase I (lasting 2 weeks) ended with teachers meeting with their coaching groups to pose We- and I-Search questions. This was an excellent opportunity for using a variety of strategies. For example, working with her coaching groups, the special education resource room teacher asked each group first to review all of their "processing" worksheets stored in their portfolio. She suggested that students underline or circle any questions that seemed most interesting and discuss them with peers. She spent time with each group, helping them to focus if their conversation meandered. As groups drafted their possible questions, she invited other groups to comment: Were the We-Search questions too "fat" or "skinny"? Were questions related to the theme of the unit? Were the subquestions relevant?

During their daily team meetings, teachers reviewed all questions proposed by every group. As an interim checkpoint, no group could exit Phase I until each teacher in the team "signed off" on the questions. Teachers carefully evaluated the questions by asking: "Do the questions relate to the unit's overarching concepts?" "Will students find enough information?" "Will every student be able to make a contribution?" Teachers' concerns were translated into written suggestions, revised questions, and scheduled appointments to work individually with groups. The scaffolding by teachers in Phase I served four basic purposes: (1) to elicit background knowledge, (2) to build background knowledge, (3) to model ways to gather information through varied materials and resources, and (4) to help students pose personally meaningful questions related to the theme of the unit. This laid the foundation for the next three phases.

Phase II. In Phase II (3 days), teachers helped students develop a search plan. Each period, the language arts teacher took the class to the media center where materials/resources on water ecology had been set aside. Before going to the media center, the language arts teacher explained: "Your whole group will have to gather information in four ways: reading, watching, asking, and doing. As a group you will have to decide who does what." By making these requirements explicit, teachers provided a type of "logistical" scaffolding, identifying the categories of resources and materials students were required to use.

Teachers also guided students to think realistically about when and in what order they would gather information. They gave students calendars to lay out their plans graphically. During coaching time, teachers checked in with each group to make sure that every student had specific responsibilities, the division of labor was fair, the materials to be used were relevant, the sequence of tasks was doable, and the materials and resources matched abilities and learning styles.

Phase III. In Phase III—gathering and integrating information—students carried out their search plans over a 2-week period. Here scaffolding took varied forms. For example, the teachers developed a rotating schedule to make sure that all groups had enough time in the media center. Teachers met with their coaching groups to review the notes students had taken on index cards. To promote integrating and processing of information, they explained, "I want you to talk about what you are learning so that your information comes alive." Teachers helped students relate information. For example, when students talked about what they learned on their field trip to the zoo, the teacher encouraged other students to share what they had read about the effect of water pollution on seals.

When teachers arranged for speakers to come to the school, they explained to students, "You only need to sign up to interview those speakers who are relevant to your questions." Teachers helped students develop a set of written questions (with lots of room between questions) before the speaker's appointment. They also tape-recorded the speakers for repeated listening. One group interview was conducted via telephone using the speakerphone. The teacher carefully worked out a management plan, so that one student at a time came up to the telephone, introduced him- or herself, and asked the question. Other students recorded answers.

The group telephone interview served as a model for Robert, who has learning disabilities. When teachers found that Robert was having difficulty finding information about the impact of pollution on fishing in Marion County, they suggested that he use telephone interviewing as a way to gather information. One teacher helped Robert first locate in the Yellow Pages and then make a list of businesses that rented fishing equipment and also of relevant government departments. Another coached Robert, helping him to rehearse what he would say during each call. Later, she reported to the other teachers, "He was shaky when he started, but by the tenth phone call, his voice became stronger, filled with confidence. He also learned what the word 'bureaucracy' meant when he was shuttled from one government office to another."

At their daily meetings, teachers regularly discussed the functioning of the cooperative groups. Before the unit started, teachers agonized over the makeup of each group, taking into account gender, racial, emotional, social, and academic factors. During Phase I, they had given each group special help in learning how to be a group: how to take on different roles, how to be attentive listeners, how to build consensus. Even so, halfway through Phase III, teachers recognized widespread problems centering on leadership (too much or too little), communication, and acceptance of responsibility. "It's obvious we need to deepen our efforts," offered the resource room teacher. After much discussion, the teachers developed a plan that involved the resource room teacher working individually with each group. She would teach them how to discuss their frustrations constructively, using "I" statements, instead of fighting. For example, she modeled how they could say, "I get upset when you say you will read a book and take notes and you don't." She plastered examples of I statements on her walls and often directed students' attention to these models.

Phase IV. In Phase IV, students were ready to redraft, revise, edit, and publish their We-Search reports based on earlier drafting. For example, at the end of Phase I, students began writing about their question—what had motivated their interest, and what they already knew. At the end of Phase II, they drafted their search plan. In Phase III, they kept a journal of the trials and tribulations of their search.

For Phase IV, students used word processing on laptop computers brought to each classroom. Teachers modified the schedule so that there would be longer block periods for writing. As teachers worked with their coaching groups during these writing periods, they circulated from group to group, reading drafts and making suggestions. Students referred to guide sheets developed by the teachers that carefully detailed what was required in each section of the report. This tool focused conversation during peer and teacher conferences. Teachers also introduced mini-lessons that focused on a particular skill. One mini-lesson showed students how to write a lead using a quote, a question, or an interesting statement to capture reader interest.

In a culminating event, students invited more than 200 family members and friends to their school to share what they had learned by exhibiting their work. Students were motivated to share their recommendations to solve real problems facing their community. Teachers created a productive work context, rearranging the schedule so students would have large chunks of time to create posters; reorganize their portfolios; write, rehearse, and video tape skits; and design experiments to accompany their published reports. At a deeper level, teachers continued to help students plan what they would do as a group and individually, assign roles, manage tasks, and work together productively so every student was a successful participant.

ASPECTS OF SCAFFOLDING IN THE CASES

These two cases reflect variations of the kinds of scaffolding discussed earlier. They show how teachers at different grade levels actively support learning in students with diverse academic needs; together they help to "unpack" the complexity of scaffolding.

Scaffolding Is Multilevel

Both cases describe multiple levels of scaffolding. The polish and virtuosity of the general classroom scaffolding in the "We-Search" story suggests several points about how preplanned, general classroom strategies can scaffold inquiry.

First, the strategies to emphasize are the ones that are sufficiently "robust" to support students with and without disabilities. Such strategies obviate the need to pull students out of class. Formats for helping students process information after conducting water testing and preparing questions before a field trip have this robust character. Second, those general scaffolding strategies are critical at every stage of the inquiry process. Finding questions of sufficient personal and social relevance to merit weeks of investigation requires as much scaffolding at this age as does developing a research plan or synthesizing information from varied sources. Finally, scaffolding is a cumulative process. Supporting all students in finding a question that is worth investigating lays the foundation for the research process; well-scaffolded information gathering brings students to the next challenges of synthesizing information and forming a policy position.

Mark's story illustrates the micro-level, in-flight scaffolding that may be required if all students are to be successful in authentic problem-centered instruction. Was the scaffolding sufficient? Where are students now? Who is still struggling and why? The teachers' conjectures about why their students could not start their personal narratives drew on their content- and subject-area knowledge and their general and particular knowledge of students. Mark's thinking that students—particularly students with learning disabilities—have difficulty accessing their knowledge of text structures is well supported by research (Englert, Tarrant, & Mariage, 1992). When that conjecture still did not explain Kevin's difficulty, Mark drew on his more particular knowledge of Kevin's relative strengths in oral and written communication.

Scaffolding Is Inclusive

The goal of scaffolding for students with disabilities in both cases is to strengthen students' participation in classroom inquiry and problem solving. In having Kevin dictate his story, Mark risked having him look "too different" to other students and also taking ownership of the writing away from him. The strategy worked, not simply because it resulted in a "good" story, but because it provided just the right amount of support to enable Kevin to produce the story orally and feel that he was as much an author as the other students.

Scaffolding Is Aimed at Promoting Higher-Level Thinking

While the cases include a myriad of examples of scaffolding, all of those instances contribute toward a unified purpose: building knowledge of water ecology in one case and building interpretations of an historical novel on the other. Students use all of the language processes—reading, writing, listening, discussing, and visualizing—as tools to help them think about water pollution and about hard choices.

Across both cases, writing is probably the most pervasive scaffolding approach. In the early phase of the "We-Search" process students write questions to guide their observation, record emerging ideas and issues to help them build ideas, and develop portfolios of accumulated information to help them answer their questions. In the "Hard Choices" unit, students write predictions to activate their reading, write about their reasons to focus them on details and consequences, make collections of ideas on chart paper to expand each child's thinking, and write alternative chapters to help them visualize the consequences of the boy's choices. Ironically, although formal writing is difficult for many children with disabilities, these teachers found that informal "writing-for-thinking" provides powerful scaffolding for these same students.

Scaffolding Is Dynamic and Evolving

Teachers in both cases revised or extended their scaffolding in response to student needs that they had not fully anticipated in their preplanning and that became visible in the context of the unit activity.

The cases suggest that scaffolding strategies evolve in different ways. Some strategies, like scribing for Kevin, are likely to be quite temporary so that students do not come to depend on others to write for them. Other scaffolding strategies emerge as temporary solutions to particular challenges of thematic units and may be integrated into subsequent unit designs as semipermanent building blocks. Many of the supports in the "We-Search" unit have this feeling. They are robust ways to support students through the research phases and may take on the quality of a routine. Because routines serve to reduce the cognitive complexity of the teaching process, this is an appropriate evolution for scaffolding—as long as teachers use the approaches mindfully, continually assessing how students are doing.

Together, these four aspects of scaffolding point to the immense skill required in order to engage diverse groups of students in authentic inquiry and interpretation processes. The cases also reveal the rewards of including all students in learning communities in which they address themes and issues that extend beyond school.

SCAFFOLDING FOR TEACHER LEARNING

The tenacity and sheer inventiveness of teacher scaffolding in these stories is the result of extensive teacher learning and a richly shared teacher knowledge base. Behind both cases are stories, told elsewhere (Morocco, Riley, Gordon, Howard, & Longo, 1993; Riley, Morocco, Gordon, & Howard, 1993; Zorfass, 1994; Zorfass & Korngold, 1992; Zorfass, Morocco, & Lory, 1991), of several years of ongoing teacher/researcher effort to identify the general scaffolding strategies that can engage young adolescents in active inquiry and the ways that teachers can expand their own deep understanding of active inquiry learning. A small part of those stories will point up the kinds of professional development and organizational support that schools will need to provide—and, in our experience, can provide—to enable teachers to scaffold meaning making at very high levels for their students.

Teachers in the "Hard Choices" case met as a group two to three times during each of the units they had planned together. In early meetings, they read, wrote, and talked about the same themes that they would be presenting to their students and became aware of the meaning-making processes they wanted to activate for their students. In later meetings they talked about their scaffolding experiences and discussed alternative ways to support students. In their own schools, they had scheduled time for weekly planning and debriefing, and support from their principal and from district administrators to focus on the challenge of including students with disabilities in complex, thematic literacy instruction.

Teachers in the middle school "We-Search" case had 5 days of professional time away from the school to design the unit. The middle school schedule included daily common planning times shared by the resource room teacher. Teachers had the full support of the school in departing from textbooks in order to use widely varied resources for gathering information, and varied technology and media for storing and representing information. Teachers had the assistance of a facilitator, trained in the development of "We-Search" curricula, to guide their planning and provide ongoing technical assistance. In both cases, teachers were part of "communities of practice" that included classroom teachers and specialists. These became collaborative networks within and across schools where knowledge of teaching could be shared continually and constructed out of teachers' collective experiences. All of these kinds of organizational and professional development helped these teachers build their knowledge of scaffolding. We propose that the model of modern literacy instruction that Monda-Amaya and Pearson offer be nested in communities of professional practice such as these, and that expertise in scaffolding and ongoing assessment have a privileged role in that community.

ACKNOWLEDGMENTS

The authors wish to acknowledge their research colleagues whose work is reflected in the teacher cases in this response. For the "Hard Choices" case, which is drawn from the work of the Teacher as Composer Project, these colleagues include Sue Gordon, Project Director; Maureen Riley, Co-Project Director; and Carol Howard, Research Assistant. The "We-Search" case was drawn from the work of the Make It Happen! Project.

REFERENCES

Bransford, J. D., Hasselbring, T., Barron, B., Kulewixz, S., Littlefield, J., & Goin, L. (1988). Uses of macro-contexts to facilitate mathematical thinking. In R. Charles & E. A. Silver (Eds.), *The teaching and assessing of mathematical problem solving* (pp. 171–190). Hillsdale, NJ: Erlbaum & National Council of Teachers of Mathematics.

Campione, J. C. (1993, November). *Integrating dynamic assessment and instruction within the classroom setting.* Address presented at the ninth annual Learning Disorders Conference, Harvard Graduate School of Education, Cambridge, MA.

Daiute, C., & Dalton, B. (1993). Collaboration between children learning to write: Can novices be masters? *Cognition and Instruction, 10*(4), 281.

Englert, C. S., Tarrant, K., & Mariage, T. (1992). Defining and redefining instructional practice in special education: Perspectives on good teaching. *Teacher Education and Special Education, 15*(2), 62–82.

Macrorie, K. (1988). *The I-Search paper* (rev. ed. of *Searching writing*). Portsmouth, NH: Boynton/Cook.

Morocco, C. C., Dalton, B., Tivnan, T., & Rawson, P. (1992, April). *The effect of assessment modality on children's performance in inquiry science.* Paper presented at the annual meeting of the American Educational Research Association, San Francisco.

Morocco, C. C., Riley, M. K., Gordon, S. M., Howard, C., & Longo, A. (1993, April). *Professional development through collaborative planning.* Paper presented at the annual meeting of the American Educational Research Association, Atlanta.

Palincsar, A. S., & Brown, A. L. (1984). Reciprocal teaching of comprehension-fostering and monitoring activities. *Cognition and Instruction, 1*(2), 117–175.

Riley, M. K., Morocco, C. C., Gordon, S. M., & Howard, C. (1993). Walking the talk: Putting constructivist theory into practice in classrooms. Issue: From the ivory tower: Psychological perspectives on schools and classrooms. *Educational Horizons, 71*(4), 187–196.

Speare, E.G. (1983). *Sign of the beaver.* New York: Houghton Mifflin.

Tateyama-Sniezek, K. M. (1990). Cooperative learning: Does it improve the academic achievement of students with handicaps? *Exceptional Children, 56*(5), 426–437.

Zorfass, J. (1994). Integrating technology into an I-search unit to support LD students. *Technology and Disability, 3*(2), 129–136.

Zorfass, J., & Korngold, B. (1992). Empowering teachers to keep students with language disorders in the mainstream. *OSERS News in Print, 5*(2), 36–39.

Zorfass, J., Morocco, C. C., & Lory, N. (1991). Make It Happen!: A school-based approach to integrating technology into the middle school curriculum. In F. Betts & V. Hancock (Eds.), *Curriculum handbook* (pp. 11.51–11.95). Alexandria, VA: Association for Supervision and Curriculum Development.

Response

Enacting Responsible Pedagogy with Students in Special Education

Laura Klenk and Annemarie Sullivan Palincsar

At the end of Ben's second year in school, we asked him if he knew any good writers. After a long, thoughtful pause, Ben responded, "My mother and my teacher." In response to the same question in the spring of his third year in school, Ben quickly and confidently responded, "Me, I am the best writer in this room." Indeed, in the course of that year, Ben had developed from a child who conceptualized writing as copying and avoided real writing at all costs to one who understood the instrumentality of writing and took great pleasure in his new-found ability. While there are many lenses through which we might examine Ben's development, we would like to explore his literacy learning from a pedagogical perspective.

Instruction and curriculum are two pedagogical issues that reside at the heart of education. In this response, we address these two issues for the purpose of guiding teachers to provide a supportive and stimulating context in which to enhance the literacy learning of students who have special learning needs. We heartily agree with the principles that Monda-Amaya and Pearson have presented in their chapter and wish to extend their discussion by illustrating how we have employed these principles (or modifications of them) in designing literacy assessment and instruction for special education students.

We begin by presenting three theoretical perspectives on literacy learning, and their attending principles, that have influenced our thinking. We then proceed to demonstrate how these principles were enacted in two instructional settings: a classroom for primary-aged, special education students, identified as learning disabled and/or emotionally impaired, who were being introduced to writing, and an upper-elementary setting in which students, similarly identified, were exploring the theme of friendship through an array of literacy activities.

THREE THEORETICAL PERSPECTIVES ON LITERACY AND LEARNING, AND ASSOCIATED GUIDING PRINCIPLES

In Figure 5.1, we present three perspectives that, in complementary ways, have significantly influenced the assessment, curriculum, and instruction that we describe in this response: cognitive, sociohistorical, and developmental. The figure describes the literacy focus suggested by each perspective, the instructional goals and guiding principles, and suggests references in the literature to work that is representative of the three perspectives.

While most children seem to become literate with relative ease, learning to read and write is a tremendous struggle for other youngsters—from all socioeconomic and cultural backgrounds. Some may have learning difficulties due to neurological trauma suffered before or during birth, or due to an accident. Others may have mild to severe delays in one or more areas of development, such as motor, speech, language, or social skills, for which there is no apparent cause. Still other children have had too few experiences with printed language to develop the important prerequisite concepts for conventional reading and writing. In any event, teachers need to be aware of patterns in normal literacy development in order to understand the difficulties of children who are not learning to read easily. What are the important concepts that young children must acquire in order to become literate? How can teachers assess children to determine their understanding of these concepts? Can the principles of integrated, meaningful, community-based literacy instruction be applied successfully to young children who are not learning to read and write with ease? These are the questions we address in the next sections. We begin with a brief review of aspects of literacy development that we have found to be problematic for young children with learning disabilities, along with suggestions for assessment of early literacy development. This is followed by a description of an emergent writing project that we conducted in a primary-grade, self-contained classroom for children identified as learning disabled.

PRINT CONCEPTS

By the time most children enter first grade, they understand that English is printed and read from left to right, and from the top of a page to the bottom. Pages are turned from the front of the book to the back, and conventional readers focus their eyes on the print, not the illustrations. Most first graders also are aware—or soon become aware—that print consists of individual letters combined into words, and words are recognized as separate units of print that have a direct match in speech. Children also need to

Figure 5.1 Theoretical Perspectives on Literacy and Learning

Literary Focus	Instructional Goals	Guiding Principles
	Cognitive Perspective	
Thinking, reasoning, and problem solving with print Reading and writing as tools rather than ends in themselves	Teaching for self-regulation Opportunities to read and write for multiple purposes	Attend to the process as well as the content of literacy learning Select strategies that are useful to learning across the curriculum Provide students with rationale for strategy instruction Model strategies and provide guided practice with authentic materials Engage students in self-evaluation of strategy use
	Sociohistorical Perspective	
Participation in Communities of Literacy Practice	Opportunities to learn from print and about print in socially supported interactions Experiences with the total enterprise of reading and writing while still learning about that enterprise	Joint activity in a community of learners with multiple roles distributed in accordance with ability and interests Teaching viewed as assisted performance accomplished through scaffolding Reading and writing used as tools to achieve meaningful ends even as children are acquiring the mechanical aspects of reading and writing
	Developmental Perspective	
Engaging young children in meaningful reading and writing through a variety of preconventional forms	Engaging children in learning essential concepts of print (e.g., directionality, print-to-speech match, phonemic awareness), while experimenting with preconventional forms of print	Teachers accept all preconventional forms of reading (e.g., reenacting stories from pictures or memory) and writing (e.g., scribbles, invented spellings) as meaningful attempts to communicate Teachers lead children into literacy communities through modeling their own engagement in reading and writing and by providing print-rich environments

Note: The cognitive perspective is represented in the work of Bereiter & Scardamalia (1987); Deshler, Schumaker, & Lenz (1984); Englert, Raphael, Fear, & Anderson (1988); Englert et al. (1991); Graham & Harris (1989); Palincsar & Brown (1989); and Pressley et al. (1990). Sociohistorical explanations of learning are found in Englert & Palincsar (1991) and Moll (1990). Examples of the developmental (emergent literacy) perspective include Allen, Michalove, & Shockley (1993); Morrow (1989); Taylor & Dorsey-Gaines (1988); Teale (1986); and Temple, Nathan, Burris, & Temple (1993).

acquire the metalinguistic knowledge, or vocabulary, of printed language (Clay, 1979). They need to know the names of upper- and lowercase letters, be able to recognize letters automatically, and know that letters not only have names, but also are associated with one or more sounds (letter–sound match). They need to learn the difference between a letter and a number, and the difference between a letter and a word. Children who have not grasped these basic concepts of letter names, directionality, letter–sound match, and metalinguistic knowledge most likely will have difficulty learning to read and write.

Teachers can easily assess children for most of these concepts by observing them closely during the course of instructional activities. Does the child hold the book right-side-up? Are the child's eyes focused on print or pictures? Does the child follow the print from left to right, either visually (with eye movements) or physically (by pointing with a finger)? Does the child demonstrate an accurate print-to-speech match when asked to "point as we read"? On an individual basis, the teacher can ask a child to count the number of words on a page with one line of print.

The importance of establishing the one-to-one correspondence between print and speech cannot be overemphasized. Some youngsters are able to memorize the simplified text in pre-primers and repetitive literature books before they make this match, and their teachers assume that they are gaining conventional reading skills. As these children encounter less familiar or nonrepetitive text, they will be less successful. Some learning disabled adults have reported that they passed from one grade to the next by memorizing stories as other children read. Because they did not want to appear incompetent, or because they mistakenly thought that this was how other children were reading, they did not ask for help. Their teachers remained unaware of the fact they were not decoding from text, and thus their failure to learn to read continued (Johnston, 1985).

When assessing children for letter-name knowledge, it is not enough to ask children to "say the alphabet." Many preschoolers are able to sing the alphabet song—usually with great pride, since this skill is highly valued by parents. However, kindergarten and first-grade teachers need to distinguish between rote memory of the alphabet and specific knowledge of letter names. Children who are unable to recognize letters presented at random, or who cannot do this quickly, are likely to have difficulty learning to read and write (Foorman, Francis, Novy, & Liberman, 1991; Walsh, Price, & Gillingham, 1988).

PHONEMIC AWARENESS

Phonemes are the individual sounds of language that we represent with letters or combinations of letters. We have already mentioned that children must learn to match letters with sounds. Generally, children who learn to read easily are able to distinguish the different sounds in words and, more important, are able to manipulate these sounds. That is, they can isolate the beginning, middle, and ending sounds of a word (phoneme segmentation), and they can combine isolated sounds into a word (phoneme blending). Most children learn to make these discriminations through rhyming and other word games, and through incidental experimentation. For example, a 5-year-old we know was leaving Sunday school with his mother, who had been busy canning fruit earlier that week. "Listen, Mom," said the little fellow, "'church' and 'cherry'—they sound the same!"

Determining a child's skill in manipulating phonemes requires close and often deliberate observation. Is the child able to produce rhyming words in songs or poems that are recited in class? When asked, can the child tell you the first or last sound of familiar words? When asked to listen to a series of sounds, can the child blend these sounds into a familiar word? Given a familiar word, can the child think of other words that begin with the same sound? Does the child invent spellings with reasonable phonetic similarities?

Researchers disagree on the relationship between phonemic awareness and learning to read—whether it is a cause-and-effect relationship and, if so, in what direction the cause–effect lies; or whether phonemic awareness is merely a strong correlate of learning to read (Bryant, 1990; Perfetti, Beck, & Hughes, 1987; Torneus, 1984). One thing is certain—youngsters who are unable to discriminate and manipulate the sounds in words will be frustrated if placed in a rigid, phonics-based curriculum.

MOTOR SKILLS

A delay in fine motor development often is manifested in children with learning disabilities as poor or illegible handwriting. Some children are unable to reproduce letters and numbers, either by copying or tracing the shapes. Alan, a fourth-grade student in a resource classroom, had not developed legible handwriting. Often he could not read his own handwriting, although he composed lengthy and highly complex, imaginative stories. Traditionally, special educators have focused their instructional efforts on the correction of handwriting problems, to the exclusion of opportunities for children like Alan to compose original text. In primary-grade special education classes, we have observed that children spend a great deal of time copying unfamiliar text from a chalkboard, or filling in worksheets with rows of letters, trying to make their own reproductions look exactly like those of the teacher or the publisher of the handwriting curriculum. We have found that regular, sustained opportunities for composing original stories provides sufficient practice for most children to develop fluent handwriting. For the exceptions like Alan, computers and child-friendly word processing programs are widely available.

SPEECH/LANGUAGE ISSUES

Literacy theorists have long been interested in the relationships between learning to speak, read, and write. We have observed several points at which speech and language development may intersect and interfere with learning to read and write. For example, fluent oral language, adequate vocabulary development, and normal development of syntax (word order or grammar) all support reading and writing (Pflaum, 1986). Children who have limited vocabularies will have greater difficulty understanding what they read even if they can sound out unfamiliar words. Incomplete syntax development may indicate more general cognitive delays, and has even more serious implications for learning to read and write. This is because good readers use their grammatical sense to anticipate and decode words, and to monitor their comprehension of text. Children who have not mastered critical elements of syntax do not have this important advantage as they encounter unfamiliar words in text.

Some children, because of delayed maturation or physical abnormalities of the speech mechanisms, are delayed in mastering accurate articulation of sounds. Children may exhibit three major kinds of articulation disorders: omissions ("ot" for "got"), substitutions ("wady" for "lady"), or distortions ("ow" for "are"). Articulation problems do not lead automatically to difficulties in reading and writing. Some children are able to discriminate sounds auditorily that they cannot articulate correctly. Teachers also must distinguish articulation disorders from dialectic differences in pronunciations. When articulation disorders cause confusion in decoding or spelling, or when they are combined with lack of phonemic awareness, difficulties in learning to read and write are almost a certainty.

EMERGENT WRITING PROJECT FOR CHILDREN WITH LEARNING DISABILITIES

Rationale

The children with whom we work in special education classes present unique combinations of problems with print concepts, phonemic awareness, oral language, speech production, and motor development. The traditional pedagogical response to such problems in the field of special education has been to train children in these specific skills. Following behaviorist learning theories, special educators have believed for decades that knowledge or skills must be broken down into the smallest components in order to be mastered by children with learning difficulties. Much of this instruction takes place in isolation from authentic reading and writing activities. A serious consequence of such instruction is that children develop limited definitions of reading and writing, and limited views of themselves as readers and writers.

When we asked youngsters in special education classes, "What is reading?" or "What do you do when you read?" they typically responded with answers such as: "[Reading is] reading group." "Like you dig in a bag and get some letters, you match 'em up." "Reading words. You have to do them [copy them] five times each." "Look at words and put your finger on them." "I do reading like *A, B,* only circle one that doesn't belong." When asked, "What is writing?" these same youngsters told us: "Handwriting"; or, "It's something you do in school. It's like handwriting; you can write sentences and spell anything"; or, "Like writing your alphabet, writing spelling words; writing your math problems." These responses clearly indicate that the children do not conceive of reading and writing as creative processes through which they can construct and communicate meaning. Rather, to these children, reading and writing are merely the mechanical processes of decoding and penmanship, and are associated with the particular activities known to the children as "schoolwork." It was our goal in this project to provide opportunities for the children to experience engagement in reading and writing beyond schoolwork—for gaining and sharing information, recreation, and personal expression. We will now describe how we incorporated the principles of meaningfulness, integration, and community in designing the writing project and how we scaffolded writing activities for children who exhibited delays in literacy acquisition.

Activities and Methods

This study took place in a class with seven children, aged 6 to 8, in grades 1 and 2. Most of the children had been identified as learning disabled or developmentally delayed in preschool or kindergarten; their difficulties in school ranged from mild to severe delays in social, cognitive, speech/language, and motor development. Writing instruction in this class consisted of penmanship activities. Each day, the children copied a short poem from the chalkboard, filled in worksheets with rows of letters, and wrote their name five times. The teacher explained that she did not do any creative writing with the class because the children did not have the necessary spelling and "pencil skills." At the beginning of the school year, several of the children had difficulty recognizing the alphabet, and none could write more than four words from memory, including names of family members. None recognized more than one word on a list of common sight words, and on a test of dictation, only three children were able to produce any letter–sound matches. Several had great difficulty reproducing letter shapes; for handwriting practice, these children were allowed to trace the poem, rather than copy it from the board. When judged either by conventional or emergent literacy standards for literacy acquisition, these children clearly had fallen far behind their age peers.

We began the project by situating writing activities in a socially meaningful context: the newspaper. For 2 weeks, the teacher led class explorations and discussions of several area newspapers. We explained to the children that they could learn from the paper even if they could not read the words, and we encouraged them to talk about what they saw in the newspapers. The children identified grocery and other advertisements, sports, weather maps, the television guide, and other features. Each child had opportunities to verbally share with the class what he or she discovered in the paper. Often, they related what they observed to their own lives—telling us about the television shows they liked to watch, about shopping trips to stores, and so on. The class also took a field trip to the local newspaper office, where they observed reporters working at their computers, the folding machine, the wire machine, and the layout tables.

Following this introduction to the newspaper, one of the researchers modeled story writing using "invented spelling"—sounding out words as she wrote and thinking aloud as she made spelling decisions. She asked the children to demonstrate on the chalkboard their own ways of writing—some wrote their names (the only word most knew how to spell), while others produced strings of random letters. The teacher and researchers emphasized to the children that they could write stories even if they did not know how to spell all the words. We gave each child a steno pad, which we called their "News Books," and explained that every day they would have time to write their own news. We instituted weekly sharing sessions, during which the children took turns coming to the front of the class to read the news they had written that week, thus establishing the foundation for a community of writers. Most often, the children were free to write about any topic of their choosing. At times, however, the teacher assigned topics based on themes from their content area classes, for example, Black history, meal worms, dinosaurs, and book reports. Twice during the school year, we published a class newspaper, which was distributed to the school district administrators, the children's families, and other teachers in the building. The children practiced reading their stories in order to visit other classrooms and share their newspaper with the rest of the student body.

In addition to conducting regular writing demonstrations for the class as a group, we also worked with the children individually to support them as they wrote their stories. Our decisions in working with the children to scaffold the writing experience were guided by principles from the cognitive, sociohistorical, and developmental perspectives and were fine-tuned to meet the individual needs of the children. To illustrate these principles and the developmental progression we witnessed during the course of the school year, we present a case study of one second grader, Randy.

Randy

Randy was 7 years old when he began second grade in this self-contained special education class. At age 4, he had been diagnosed as having "pervasive developmental delays." This diagnosis later was changed to autism. Randy had particular difficulty with expressive language and the pragmatics (social skills) of language use, and he avoided verbal interactions with other children and with adults. He possessed a remarkable ability to memorize and repeat, verbatim, lengthy portions of script from his favorite television cartoons. His interactions with teachers and peers often were loaded (inappropriately) with "cartoon talk." As for literacy development, he recognized 41 of 54 letters on a letter recognition test. He did not recognize any sight words in isolation and was unable to spell any words except his name. Randy could make no accurate letter–sound matches on a dictation test, indicating that he had not yet developed a useful sense of phonemic awareness. The precision of Randy's penmanship far outweighed that of all of his classmates. Some of his first stories consisted of rows of neatly printed random letter strings, but typically he filled his News Book with page after page of illustrations—mostly of vehicles (cars, boats, trains, rockets) and Superman. Randy seemed to lack a sense of story structure. When asked to read from his News Book, he rendered slogans or statements of opinion, rather than stories. For example:

> If you want any work, just work on buildings. [See Figure 5.2]
>
> If someone gives you drugs or cigarettes, just say NO!
>
> Don't smoke in buildings. Just smoke at home.
>
> Bad guys are too mean. If you see them rob a bank call the police.
>
> If you are blinded by the sun, just wait until the blinding is gone.

Despite these developmental delays, Randy enjoyed drawing pictures and writing in his News Book. We responded to these efforts initially by

Figure 5.2 "If you want any work, just work on buildings."

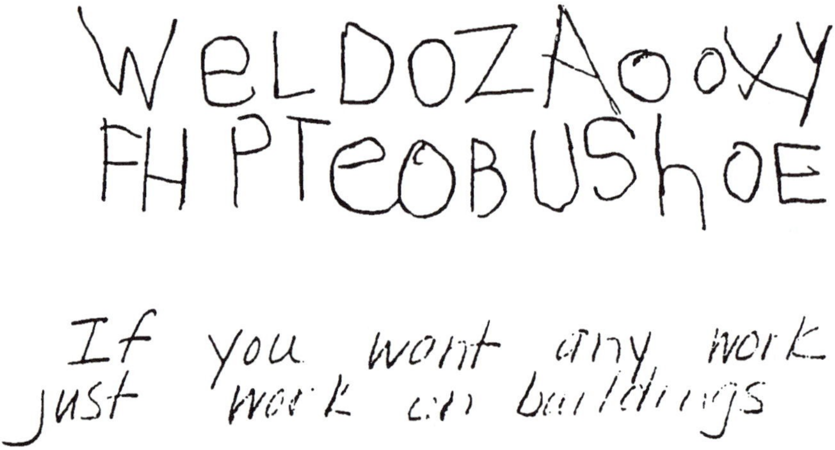

encouraging Randy's use of expressive oral language, frequently asking him to "tell us more" about his stories. After several weeks had gone by, and Randy remained reluctant to engage in extended conversations about his writing, we shifted our focus and began suggesting to Randy that he write captions for his illustrations. Some days, he would write a string of letters on his own as a one-word label or brief line from a cartoon (e.g., "Ren says, 'Shut up, you fool.'"). Other days, Randy simply dictated a caption to his teacher, who transcribed it in conventional spelling on the News Book page ("This is a car" or "Freight Train") (see Figure 5.3).

When it occurred to us that Randy's reliance on cartoons inhibited him from developing more complete stories, we began to encourage him to talk and write about his own daily experiences. We would ask, "What did you do for fun over the weekend/after school last night?" As he gained some confidence for telling his own stories, we pressed further for him to think about writing. "That is a very interesting story. Is that what you want to write about today?" When Randy decided on a topic, we encouraged him to generate and plan his stories orally before writing. "How are you going to start your story? What will you tell about next?" Shortly before the winter holidays, Randy began to talk about the Christmas tree in his house. In fact, he explained, there were two trees decorated in his home. We told Randy that other people in the class might find this interesting and suggested that he write about it in his News Book. With help from us in sounding out words, matching letters to the sounds, and holding the story in

Figure 5.3 "Car."

memory as he concentrated on the physical task of transcription, Randy produced the story shown in Figure 5.4.

In this session, Randy demonstrated that he knew at least one sight word (THE) and that he listened carefully to his own speech to make letter–sound matches. For example, Randy spoke with an exaggerated nasal tone, thus producing /z/ as the first sound in "THE." His spacing indicated a sense of word boundaries, though not totally accurate yet. He was definitely inventing spellings for each word as he proceeded through the story. Tree is spelled simply "T" the first time, but "TR" the second time. It is doubtful that Randy would have sustained this level of effort without the individual support we offered.

As the weeks and months passed, it became easier for us to engage Randy in conversations and story writing from his own experience. His spelling progressed from using one consonant sound per word or syllable, to including several consonants and even vowels. By listening to his story and holding it in memory as he worked on spelling, we continued to assist Randy as he wrote. We encouraged him to think about letter–sound associations, offering suggestions when he was completely stuck. Like many of his classmates, Randy continued to add simple labels or captions to his illustrations when working on his own.

Randy's progression of spelling development resembles that of 4- and 5-year-old children who do not have learning disabilities. He made slow but steady progress in spelling, adding vowels and even some sight words to his stories. As with most other children, his progress in writing was "recursive"; that is, he often would revert to nonphonetic letter strings or illustrations even after having produced phonetic inventions on a previous day. Several times, we observed that Randy revised his writing, adding details or additional information in order to satisfy his audience's curiosity or his own sense of what was important in the story. As we continued to engage him in discussions of his stories, Randy's oral and written stories became more elaborated and natural. Late in the school year, Randy was independently creating humorous stories and pictures about his personal experiences, stories that delighted and entertained children and adults alike (see Figure 5.5).

Learning from Randy's Experience

Earlier in this chapter, we reviewed some developmental concepts that are important to literacy acquisition. Randy's story illustrates how developmental delays in speech/language, phoneme awareness, and other print concepts hinders literacy acquisition. While Randy's involvement in this emergent writing project did not magically bring him to grade level in reading

Figure 5.4 "The little tree is in the bedroom. The big tree is in the basement."

Figure 5.5 "I am late for school."

or writing, his story also illustrates that even children with severe delays can participate in meaningful literacy activities and can make progress toward becoming conventional, independent readers and writers through their engagement in these activities.

At the end of the year, Randy confused the same letters as at the start of the year. He still was not able to recognize common sight words in isolation, even though he had been using some of these words in his writing. On the pretest, Randy had been unable to spell a single word. At the end of the year, he spelled four words accurately, and, more significant, he attempted a dozen other words—many of them names of his classmates, which he spelled with only minor omissions. His score on the dictation test improved from zero to 15 accurate letter–sound matches. With regard to his expressive language, Randy became more engaged in class discussions, and his interactions were less stilted. Other children in the class sought him out as an illustrator for their own stories, and he enjoyed the friendly laughter with which they received his stories. Cartoons continued to influence Randy's writing and illustration. When the children wrote and published their own storybooks, Randy concluded his story with Woody Woodpecker's famous laugh ("That's all, folks"), to the great amusement of his classmates, who asked him to repeat his story many times.

What are the most important lessons that we have learned from working with Randy and his classmates? First, teachers cannot wait for children to acquire basic concepts of print before allowing them to read and write "their own way." Following the dictate of "starting where the child is" should not preclude learning disabled youngsters from composing and reading original text. To the contrary, we advocate allowing children to acquire basic concepts from their engagement in meaningful literacy activities. Clearly, some children will continue to struggle in the quest to read and write independently and conventionally—but this does not mean that they should be denied opportunities to write often, and for many different reasons. Randy wrote a lengthy informational story about dinosaurs for the class newspaper, revealing his capacity to learn content material. He learned to share anecdotes from his own life with his classmates; we believe that he was beginning to value his own stories just as we did. He honed his sense of humor, gaining respect from his peers for his ability to make them laugh as well as for his skill in illustrating stories.

As for instructional implications, we were able to scaffold the writing experience for Randy by working with his interests (cartoons) and focusing first on the content of his stories. In so doing, we were able to effect a change not only in his writing, but in his oral language skills as well. In accord with principles of emergent literacy, we accepted Randy's "own way" of writing—drawing pictures and printing random letter strings—and by guiding and supporting him into the risky venture of inventing spellings. Thus Randy was able to experience reading and writing as problem solving with print, not merely as "schoolwork."

In the next section, we describe our research working in an upper-elementary special education class.

AN UPPER-ELEMENTARY CONTEXT

The 10 children in this class were between the ages of 8 and 12 and were considered to be third and fourth graders. Seven of the children were from racial minority families and five were girls. Their reading and writing achievement was considerably below grade level, with reading achievement assessed to range from mid-first to mid-second grade, based on the results of the Qualitative Reading Inventory (Leslie & Caldwell, 1990). Their writing achievement was also significantly below grade level; 70% of the children used preconventional forms of writing, while the remaining children wrote in conventional forms. Regarding their awareness and experience with literature, only two of the 10 children were able to identify a favorite story during interviews that were administered prior to beginning the unit of instruction, and, when read a story aloud and asked to retell it, the majority of the children included only one story element in their retelling.

The goal of the instruction in this classroom was to increase interest, engagement, and achievement in reading and writing. The unit of instruction was designed around the theme of friendship.[1] We will first describe the broad strokes of the curriculum and then detail its enactment, referring to the principles described in the first section of this response. The instructional activities included: (1) interactive readings from literature on friendship; (2) personal written responses to the literature; (3) supported retelling of the literature for the purpose of preparing a performance to share the literature with others; (4) performance related to the literature; and (5) journal writing on the topic of friendship.

The selected literature included fantasy, realistic fiction, and nonfiction—all of which addressed different facets of friendship.[2] Our goal was for the students to acquire increased understanding of and shared experiences with the theme of friendship. The texts also were selected because they represented an array of text structures; for example, while each story contained typical story elements (characters and setting), each also was organized using cause and effect, problem/ solution, and sequences of events. Finally, the literature featured characters that were diverse with respect to race.

The specific instructional activities included the following. In preparation to read each story, the students generated predictions, based on the title, the cover illustrations, and—with each new story—their developing understanding of friendship. The preparation was followed by an interactive reading of the story (the text was read aloud by the teacher as children followed along), during which the students were encouraged to comment on the developments in the text and to relate the story not only to their personal experiences as friends but also to the other stories they had read in the friendship series. The teacher scaffolded these discussions by initially modeling interactions with the story, for example, commenting on how the story reminded her of a friendship that she had, how the story suggested a different aspect of friendship, or how the friendship depicted in one story compared with that in another. In each case, the teacher was attentive to justifying her statement by drawing upon the literature or personal experiences. Over time, the teacher made fewer of these comments and, instead, simply paused opportunistically to give the students the chance to comment or raise issues.[3]

The interactive reading of the text was followed by each student generating a personal response to the piece of literature; the children were encouraged to write about the way(s) in which the story added to or changed their ideas about friendship. These responses were for personal use and were written using whatever forms of writing the students had in their repertoire; the teacher provided the same types of support described earlier in this chapter (e.g., holding ideas in memory for the child, reminding the child where the spellings could be found in environmental print, assisting children to sound out words that were phonetically regular).

The day after the interactive reading and personal response to the story, the group engaged in a teacher-led retelling of the story for the purpose of teaching the students to make use of the story structure to support their recall and retelling of the story. For example, the students always began their retellings by identifying the characters, setting (where appropriate), and the problem in the story. They then completed, as a group, a graphic that best depicted the story's events. The students determined, through discussion, the story's key ideas or events to be captured in the retelling. While these retellings initially were heavily directed and led by the teacher, over the course of the 6-week unit of study, the students required less teacher assistance.

Following the retelling, the children prepared a script for a performance of the story; the performances varied from a puppet show to a dramatic reenactment of the story. In some cases, the class drew a mural depicting the events and, with the assistance of the mural, narrated the story. The purpose of this activity was to provide the students an array of opportunities for making the story their own. Converting the retellings to scripts provided the students with multiple opportunities to determine what was most salient about the stories and how best to communicate these ideas in their own words. In addition to writing in response to the literature, the students maintained a "friendship journal" for the purpose of reflecting on themselves as friends and on what they valued in friendships. These writings were more extensive than the brief responses made following the stories and were read aloud to the class for the purpose of soliciting feedback from others about their writing and their ideas. To draw the unit to a close, the class formed a critics' circle. In preparation, the children wrote their opinions of each of the six stories read, presented their critiques, and then voted for their favorite story, to which they awarded the Class Caldecott Award.

Learning from the Friendship Unit

How does the friendship unit represent the principles of literacy instruction to which we referred early in this response? A number of features of the instruction were designed to enhance self-regulation, including the interactive reading, the instruction of story elements and story structure to guide the retellings, and the opportunities to write and receive feedback on one's writing. In addition, from a cognitive perspective, the children read and wrote for a broad range of purposes, including indicating their understandings of the stories, expressing their own opinions, creatively representing the stories to others, and reflecting on their own beliefs about friendship. The context in which this instruction occurred was designed to reflect socio-historical tenets to the extent that the children constituted a community of readers, writers, and performers. They experienced reading and writing in holistic and integrated ways. They assisted one another in each of these activities, using their distributed expertise; children who were facile with printing prepared the cue cards that had been generated by the group as a whole, and children who were budding artists prepared the props for plays and the murals. Finally, from a developmental perspective, instruction began with the children—both in terms of their concerns (friendship) and in terms of their current literacy levels.

What were the outcomes of this instruction? At the conclusion of this unit of study, each child successfully identified and retold, using all of the story elements, a favorite story. The sheer amount of writing in which the children engaged increased significantly. In addition, their writings and the discussions held during the readings indicate that they made cumulative use of the ideas about friendship that they encountered across the stories. Finally, interest in the stories themselves prompted the children to engage independently in repeated, independent readings.

CONCLUSION

Our work with children in special education classes has convinced us that these children benefit from literacy instruction based on many of the features espoused by Monda-Amaya and Pearson in their model of modern literacy instruction. First, reading and writing instruction was situated within socially meaningful activities (the newspaper, journal writing, and collaborative sessions in the friendship unit). We recognized the need to individualize the scaffolds we provided for reading and writing, and observed that the children discovered important concepts of print and embraced conventions of print as they read and wrote for each other. Second, we recognized the importance of social interactions—between teacher and student, as well as among children. The children wrote and read not just as an exercise to be evaluated by their teachers, but for personal expression and to inform and entertain their peers and other members of their school and home communities. These social interactions were vital to the establishment of a community of learners, the third feature of the model. We extended the community beyond the classroom walls—"reading" the newspaper connected the children to their lives outside of school and demonstrated the practical use of print. On their visit to the newspaper office, the children observed adults for whom writing plays a prominent role in earning their livelihoods. Throughout the friendship unit, the students interwove their daily experiences and dilemmas in making and sustaining friendships within their classroom as well as within the school and in their neighborhoods.

Special education teachers currently face many challenges and choices in determining how they will approach literacy instruction. Concurrent with the rising popularity of holistic approaches, highly structured and isolated phonics-based curricula remain popular as remedial approaches in many school districts.[4] Despite empirical evidence supporting the need for and effectiveness of teaching students to be self-regulating, the value of strategy instruction has yet to be realized in many remedial and special education settings. In our own work, we have demonstrated that literacy instruction for youngsters with learning difficulties can be adapted to accommodate their special needs without compromising the important social and communicative goals of literacy.

ACKNOWLEDGMENTS

The two research projects referred to in this chapter were supported by a grant from the Office of Special Education Programs (H023C90076-90) awarded to A. S. Palincsar and C. S. Englert (co-principal investigator), T. Raphael, and J. Gavelek. The reader is referred to Englert, Raphael, and Mariage (1994) for an extensive description of additional instructional activities examined in special education settings that were informed by the perspectives identified in this chapter. The research on the friendship unit was conducted in collaboration with Andrea Parecki, whom we gratefully acknowledge.

NOTES

1. This theme emerged from the students' observations that they were not very adept at developing and maintaining friendships and that, in fact, they had a hard time getting along with one another. The interviews we administered before beginning instruction also revealed that the ideas these children were able to generate about friendship were very thin, most children commenting only that they play with friends.

2. Titles included *Morgan and Yew, Amos and Boris, Jamaica Tag Along, Team Mates, A Place for Everyone,* and *Elizabeth and Larry.*

3. Book club research conducted by Urba (1994), drawing on the work of Raphael and McMahon, supports the benefits of teacher scaffolding of literature-based discussions in special education settings.

4. Examples include Project Read and other programs based on the Orton-Gillingham approach to reading.

REFERENCES

Allen, J., Michalove, B., & Shockley, B. (1993). *Engaging children: Community and chaos in the lives of young literacy learners.* Portsmouth, NH: Heinemann.

Bereiter, C., & Scardamalia, M. (1987). An attainable version of high literacy: Approaches to teaching higher-order skills in reading and writing. *Curriculum Inquiry, 17*(1), 9–30.

Bryant, P. E. (1990). Phonological development and reading. In P. D. Pumfrey & C. D. Elliott (Eds.), *Children's difficulties in reading, spelling, and writing: Challenges and responses* (pp. 63–82). London: Falmer Press.

Clay, M. M. (1979). *The early detection of reading difficulties.* Auckland, New Zealand: Heinemann.

Deshler, D. P., Schumaker, J. B., & Lenz, B. K. (1984). Academic and cognitive interventions for LD adolescents. *Journal of Learning Disabilities, 17,* 108–117.

Dyson, A. H. (1993). *Social worlds of children learning to write in an urban primary school.* New York: Teachers College Press.

Englert, C. S., & Palincsar, A. S. (1991). Reconsidering instructional research in literacy from a sociocultural perspective. *Learning Disabilities Research and Practice, 6,* 225–229.

Englert, C. S., Raphael, T. E., Anderson, L. M., Anthony, H. M., & Stevens, D. D. (1991). Making writing strategies and self-talk visible: Cognitive strategy instruction in regular and special education classrooms. *American Educational Research Journal, 28,* 337–372.

Englert, C. S., Raphael, T. E., Fear, K. L., & Anderson, L.M. (1988). Students' metacognitive knowledge about how to write informational texts. *Learning Disability Quarterly, 11*(1), 18–46.

Englert, C. S., Raphael, T. E., & Mariage, T. V. (1994). Developing a school-based discourse for literacy learning: A principled search for understanding. *Learning Disability Quarterly, 17*(1), 2–32.

Foorman, B. R., Francis, D. J., Novy, D. M., & Liberman, D. (1991). How letter–sound instruction mediates progress in first grade reading. *Journal of Educational Psychology, 83*(4), 456–469.

Graham, S., & Harris, K. R. (1989). Improving learning disabled students' skills at composing essays: Self-instructional strategy training. *Exceptional Children, 56*(3), 201–216.

Johnston, P. H. (1985). Understanding reading disability: A case study approach. *Harvard Educational Review, 55*(2), 153–177.

Leslie, L., & Caldwell, J. (1990). *Qualitative reading inventory.* New York: HarperCollins.

Moll, L. (Ed.). (1990). *Vygotsky and education.* New York: Cambridge University Press.

Morrow, L. M. (1989). *Literacy development in the early years: Helping children read and write.* Englewood Cliffs, NJ: Prentice-Hall.

Palincsar, A. S., & Brown, A. L. (1989). Classroom dialogues to promote self-regulated comprehension. In J. Brophy (Ed.), *Advances in research on teaching* (pp. 35–72). Greenwich, CT: JAI Press.

Perfetti, C.A., Beck, I., & Hughes, C. (1987). Phonemic knowledge and learning to read are reciprocal: A longitudinal study of first graders. *Merrill-Palmer Quarterly, 33*(3), 283–319.

Pflaum, S. W. (1986). *The development of language and literacy in young children.* Columbus, OH: Merrill.

Pressley, M., et al. (1990). *Cognitive strategy instruction that really improves children's academic performance* (1st ed.). Cambridge, MA: Brookline Books.

Taylor, D., & Dorsey-Gaines, C. (1988). *Growing up literate: Learning from inner-city families.* Portsmouth, NH: Heinemann.

Teale, W. H. (1986). The beginnings of reading and writing: Written language development during the preschool and kindergarten years. In M. R. Sampson (Ed.), *The pursuit of literacy: Early reading and writing* (pp. 1–29). Dubuque, IA: Kendall-Hunt.

Temple, C., Nathan, R., Burris, N., & Temple, F. (1993). *The beginnings of writing.* Newton, MA: Allyn & Bacon.

Torneus, M. (1984). Phonological awareness: A chicken and egg problem? *Journal of Educational Psychology, 76,* 1346–1358.

Urba, J. (1994). *Changing the nature of special education students' talk in literature discussion groups: The evolution of a literacy activity.* Paper presented at the annual meeting of the American Educational Research Association, New Orleans.

Walsh, D. J., Price, G. G., & Gillingham, M. G. (1988). The critical but transitory importance of letter naming. *Reading Research Quarterly, 23*(1), 108–122.

* *CHAPTER 6* *

Curriculum in Early Childhood Education: Redefining the Specialization

Christine Burton Maxwell

Controversy about the specific goals, content, and methods of the early childhood curriculum has raged throughout the generations. The main debate focuses on which developmental and educational aims and corresponding experiences are of most worth for young children: the nurturance of social and emotional competence or the promotion of early academic achievement (Zigler, 1990). Other issues, such as the appropriate settings for early education and bringing curricular cohesion to the full age span of early education offerings, are offshoots of the curriculum question (Caldwell, 1991; Kagan, 1991).

THE HISTORICAL LANDSCAPE OF EARLY CHILDHOOD CURRICULUM

Three aspects of the field's recent past are particularly instructive in explaining current curriculum issues and trends. These include: (1) a long-term reliance on the "traditional" nursery and kindergarten approach as early childhood education's defining core, (2) the advent of Head Start in the 1960s and an emergent emphasis on early education as cognitive intervention, and (3) the burgeoning in the 1980s of early childhood programs across an increasingly diverse array of settings, including community child-care centers and public school preschools.

The traditional nursery and kindergarten approach has contributed significantly to the mainstream curriculum patterns we see today (Evans, 1975). The specific defining feature of the traditional approach is commitment to nurturing children's social and emotional development. Particular emphasis is placed on the general goals of learning to control personal feelings and to cope with peers (McCarthy, 1983). Indeed, according to McCarthy (1983), "if the child learned something beyond these skills, it was quite acceptable, but not considered extremely important" (p. 275).

In the traditional nursery and kindergarten approach, quality early education was equated with the overall provision of a positive, holistic child development experience (Evans, 1975). Child development was the general organizing framework for curriculum, with instructional methods focused on self-initiated free play and creative expression within a flexible, benevolent educational environment. The ages 3 through 5 years, the period prior to the beginning of "formal" schooling, defined the age range of predominant concern.

During the 1960s, the traditional nursery and kindergarten approach underwent transition as a number of scientific and societal forces came onto the scene (Shonkoff & Meisels, 1990). Foremost among these was the accumulation of theoretical and empirical knowledge documenting the importance of the preschool years in influencing the long-term trajectory of children's intellectual or cognitive development.

The field's traditional embrace of social-emotional development as its primary aim thus gave way to an emphasis on children's early cognitive development (Evans, 1975). Although the primary goal remained the promotion of child development, more emphasis shifted to a vertical, futurist orientation in which children are prepared for upcoming developmental stages and experiences, particularly upcoming school experiences.

In addition, during the 1960s, early educators' attention increasingly became directed toward the construction of more explicitly articulated, theoretically derived curriculum models and the more conscious extension of such early childhood curricula into the primary school years (Evans, 1975). The advent of Head Start, based on this emerging theory and research, was strongly instrumental in reshaping mainstream orientations to early childhood curricula. Exemplified by the Head Start Follow-Forward initiative, quality early childhood education became recognized as a critical component of a *long-term* educational continuum (Zigler, 1990).

As dramatic as these early childhood curriculum developments of the 1960s were, they were in many ways outmatched by the social events of the 1980s. Unprecedented numbers of single and married mothers entered the work force, requiring that their young children receive out-of-home, child-care services. Concern for the impact of the country's escalating poverty rate on young children's learning and development was encouraged by the popularization of research findings documenting the academic and social benefits that preschool intervention can yield for young children of economic poverty (Kagan, 1991). This concern was magnified by public alarm over the general status of American educational outcomes.

Taken together, the social trends of the 1980s and 1990s resulted in the unheralded expansion of early childhood education programs. Many of these programs followed the current trend toward a "push-down" curriculum where a didactic, teacher-directed curriculum was the mainstay. Teaching abstract, decontextualized basic skills ushered in the use of standardized testing for such purposes as school entrance, retention, and ability grouping (Freeman, 1990).

Among traditional early childhood educators, the new school-based practices represented an assault on the field's long-standing child development orientation (Bredekamp, 1987). Inappropriate curriculum was being inflicted on younger and more vulnerable children.

CURRENT STATUS OF EARLY CHILDHOOD CURRICULUM

Emergence of Developmentally Appropriate Practice

Recent movements to articulate professional criteria for quality early childhood curriculum actually began as a defense strategy to counter these trends toward more academic curriculum (Bredekamp, 1987). The National Association for the Education of Young Children (NAEYC) published its first major curriculum position statement, *Developmentally Appropriate Practice in Early Childhood Programs Serving Children from Birth Through Age 8* (Bredekamp, 1987), with the primary goal of reasserting the child development orientation of early childhood education by setting forth more explicit definitions of the specialization's key conceptual parameters.

During the decade since the publication of the NAEYC statement, similar curriculum guidelines with similar rationales have been produced by a host of other national professional organizations (National Association of State Boards of Education, 1988; National Association of Elementary School Principals, 1990; National Black Child Development Institute, 1987; National Association for the Education of Young Children and National Association of Early Childhood Specialists in State Departments of Education, 1992). As a set of principles to guide the design of curriculum in early childhood education, the current dominant position statements evidence substantial commonalities. Katz (1991) and others have pointed out that these commonalities in the curriculum standards typically are telegraphed into a shared list of descriptors, including such terms as "child-initiated," "unstructured," "play-based," "nondidactic," and "concrete, integrated, hands-on learning." The umbrella term that has come to symbolize current standards for early childhood curriculum, however, is "developmentally appropriate practice."

In its most basic interpretation, "developmentally appropriate practice" connotes the belief that a quality early childhood curriculum is one that is matched to each child's level of learning and development (Elkind, 1991). It is posited that this match should be accomplished with regard to both the child's general age-related patterns of development and his or her unique individual patterns of development (Bredekamp, 1987). Among the aspects of learning and development cited in the standards as calling for such a deliberately designed child–curriculum match are children's needs, interests, learning styles, developmental paces, and cultural/linguistic orientations.

All aspects of the principles stand, at least at face value, in opposition to educational approaches that emphasize teacher-controlled, skills-oriented instruction. Beyond such surface appeal, however, the central curriculum controversy facing the field of early education today is whether the current standards for developmentally appropriate practice hold potential for delineating a comprehensive, cohesive foundation for curriculum design and implementation. This question is forcing early childhood educators to revisit perennial curriculum issues, as well as to infuse new complexities into the field's ongoing curriculum debates.

Dimensions of Developmentally Appropriate Practice

The consideration of developmentally appropriate practice thus is being moved beyond what started as a concern for advocacy to intensified efforts to explicate more clearly the standards' underlying premises and practical implications. Following traditional curriculum theory, this explication has been focused through a philosophical and theoretical summary of the developmentally appropriate practice standards along three interrelated dimensions: (1) assumptions about the nature of young children as learners, (2) assumptions about the nature of learning processes in young children, and (3) assumptions about the appropriate aims for early education and the types of learning and development that are most worthy of educational concern (Elkind, 1991).

Images of the child as a learner. The central image of the child underlying the principles of developmentally appropriate practice for early childhood education is that of a "creative scientist." This guiding metaphor for the child as a learner derives from the field's overarching reliance on cognitive-developmental theory. Although other constructivist orientations are gaining influence (e.g., Vygotsky), the work of Piaget and associated cognitive-developmental psychologists has continued to predominate since the 1960s and still defines the generally accepted theoretical core for early childhood curriculum.

Viewed as a creative scientist, the child is assumed to be naturally curious. This natural curiosity presumably motivates the child to seek an ever-increasing understanding and mastery of his or her physical, social, and moral environments, including the school environment. More specifically, the child's natural curiosity is believed to provide the foundation for his or her intrinsic motivation to learn and to persist in learning as long as the learning is "relevant" and personally meaningful (Bredekamp, 1987).

In emphasizing the significance of meaningful experiences in fueling children's learning, the cognitive-developmental foundations of current early childhood curriculum standards highlight the role of children in constructing their own learning outcomes (Elkind, 1991). Children of different cognitive-developmental stages are respected for the qualitatively different thinking and problem-solving abilities that they bring to learning experiences.

For the early childhood educator, predictability of the general responses that children will have to various potential learning opportunities—and guidance in structuring learning opportunities that children are likely to find meaningful and motivating—stems from the universality of the cognitive-developmental stages. Children in the preoperational stage of development, the stage coinciding with the preschool and early primary years, process information, construct knowledge, and solve problems in ways that reflect their nonabstract, perception-bound mental abilities (Gullo, 1992). In light of this, children of this age range are expected to derive the greatest meaning from playful learning experiences that involve the active manipulation of concrete and real materials, as well as from projects that reflect their natural childhood interests while inviting the functional application of their emerging mental competencies (Bredekamp, 1987). In short, as the principles of developmentally appropriate practice declare, young children need abundant opportunities for self-initiated exploration, experimentation, and creation if they are to learn effectively.

Beliefs about the nature of the learning process. Current early childhood curriculum standards clearly are based on a general belief that learning is a creative, constructive process rather than an accumulation of information and skills (NASBE, 1988). Three relatively more specific, interrelated beliefs about the nature of the learning process in young children further shape the thrust of current curriculum recommendations. These include the assumptions that: (1) learning and development occur through young children's interactions with materials, adults, and other children; (2) learning and development occur in an integrated manner; and (3) although following broad universal sequences, young children's learning and development advance through highly individual patterns and paces (Bredekamp, 1987; Bredekamp & Rosegrant, 1992).

Reflecting their cognitive-developmental foundation, the principles of developmentally appropriate practice emphasize that learning occurs through young children's interactions with their physical and social worlds. As Elkind (1991) has noted, the learning process results in the creation of knowledge that reflects both the child's own mental activity or subjective world, and the material or people with which the child has dealt in the external world. When confronted with an experience that does not fit neatly within their current ways of thinking, children are presumed to adapt by constructing new knowledge or by generalizing their existing knowledge to fit the discrepant situation. It is recommended that the early childhood curriculum provide a "modicum" of discrepancy to provide the optimal opportunity for children to "stretch" and create knowledge (Gullo, 1992).

Instructionally, the interactionist orientation of current early childhood curriculum standards implies that teachers serve primarily as facilitators and mediators of children's learning rather than as direct transmitters of knowledge. In this regard, the standards likewise argue for the importance of facilitating learning and development in an *integrated* manner, given the integrated nature of children's learning and development across both the developmental domains and traditionally segregated content areas. As the NAEYC position statements declare, developmentally appropriate curriculum provides for all areas of a child's development—physical, emotional, social, and cognitive—through an integrated approach. Indeed, children learn best when their social and emotional needs are met (Bredekamp, 1987). Furthermore, "curriculum allows for focus on a particular topic or content while allowing for integration across traditional subject-matter divisions," and "children's learning is not compartmentalized into subject matter distinctions" (National Association for the Education of Young Children and National Association of Early Childhood Specialists in State Departments of Education, 1992, pp. 20–21). The purpose of integrating curriculum is to facilitate the natural way children learn and to help children make connections between different disciplines or subject-matter areas (Bredekamp & Rosegrant, 1992).

The third broad assumption about the learning process that has shaped the principles of developmentally appropriate practice is a profound respect for natural variations in the pace of young children's learning and development. Young children are presumed to learn and develop through the same *basic* stages. Yet, given similar educational experiences, young children nevertheless are expected to learn and develop at very different rates because of differences in their maturation rates, prior experiences, and other individual characteristics (Bredekamp, 1987; Gullo, 1992).

This belief in the uniqueness of children's learning and developmental rates is reflected in guidelines that call for a "responsive" curriculum that "allows" children to move at their own pace in acquiring important educational competencies (Bredekamp, 1987). Furthermore, early childhood educators are cautioned not to be too hasty in making judgments about young children's learning potential. The vast ability differences often found among very young children are presumed to even out somewhat by the time the children reach age 8 unless they are reinforced by labeling, ability grouping, and other stigmatizing instructional strategies (Gullo, 1992).

Instructional goals and content. In contrast to their strong focus on describing recommended processes for early childhood education, curriculum standards have been relatively silent on questions of appropriate goals and content (Bredekamp & Rosegrant, 1992). This skew in the standards actually is not surprising. As a foundation for prescribing practice, the child development theory that underlies the principles of developmentally appropriate practice translates much more readily into definitions of the "how" rather than the "what" of early education.

Despite this often criticized emphasis on process, however, the principles of developmentally appropriate practice do present at least an implicit outline of the types of learning that are considered to be of most worth for young children. At the very global level, following the "whole child" orientation, the stated aim for curriculum is to develop children's knowledge and skills in all developmental areas—physical, social, emotional, and intellectual. Within this sweeping statement, more specific emphasis is placed on the goals of promoting young children's general problem-solving and critical thinking abilities, along with the positive emotional and social dispositions required to support the development and use of these abilities (Bredekamp, 1987).

Still, in outlining desirable educational outcomes the principles of developmentally appropriate practice are particularly vague in describing recommended goals and content for the various subject-matter areas. As the following examples reveal, the goals that are suggested in this regard tend to focus on applied, process-oriented outcomes. The suggested goal for early childhood math, for instance, is "to enable children to use math through exploration, discovery, and solving meaningful problems" (Bredekamp, 1987, p. 71). The goals of the early childhood language and literacy program are for children "to expand their ability to communicate verbally and through reading and writing, and to enjoy these activities" (Bredekamp, 1987, p. 70). Finally, an example that summarizes well the general early childhood stance toward subject-matter guidelines, the recommended goal for science is basically to "do science"—that is, to learn through science projects "to apply thinking skills such as hypothesizing, observing, experimenting, and verifying" (Bredekamp, 1987, p. 72).

Specific guidelines for appropriate curriculum content and assessment in programs serving children ages 3 through 8 years were issued jointly by the National Association for the Education of Young Children and National Association of Early Childhood Specialists in State Departments of Education (1992). The express intent of these guidelines is to address the "early childhood error" of paying inadequate attention to the content of the curriculum. Yet, rather than articulate substantive recommendations regarding subject-matter content, the new position statement sets forth a framework for local decision making about appropriate early childhood curriculum content. Among the key proposals of this framework are recommendations that: (a) curriculum content for young children have "intellectual integrity" and meet the recognized standards of the relevant subject-matter disciplines; (b) the content of the curriculum be worth knowing and important for young children to learn to function capably in their world; and (c) in all subject-matter disciplines, the curriculum address the interrelated development of knowledge and understanding, processes and skills, dispositions, and attitudes (NAEYC & NAECS/SDE, 1992).

Accumulated experience and research indicate that children's transitions through the early childhood period and into more advanced developmental and educational periods are facilitated by the successful negotiation of several key developmental tasks. These include the acquisition of fundamental competencies in literacy and mathematical thinking, the development of positive relationships with school peers and adult teachers, a positive image of oneself as a student, a sense of self-efficacy, and a correspondingly self-regulated, persistent approach to problem solving (Entwisle & Alexander, 1989). Indeed, by the end of third grade, children's progress in negotiating these tasks forecasts quite accurately the achievement trajectories that the children will follow the rest of their school years (Alexander & Entwisle, 1988; Katz & Chard, 1989; Parker & Asher, 1987).

A comprehensive array of developmental and learning expectations with documented significance for young children's present and long-term functioning recently has been elaborated by Meisels and his associates in the form of a developmental assessment system for preschool through third-grade children (Jablon, Marsden, & Meisels, 1993). Figure 6.1 summarizes the categories of knowledge, behaviors, skills, and attitudes that are included in this state-of-the-art delineation of desired developmental and learning outcomes. Commonalities with current professional standards are evident in the emphasis on the acquisition of general problem-solving capabilities and functional competencies within the various categories of learning and development. An added contribution of this work to the field is that each goal is explicated across a 6-year developmental continuum. These continua highlight the likely pathway of a child's progress within each category of learning and development, and describe the qualitatively

Figure 6.1 Early Childhood Curriculum Goals by Developmental Domain

Personal and Social Development	
Self-concept	Positive sense of self Initiative and self-direction
Self-control	Observes rules and routines Handles materials purposefully Manages transitions
Learning approach	Eager and curious Chooses activities appropriately Flexible and inventive Sustains interest
Social interactions	Comfortable peer relations Comfortable adult relations Empathetic and caring
Group participation	Participates in classroom community Plays fairly
Conflict resolution	Seeks help when needed Uses discussion/compromise
Language and Literacy	
Listening	Listens with understanding Follows directions
Speaking	Speaks to convey meaning Uses language for diverse purposes
Literature & reading	Listens with interest to oral text Shows interest in reading Retells/interprets information from stories Makes predictions about text Constructs meaning from print Reads for diverse purposes
Writing	Uses age-appropriate writing Writes for diverse purposes Composes stories Reads and edits own writing
Spelling	Uses age-appropriate spelling, with increasing approximations of standard spelling
Mathematical Thinking	
Thinking approach	Solves problems strategically Communicates mathematical thinking
Patterns/relationships	Recognizes and produces patterns Uses patterns for predicting Sorts, classifies, and orders
Number concepts & operations	Recognizes numerals Understands quantity Uses counting strategies Uses addition/subtraction strategies Uses simple multiplication/division strategies

(continued)

Figure 6.1 *(continued)*

Mathematical Thinking *(continued)*	
Geometry & spatial relations	Identifies and classifies shapes Understands position words Explores 2- and 3-dimensional constructions Solve spatial problems
Measurement	Uses comparative words Measures using nonstandard & standard measures Uses common measuring instruments Understands and tells time Understands monetary coins & bills
Probability/statistics	Collects and records data Uses graphs and charts to predict
Scientific Thinking	
Observing	Uses senses to observe Classifies/compares living & nonliving things
Questioning & predicting	Expresses wonder about the world Engages in purposeful, active investigation
Explaining	Draws conclusions from investigations Applies scientific concepts to new situations Communicates scientific "findings" through diverse methods
Social Studies	
Self, family, & community	Recognizes human differences Understands concept of family Understands concept of community
People & the environment	Understands interrelationships between people & their environment Makes and reads simple maps
The Arts	
Expression / representation	Uses the arts to express self Enjoys creating through the arts
Artistic appreciation	Shows interest in art works Interprets artistic products
Physical Development	
Gross motor development	Moves with control and balance Performs gross motor tasks
Fine motor development	Shows strength, control, and eye-hand coordination in fine motor tasks Uses fine motor skills for functional purposes (e.g., writing)

Source: Summarized from Jablon et al. (1993).

different forms that accomplishments within each category can take at different developmental stages.

EARLY CHILDHOOD CURRICULUM FOR EMERGING CIRCUMSTANCES

Where do current curriculum standards leave the early childhood field with regard to "what should be," the central philosophical question that underlies all instructional decisions? This question implores early educators to define, and to reflectively redefine, what is most important for young children to gain through their experiences in educational settings. Responses must take into account the general patterns of young children's learning and development, as well as the specific circumstances of individual children's current and future lives.

As previously noted in this chapter, the demographic characteristics and circumstances of American children and families have been undergoing a virtual revolution since the 1970s. The implications are significant. For example, a recent national survey found that 42% of kindergarten teachers said that children were less "ready for school" than 5 years ago; 51% of kindergarten children were perceived to have serious language proficiency problems, while 43% were perceived to have serious emotional concerns (Boyer, 1991). Because of societal changes, significant numbers of children appear to be coming into preschool and primary education without the basic foundations traditionally deemed necessary for school success. In addition, because the social, cultural, linguistic, and economic distance between children and their teachers is increasing, teachers also may be increasingly prone to *judge* their students as intellectually and emotionally disadvantaged (Alexander & Entwisle, 1988). Both explanations hold far-reaching implications for curriculum development in early childhood education.

On the bottom line, the adverse impact of current social circumstances on children's learning and development has been channeled through a pervasive attenuation of the consistent, caring relationships that are available to both the children and their parents (Hamburg, 1992). It is in the context of considering the role of caring relationships in fostering early learning and development, then, that contemporary approaches to early childhood curriculum must be reviewed (Garbarino, 1989).

What would this mean for curriculum content? Most broadly, it would require both the setting of new priorities and the reinterpretation of traditional early education goals and activities. Young children's basic social-emotional well-being, or mental health, would be emphasized as a necessary starting point around which educational experiences in the preschool, kindergarten, and primary grades would be designed (Erickson & Pianta, 1989; Garbarino, Dubrow, Kostelny, & Pardo, 1992). Establishing a sense of trust in the consistency and benevolence of adult relationships, once taken for granted, would be a key educational objective, as would provisions for ensuring that all children have access to such relationships within their formal educational environments. Similarly, promoting children's sense of control in shaping their own experiences and in solving personally meaningful problems would be a central educational aim, often requiring strategies for overcoming widespread learned helplessness among children (Dweck & Elliot, 1983). Finally, assisting children in developing both the expectations and the skills to form positive peer relationships would be given heightened emphasis as a legitimate and central "content area" within the early education curriculum (Burton, 1987). Again, cognitive-behavioral intervention strategies, such as social problem-solving interventions and attribution retraining, would be needed in many cases to help children redefine the "working models" of peer relationships with which they enter school and other early childhood programs (e.g., Dodge, Murphy, & Buchsbaum, 1984; Erickson & Pianta, 1989).

These social-emotional outcomes must be attained if children's experiences and interactions in early childhood classrooms are to be cognitively and academically productive. However, other revisions and reprioritizations in mainstream early education goals and content also would be suggested by research that has accumulated around such conceptual frameworks as the organizational developmental perspective (Cicchetti, Toth, & Hennessy, 1989) and the constructs of resiliency and protective factors (National Commission on Children, 1991; Werner, 1990). Active, self-directed learning among young children in such cognitive content areas as mathematics requires a fundamental ability to perceive order within the classroom structure, as well as the ability to explore and problem solve in developmentally appropriate yet systematic ways. Progress in literacy development, including reading and writing, is likewise contingent upon a foundation of oral language competence (Genishi, 1992). As noted, data indicate that increasing numbers of children, especially those exposed to chaotic and stress-laden family circumstances, are not receiving early opportunities to acquire these basic competencies (Boyer, 1991; Cicchetti, Toth, & Hennessy, 1989). A new premium must therefore be placed on infusing the early childhood curriculum with: (1) focused efforts to promote children's general opportunities and abilities to play and explore in *planful, systematic ways;* and (2) focused and diverse efforts to promote children's expressive and receptive oral communication abilities (Genishi, 1992). With regard to the former point, Zimiles (1991) has summed it up by saying that children need "to have ample opportunity to be heard, to learn to expect to be heard, and to have extensive exposure to communicative adults. In such cases, conversing and exchanging become prime elements of the curriculum" (p. 32).

SUMMARY AND CONCLUSION

The principles of developmentally appropriate practice, the extant summary of early childhood curriculum standards, have been translated into broad prescriptions for early childhood curriculum. What is prescribed are classrooms that resemble busy labs for learning. Children are actively exploring and experimenting in learning centers stocked with manipulative materials or are working on interesting, applied projects. Groupings of children are flexible—children work less often as a whole group and more often in peer groups where children collaborate and depend on each other as learning resources. Teachers' central roles are likewise to serve as resources and facilitators of children's learning, structuring the learning environment and sensitively monitoring and stimulating each child's individual progress.

Beyond the classroom level, traditional age and grade-level distinctions increasingly are dropped in favor of ungraded program organizations that respect the natural variations in young children's learning rates. Schools and other educational programs themselves often are organized into early childhood units to emphasize and protect the unique, "specialty" status of curriculum and instruction for children age 8 years and younger (NASBE, 1988).

The field's reliance on general child development theory to conjure such appealing images of quality early childhood curriculum must now be traded for more complex theories of practice that assist educators in linking their curricula to the increasingly diverse and complex characteristics of young children (Bowman, 1993; Wolery, Strain, & Bailey, 1992). These models must draw upon both developmental theory and the knowledge bases of the subject-matter disciplines. Beyond this, though, the mainstream early childhood specialization must be redefined to include approaches traditionally associated with intervention-related disciplines, including early childhood special education and developmental psychopathology (Burton, Hains, Hanline, McLean, & McCormick, 1992). Given the field's philosophical intent to respond to the dramatic variance in young children's individual needs and characteristics, the guiding question for this redefinition must be, "What early education experiences should be provided for whom to best facilitate their present and long-term well-being?" (Powell, 1987).

REFERENCES

Alexander, K., & Entwisle, D. (1988). Achievement in the first two years of school: Patterns and processes. *Monographs of the Society for Research in Child Development, 53*(2).

Bowman, B. (1993). Early childhood education. In L. Darling-Hammond (Ed.), *Review of research in education* (pp. 101–134). Washington, DC: American Educational Research Association.

Boyer, E. L. (1991). *Ready to learn: A mandate for the nation.* Princeton, NJ: Carnegie Foundation for the Advancement of Teaching.

Bredekamp, S. (Ed.). (1987). *Developmentally appropriate practice in early childhood programs serving children from birth through age 8.* Washington, DC: NAEYC.

Bredekamp, S., & Rosegrant, T. (Eds.). (1992). *Reaching potentials: Appropriate curriculum and assessment for young children.* Washington, DC: NAEYC.

Burton, C. (1987). Problems in children's peer relations: A broadening perspective. In L. G. Katz (Ed.), *Current topics in early childhood education* (Vol. 7, pp. 59–84). Norwood, NJ: Ablex.

Burton, C. B., Hains, A. H., Hanline, M. F., McLean, M., & McCormick, K. (1992). Early childhood education and intervention: The urgency of professional unification. *Topics in Early Childhood Special Education, 11*(4), 53–69.

Caldwell, B. M. (1991). Continuity in the early years: Transitions between grades and systems. In S. L. Kagan (Ed.), *The care and education of America's young children: Obstacles and opportunities* (pp. 69–90). Chicago: University of Chicago Press.

Cicchetti, D., Toth, S., & Hennessy, K. (1989). Research on the consequences of child maltreatment and its application to educational settings. *Topics in Early Childhood Special Education, 9*(2), 33–55.

Dodge, K. A., Murphy, R. R., & Buchsbaum, K. (1984). The assessment of intention–cue detection skills in children: Implications for developmental psychopathology. *Child Development, 55,* 163–173.

Dweck, C., & Elliot, E. (1983). Achievement motivation. In P. H. Mussen (Ed.), *Handbook of child psychology* (4th ed., pp. 643–691). New York: Wiley.

Elkind, D. (1991). Developmentally appropriate practice: A case of educational inertia. In S. L. Kagan (Ed.), *The care and education of America's young children: Obstacles and opportunities* (pp. 1–16). Chicago: University of Chicago Press.

Entwisle, D., & Alexander, K. (1989). Children's transition into full-time schooling: Black/White comparisons. *Early Education and Development, 1*(2), 86–104.

Erickson, M. F., & Pianta, R. C. (1989). New lunchbox, old feelings: What kids bring to school. *Early Education and Development, 1*(1), 35–49.

Evans, E. D. (1975). *Contemporary influences in early childhood education.* New York: Holt, Rinehart & Winston.

Freeman, E. (1990). Issues in kindergarten policy and practice. *Young Children, 45*(4), 29–34.

Garbarino, J. (1989). Early investment in cognitive development as a strategy for reducing poverty. *Early Education and Development, 1*(1), 64–76.

Garbarino, J., Dubrow, N., Kostelny, K., & Pardo, C. (1992). *Children in danger.* San Francisco: Jossey-Bass.

Genishi, C. (1992). Developing the foundation: Oral language and communicative competence. In C. Seefeldt (Ed.), *The early childhood curriculum: A review of current research* (pp. 85–117). New York: Teachers College Press.

Gullo, D. F. (1992). *Developmentally appropriate teaching in early childhood.* Washington, DC: National Education Association.

Hamburg, D. (1992). *Today's children: Creating a future for a generation in crisis.* New York: Random House.

Jablon, J., Marsden, D., & Meisels, S. (1993). *The work sampling system: Omnibus guidelines for the developmental checklists.* Ann Arbor, MI: Rebus Planning Associates.

Kagan, S. L. (Ed.). (1991). *The care and education of America's young children: Obstacles and opportunities.* Chicago: University of Chicago Press.

Katz, L. G. (1991). Pedagogical issues in early childhood education. In S. L. Kagan (Ed.), *The care and education of America's young children: Obstacles and opportunities* (pp. 50–68). Chicago: University of Chicago Press.

Katz, L. G., & Chard, S. C. (1989). *Engaging children's minds: The project approach.* Norwood, NJ: Ablex.

McCarthy, J. (1983). Curriculum in early childhood education: The state of the art. *Contemporary Education, 54*(4), 275–278.

National Association for the Education of Young Children and National Association of Early Childhood Specialists in State Departments of Education. (1992). Guidelines for appropriate curriculum content and assessment in programs serving children ages 3 through 8. In S. Bredekamp & T. Rosegrant (Eds.), *Reaching potentials: Appropriate curriculum and assessment for young children* (pp. 9–27). Washington, DC: NAEYC.

National Association of Elementary School Principals. (1990). *Early childhood education and the elementary school principal: Standards for quality programs for young children.* Alexandria, VA: Author.

National Association of State Boards of Education. (1988). *Right from the start.* Alexandria, VA: Author.

National Black Child Development Institute. (1987). *Safeguards: Guidelines for establishing programs for four-year-olds.* Washington, DC: Author.

National Commission on Children. (1991). *Beyond rhetoric: A new American agenda for children and families.* Washington, DC: Author.

Parker, J., & Asher, S. (1987). Peer acceptance and later personal adjustment: Are low accepted children "at risk"? *Psychological Bulletin, 102,* 357–389.

Powell, D. R. (1987). Comparing preschool curricula and practices: The state of research. In S. L. Kagan & E. F. Zigler (Eds.), *Early schooling: The national debate* (pp. 190–211). New Haven, CT: Yale University Press.

Shonkoff, J. P., & Meisels, S. J. (1990). Early childhood intervention: The evolution of a concept. In S. J. Meisels & J. P. Shonkoff (Eds.), *Handbook of early childhood intervention* (pp. 3–31). New York: Cambridge University Press.

Werner, E. (1990). Protective factors and individual resilience. In S. J. Meisels & J. P. Shonkoff (Eds.), *Handbook of early childhood intervention* (pp. 97–116). New York: Cambridge University Press.

Wolery, M., Strain, P., & Bailey, D. (1992). Reaching potentials of young children with special needs. In S. Bredekamp & T. Rosegrant (Eds.), *Reaching potentials: Appropriate curriculum and assessment for young children* (pp. 92–111). Washington, DC: NAEYC.

Zigler, E. F. (1990). Foreword. In S. J. Meisels & J. P. Shonkoff (Eds.), *Handbook of early childhood intervention* (pp. ix–xiv). New York: Cambridge University Press.

Zimiles, H. (1991). Diversity and change in young children: Some educational implications. In B. Spodek & O. N. Saracho (Eds.), *Issues in early childhood curriculum* (pp. 21–45). New York: Teachers College Press.

Response

Curriculum in Early Childhood Education: Moving Toward an Inclusive Specialization

Lawrence J. Johnson and Victoria W. Carr

As we read Maxwell's chapter we were struck by the amount of agreement between what is considered best practice in early childhood (EC) and early childhood special education (ECSE). In part, this agreement is reflective of the congruence between the two fields in that EC and ECSE professionals are engaged in the same basic functions when designing and implementing educational experiences for young children (Kilgo, LaMontagne, Johnson, Cooper, Cook, & Stayton, 1994). In fact, many have questioned why EC and ECSE are treated as separate entities (e.g., Burton, Hains, Hanline, McLean, & McCormick, 1992; Kemple, Hartle, Correa, & Fox, 1994; Miller, 1992). As Thorpe (1992) has asserted, "best practices in early childhood and early childhood special education are not different" (p. 14). In recognition of this view, there are increasing efforts to build bridges between these perspectives to develop a unified vision for early childhood education (Bredekamp, 1992a; Johnson, 1992). For example, the Division of Early Childhood of the International Council for Exceptional Children (DEC) and the National Association for the Education of Young Children (NAEYC) have established a liaison committee to explore common issues. States are increasingly moving in a direction that blurs the line between EC and ECSE. Currently, 15 states (Connecticut, Delaware, Florida, Georgia, Indiana, Kansas, Kentucky, Maine, Massachusetts, New Mexico, North Carolina, Oklahoma, Pennsylvania, South Carolina, & Wyoming) have generic teaching certification standards for early childhood that allow early childhood teachers to teach all children, including those with an identified disability (Heekin & Tollerton, 1994).

Although EC and ECSE increasingly are moving toward a unified vision, there are fundamental differences related to (a) child-centered, versus

 ISBN 0-8077-3562-0 (pbk), ISBN 0-8077-3563-9 (cloth).

family-centered, services, and (b) the impact of variations in development on the child's disposition. As might be expected, these are the issues that we wish to focus on and discuss in relation to their impact on curriculum. In addition to these fundamental differences, there is an important contextual difference related to the historical focus of reform efforts within EC and ECSE that we believe is critical to a more complete understanding of differences between EC AND ECSE interpretations of curriculum.

REFORM EFFORTS

A contextual dimension that differentiates EC and ECSE is the manner in which reform has been interpreted by these groups. From the broadest educational perspective, the push for educational reform has been driven by a growing recognition that an increasingly diverse population of students and their families are entering the educational system who are not being adequately served by it. It has become obvious that fundamental and systemic changes must take place before the educational system is ready to embrace this diversity so that all children and families have the opportunity to be successful and supported (McKenzie, 1993). This concept of diversity includes children and families who traditionally have challenged the educational system, particularly those who are "at risk" or those who have an identified disability. From this perspective, curriculum must be sensitive to and supportive of diversity, and must possess adaptation and accommodation as its central features.

This view of reform parallels the inception of ECSE as a field. DeWeerd (1981) discussed how in the 1950s services for young children with disabilities typically were limited to children with sensory or physical disabilities. The remainder of children with disabilities were "hidden populations" kept at home and out of sight. Parents with children experiencing mild delays often were told to be patient and "wait and see" if the problem persisted long enough to warrant treatment. In addition, children and families who did not fit into regular program routines often were dismissed or excluded from programs because expectations for these programs did not include serving challenging populations (Peterson, 1987). In the 1960s, this orientation shifted to one that focused on the importance of early experiences for the long-term development of young children, particularly those who were at risk or had a disability. Attention was directed at developing services that were responsive to the needs of children and their families who previously had not been adequately served in traditional early childhood programs. Out of this orientation emerged Head Start and eventually ECSE.

A foundational component of Head Start and ECSE has been the provision of services to accommodate the needs of diverse learners, which has had an important influence on the development and implementation of curriculum. As we will discuss in greater detail later, the primary theme within this curriculum has been functionality. From this perspective, curriculum becomes the tool to help the teacher facilitate those skills that enable the child to be more successful in his or her current or subsequent environment (Bailey & Wolery, 1984; Cook, Tessier, & Klein, 1992). In addition, in recognition of the environmental influences impinging on children and their families served by these programs, effort also has been directed at involving parents in the curriculum. This involvement has evolved from a view of parents as teachers to that of decision makers and partners (Turnbull & Turnbull, 1990).

Within EC, reform has taken a different path. In reaction to an increasing trend toward emphasis on the development of academic skills in early childhood programs, curricular reform efforts have focused on placing the child at the center of the curriculum under the rubric of developmentally appropriate practice (DAP) (Bredekamp, 1992b). Children are seen as the critical agents in the learning process by constructing knowledge, developing skills, gaining insights, shaping understanding, and developing values through exploration and experimentation with their environment. The teacher is seen as a facilitator who creates an environment that maximizes child experiences and gently guides by questioning and making suggestions as children interact with the environment. Within the EC framework, the curriculum is child centered and built upon a child's thinking and psychological processes.

The emphasis on DAP was a critical milestone for education, providing a powerful tool to combat political and social forces calling for a more academic orientation to preschool, kindergarten, and the primary grades. The NAEYC position statement on DAP provided a sound theoretical foundation that clearly established that an emphasis on academics was antithetical to the needs of young children. As Kagen (1994) proclaimed, the stance that NAEYC took on DAP will be described in the future as one of the most important historical events in education. We agree with this assessment and believe that had NAEYC not taken such a strong stance on DAP, the emphasis on academics in EC would not have been adequately challenged. However, this emphasis focused attention on the child rather than the family, which is in contrast with the predominant view of ECSE. In addition, because of the effort directed toward combating an emphasis on academics, concerns related to increasing diversity have not received the same attention as in the broader educational community.

CHILD CENTERED VERSUS FAMILY CENTERED

Early in the chapter, Maxwell acknowledges the recent dynamic nature of early childhood by highlighting the "advent of Head Start in the 1960s" and "the burgeoning in the 1980s of early childhood programs across an increasingly diverse array of settings." Noticeably absent from her discussion is the passage of PL 99–457 in 1986 (later incorporated into PL 101–476, the Individuals with Disabilities Act), which has been described by many as the most important legislation ever enacted for young children with disabilities (e.g., Gallagher, Trohanis, & Clifford, 1989; Safer & Hamilton, 1993; Smith, 1988). As efforts to bridge EC and ECSE into a unified vision mature, we believe that the impact of this law will be characterized as revolutionary for *all* young children and their families.

PL 99–457 contained two components: (1) a mandatory component that extended the provision of services to all eligible children 3 years of age or older by 1991; and (2) a component that provided incentives for states to serve infants and toddlers with disabilities. Two reasons this legislation has been characterized as revolutionary are the velocity of its implementation nationally and the expansiveness of its impact on young children and their families. For example, when PL 99–457 was passed, only 25 states were providing services for children with disabilities below 6 years of age; in 1992 all states were providing services. Moreover, in 1986 the states reported serving 20,000 infants, and in 1991 they reported serving 250,000, representing a 1,250% increase in the number of infants being served (Smith & McKenna, 1994).

Among the many requirements of PL 99–457 is the concept of an Individualized Family Service Plan to provide a guide for services to the child within the context of the family. This was a pivotal shift that made services family, as opposed to child, centered. From this perspective, the family is the primary context from which intervention and curriculum are developed (Sandall, 1993). As a result, family members are fundamental partners in the development, implementation, and prioritization of services. Moreover, because every family is unique with respect to its structure, values, beliefs, and coping styles, the curriculum must embrace diversity and be responsive to family needs (McGonigel, 1991). This requires a flexible approach that has respect for family autonomy and empowerment as its central core.

As Place (1994) has asserted, what made PL 99–457 so unique and important was its recognition of the critical role of the family in the education of young children. Bredekamp (1992a) notes that while professionals in EC and ECSE agree in principle regarding the importance of families, ECSE has been more focused on being family centered and provides the template for the broader EC community. Clearly, a major difference between EC and ECSE is the degree to which services are family focused. Although being family focused is considered best practice in ECSE regardless of the child's age, it would be a mistake to assume that the emphasis on families within ECSE is equal across programs serving different age groups. In general, programs serving infants and toddlers are much more family focused than their preschool and primary-grade counterparts. In fact, as the age of the child increases, the differences between EC and ECSE programs lessen with regard to being family focused. It is also important to note that while there are differences between the degree to which EC and ECSE programs are family focused, EC programs in general are far more family focused than programs in the broader educational community.

THE IMPACT OF VARIATIONS IN DEVELOPMENT

An underlying theoretical perspective in EC is that all children have a disposition to explore. This belief stems from the constructivist developmental theories of Piaget and Vygotsky. According to these theories, children's voluntary or intentional actions in response to their environment result in developmental growth. The insights and discoveries that children gain from exploration of their environment promote the evolution of new cognitive schemata and new developmental behaviors. The role of the teacher is to design an environment conducive to exploration and then facilitate such exploration. While we agree with this perspective, we do not believe that the impact of variations in children's disposition to explore has been given careful consideration.

The assumption that children actively engage in interactions with their environment is not equally true of all children. Clearly, children have varying degrees of exploratory behaviors. If these differences are not recognized, experiences are unlikely to be matched to children's needs. It is widely accepted that a quality early childhood education is one that is matched to each child's level and degree of learning and development (Elkind, 1991). Bredekamp (1993) emphasized that early childhood education must develop goals that are individually appropriate for children. She also suggested that the assumption of normative age appropriateness has always been flawed, especially now that early childhood programs are serving economically, culturally, linguistically, and developmentally diverse populations. This diversity, coupled with individual temperamental differences, certainly influences a child's disposition to engage in classroom activities and may impede a child's ability to actively explore his or her environment and gain meaning from that exploration.

If exploration is the foundation for the curricular system in early childhood education, we must address differences in children's abilities to explore or we will create uneven playing fields. The additive effects of ignoring variations in children can lead to increased risks of delay and can limit opportunities for children to develop their gifts and abilities, creating further gaps between children. Children who are already developmentally delayed or "at risk" will have marked differences from other children in relation to social interactions, cognitive development, motor skills, and/or symbolic play. Undoubtedly, these children will fall further behind if we do not address and accommodate their variations in development (Wolery, Strain, & Bailey, 1992).

Adults can provide children with curricular experiences that promote or hinder their development and learning (DEC, 1993). For example, Johnson, Christie, and Yawkey (1987) described four ways adults can participate in play. For intervention purposes, adults can engage in parallel play, become co-players, act as play tutors, or speak to the reality of the play. Adult parallel play is noninteractive. Acting as a co-player, an adult can assume a role in a child-led play routine, which can increase the level and persistence of play. A play tutor structures the situation and provides prompts and reinforcements for appropriate interactions. This type of intervention can facilitate gains in cognitive development and scaffold higher levels of development in all areas. An adult also might act as a spokesperson for reality with children who have highly developed play skills when the children's play becomes repetitious or antisocial (Johnson, Christie, & Yawkey, 1987).

Furthermore, we cannot assume that designing an environment that is conducive to exploration and social interactions will be sufficient to meet the needs of all children in the classroom. Bredekamp (1993), Wetherby (1992), and others concur with Johnson, Christie, and Yawkey (1987) that child-initiated, adult-supported play is the optimal vehicle for developmental growth. The curricular approach is to follow the child's lead, building on the child's scripts and routines to scaffold language and extend play. However, an individually appropriate education often requires specific questioning, coaching, intervention, or adaptation strategies initiated by the teacher or co-player. This is done to facilitate joint attention or engagement with other individuals or materials within the environment until the individual is capable of accessing the environment independently. The environment then becomes individually appropriate.

Individual appropriateness as described in *Reaching Potentials: Appropriate Curriculum and Assessment for Young Children* (Bredekamp & Rosegrant, 1992) addresses the uniqueness of each individual with regard to patterns, developmental growth, personality, learning style, and family background. The curriculum as well as the child's experiences and interactions with materials, ideas, and people should be dynamic and correspond to the child's abilities and needs while challenging the child's thinking skills. This premise of individual appropriateness leads to a concern surrounding the potential conflicts around what is functional for the child and what is developmentally appropriate. As we have previously defined, the concept of what is functional for a child focuses on strategies or activities that will help a child become more successful in his or her current environment and ease the transition into subsequent environments (Bailey & Wolery, 1984). Unfortunately, the notion of functionality sometimes leads to a deficit orientation in which professionals focus on remediating deficits in an attempt to help the child to be more successful. We would argue that this is a narrow interpretation of functionality. Professionals instead must ask how the child's abilities can be nurtured within the curricular and ecological framework that constitutes the child's environment. We must seek ways to help a child succeed, not remediate deficits.

Individual appropriateness is defined by an individual education plan (IEP) or individual family service plan (IFSP) for children with disabilities. The IEP and IFSP have specific goals and objectives that must be met. These documents must include a child's present levels of functioning, annual goals, short term instructional objectives, appropriate educational and related services, justification for placement, and the persons responsible for implementing the plan. An IFSP also would include family goals such as concerns, priorities, and resources (Turnbull & Turnbull, 1990). Teaching strategies used to reach individually appropriate goals as identified by the IEP/IFSP should be rooted primarily in the social interactions between children and adults as well as between children and their peers (Cook, Tessier, & Klein, 1992).

Since early childhood curricular decisions should reflect a child's diverse learning abilities and interests, while enhancing opportunities for developmental growth, ongoing assessment of a child's abilities can provide practitioners with relevant information for designing classroom experiences (Carr, 1995). Adaptations for children with disabilities and meeting IEP goals require collaboration among teachers, family members, and other service providers (Gallagher, LaMontagne, & Johnson, 1994; Johnson & Pugach, 1996; Pugach & Johnson, 1995). Yet, as Wolery, Strain, and Bailey (1992) proclaim, young children with special needs are a diverse group with vastly different needs from one another. Teachers who work with children with special needs and their families must be able to implement general curricula for all children and also be competent in adapting to the diverse needs of all children. This requires that teachers have the skills and willingness to collaborate. Such an approach is best implemented within the framework of an emergent and transformational curriculum.

A current trend in EC with great potential for accommodating the needs of children and families that have challenged the system is a move toward an emergent curriculum (Jones & Nimmo, 1994). Based on the Italian Reggio Emilia approach, the emergent curriculum is family centered, community centered, project-based, and dynamic. Rather than conceptualizing the curriculum as a linear progression of ideas, it is seen as a dynamic process based on continuous revision (Edwards, Gandini, & Forman, 1993). Different from the thematic approach, concrete projects often evolve on their own as a result of careful observation of children's interests and questions. Other sources of emergent curriculum include teachers' interests, developmental tasks to be mastered, curriculum resource materials, and routine or unexpected events in the community or natural world (Jones & Nimmo, 1994). The flexibility of this curricular approach lends itself to collaboration among staff, parents, and children. Practitioners need to continually observe and assess a child's progress, collaborating to change instructional strategies or adapt the curriculum as necessary. This orientation requires that the IEP or IFSP be viewed more as a tentative plan rather than a prescriptive guide.

A meaning-centered and integrated transformational approach to curriculum also places a child in the center of the sociocultural context. This approach, like the emergent curricular approach, assumes that the learner affects and changes the curriculum. This assumption supports the individual within the framework of developmentally appropriate practices since a child's needs are considered from an ecological perspective (Bronfenbrenner, 1979) and collaborative planning between the child and teacher is valued. The transformational classroom is seen as a dynamic community in which the teacher provides many opportunities for adult and peer interactions (Rosegrant & Bredekamp, 1992). These interactions provide wonderful opportunities for implementing IEP or IFSP goals and objectives.

CONCLUDING THOUGHTS

Both EC and ECSE are in the process of moving toward a unified vision for the provision of services to young children and their families (Bredekamp, 1992a; Johnson, 1992; Thorpe, 1992). The degree to which these fields become unified still remains to be seen. Collaboration is difficult and there are fundamental differences between EC and ECSE that must be rectified before we can achieve a unified vision of services for young children and their families. Although there is much yet to be done, stakeholders must acknowledge how far we have come. As we have previously stated, after reading Maxwell's chapter we were struck by the amount of information with which we agreed. Clearly EC provides the curricular foundation for meeting the needs of young children and their families. However, if we are to move toward a unified vision of early childhood education that is inclusive of children and families who challenge that system, changes in current practices are needed. We must shift from being primarily child centered to being family centered and place greater emphasis on understanding how to differentiate curriculum to accommodate the needs of children with variations in development.

REFERENCES

Bailey, D. B., & Wolery, M. (1984). *Teaching infants and preschoolers with handicaps.* Columbus, OH: Merrill.

Bredekamp, S. (1992a). A unified commitment to best practice: Counter point. In L. J. Johnson (Ed.), *Policy issues: Creating a unified vision. Proceedings of the Summer Institute for the Ohio Early Childhood Special Education: Higher Education Consortium* (pp. 21–28). Cincinnati, OH: University of Cincinnati.

Bredekamp, S. (Ed.). (1992b). *Developmentally appropriate practice in early childhood programs serving children birth through age 8.* Washington, DC: NAEYC.

Bredekamp, S. (1993). The relationship between early childhood education and early childhood special education: Healthy marriage or family feud? *Topics in Early Childhood Special Education, 13*(3), 258–273.

Bredekamp, S., & Rosegrant, T. (Eds). (1992). *Reaching potentials: Appropriate curriculum and assessment for young children.* Washington, DC: NAEYC.

Bronfenbrenner, U. (1979). *The ecology of human development.* Cambridge, MA: Harvard University Press.

Burton, C. B., Hains, A. H., Hanline, M. F., McLean, M., & McCormick, K. (1992). Early childhood education and intervention: The urgency of professional unification. *Topics in Early Childhood Special Education, 11*(4), 53–69.

Carr, V. (1995). *Assessing play to transform the emergent curriculum: Meeting the diverse needs of children in inclusive settings.* Unpublished manuscript, University of Cincinnati.

Cook, R. E., Tessier, A., & Klein, M. D. (1992). *Adapting early childhood curricula for children with special needs* (3rd ed.). New York: Macmillan.

DeWeerd, J. (1981). Early education services for children with handicaps—Where have we been, where are we now, and where are we going? *Journal of the Division for Early Childhood, 4*(2), 15–24.

Division for Early Childhood. (1993). *DEC recommended practices: Indicators for quality in programs for infants and young children with special needs and their families* (Stock No. D417). Reston, VA: Council for Exceptional Children.

Edwards, C., Gandini, L., & Forman, G. (1993). *The hundred languages of children: The Reggio Emilia approach to early childhood education.* Norwood, NJ: Ablex.

Elkind, D. (1991). *Perspectives on early childhood education: Growing with young children toward the 21st century* (Stock No. 0351-9-00). Washington, DC: National Education Association.

Gallagher, J. J., Trohanis, P. L., & Clifford, R. M. (1989). *Policy implementation and PL 99–457: Planning for young children with special needs.* Baltimore: Brookes.

Gallagher, R. J., LaMontagne, M. J., & Johnson, L. J. (1994). Early intervention: The collaborative challenge. In L. J. Johnson, R. J. Gallagher, M. J. LaMontagne, J. B. Jordan, J. J. Gallagher, P. L. Hutinger, & M. B. Karnes (Eds.), *Meeting early intervention challenges: Issues from birth to three* (2nd ed., pp. 279–288). Baltimore: Brookes.

Heekin, S., & Tollerton, D. (1994). *Section 619 profile* (5th ed). Chapel Hill, NC: National Early Childhood Technical Assistance System.

Johnson, J. E., Christie, J. F., & Yawkey, T. D. (1987). *Play and early childhood development.* Glenview, IL: Scott, Foresman.

Johnson, L. J. (1992). Policy issues: Creating a unified vision. In L. J. Johnson (Ed.), *Policy Issues: Creating a Unified Vision. Proceedings of the Summer Institute for The Ohio Early Childhood Special Education: Higher Education Consortium* (pp. i–ii). Cincinnati, OH: University of Cincinnati.

Johnson, L. J., & Pugach, M. C. (1996). The emerging third wave of collaboration: Expanding beyond individual problem solving to create an educational system that embraces diversity. In W. Stainback & S. Stainback (Eds.), *Controversial issues confronting special education: Divergent perspectives* (2nd ed., pp. 197–204). Boston: Allyn & Bacon.

Jones, E., & Nimmo, J. (1994). *Emergent curriculum.* Washington, DC: NAEYC.

Kagen, L. (1994). *Collaboration in early childhood.* Presentation at the 1994 Summer Institute for the Ohio Early Childhood Special Education: Higher Education Consortium, Maumee Bay, OH.

Kemple, K., Hartle, L., Correa, V., & Fox, L. (1994). Preparing teachers for inclusive education: The development of a unified teacher education program in early childhood and early childhood special education. *Teacher Education and Special Education, 17*(1), 38–51.

Kilgo, J., LaMontagne, M., Johnson, L., Cooper, C., Cook, M., & Stayton, V. (1994). A national study of recommended practices from early childhood and early childhood special education: Important implications for personnel preparation programs of the future. Unpublished manuscript.

McGonigel, M. (1991). Philosophy and conceptual framework. In M. McGonigel, R. Kaufmann, & B. Johnson (Eds.), *Guidelines and recommended practices for the individualized family service plan* (2nd ed.; pp. 7–14). Bethesda, MD: Association for the Care of Children's Health.

McKenzie, F. (1993). Equity: A call to action. In G. Cawelti (Ed.), *Challenges and achievements of American education* (*1993 Yearbook of the Association for Supervision and Curriculum Development;* pp. 9–18). Alexandria, VA: ASCD.

Miller, P. (1992). Segregated programs of teacher education in early childhood: Immoral and inefficient practice. *Topics in Early Childhood Special Education, 11*(4), 39–52.

Peterson, N. (1987). *Early intervention for handicapped and at-risk children.* Denver, CO: Love.

Place, P. (1994). Social policy and family autonomy. In L. J. Johnson, R. J. Gallagher, M. J. LaMontagne, J. B. Jordan, J. J. Gallagher, P. L. Hutinger, & M. B. Karnes (Eds.), *Meeting early intervention challenges: Issues from birth to three* (2nd ed., pp. 265–278). Baltimore: Brookes.

Pugach, M. C., & Johnson, L. J. (1995). *Collaborative practitioners: Collaborative schools.* Denver, CO: Love.

Rosegrant, T., & Bredekamp, S. (1992). Planning and implementing the transformational curriculum. In S. Bredekamp & T. Rosegrant (Eds.), *Reaching potentials: Appropriate curriculum and assessment for young children* (pp. 74–93). Washington, DC: NAEYC.

Safer, N., & Hamilton, J. (1993). Legislative context for early intervention. In L. Brown, S. Thurman, & L. Pearl (Eds.), *Family-centered early intervention with infants & toddlers: Innovative cross-disciplinary approaches* (pp. 1–19). Baltimore: Brookes.

Sandall, S. (1993). Curricula for early intervention. In L. Brown, S. Thurman, & L. Pearl (Eds.), *Family-centered early intervention with infants & toddlers: Innovative cross-disciplinary approaches* (pp. 129–172). Baltimore: Brookes.

Smith, B. J. (1988). Early intervention public policy: Past, present, and future. In J. Jordan, J. Gallagher, P. Hutinger, & M. Karnes (Eds.), *Early childhood special education: Birth to three* (pp. 213–228). Reston, VA: ERIC Clearinghouse on Handicapped and Gifted Children.

Smith, B. J., & McKenna, P. (1994). Early intervention public policy: Past, present, and future. In L. J. Johnson, R. J. Gallagher, M. J. LaMontagne, J. B. Jordan, J. J. Gallagher, P. L. Hutinger, & M. B. Karnes (Eds.), *Meeting early intervention challenges: Issues from birth to three* (pp. 251–264). Baltimore: Brookes.

Thorpe, E. (1992). A unified commitment to best practice: Point. In L. J. Johnson (Ed.), *Proceedings of the Summer Institute for the Ohio Early Childhood Special Education: Higher Education Consortium* (pp. 12–27). Cincinnati, OH: University of Cincinnati.

Turnbull, A. P., & Turnbull, H. R., III. (1990). *Families, professionals, and exceptionality: A special partnership* (2nd ed.). Columbus, OH: Merrill.

Wetherby, A. M. (1992). *Communication and language intervention for preschool children.* Buffalo, NY: EDUCOM.

Wolery, M., Strain, P. S., & Bailey, D. B., Jr. (1992). Reaching potentials of children with special needs. In S. Bredekamp & T. Rosegrant (Eds.), *Reaching potentials: Appropriate curriculum and assessment for young children* (pp. 92–109). Washington, DC: NAEYC.

* *CHAPTER 7* *

Challenges for the Special Education–Curriculum Reform Partnership

Marleen C. Pugach and Cynthia L. Warger

Few would discount it—in fact many would claim we are only stating the obvious—when we point out that many social wars have been waged in the schools. Throughout the years, policy makers, with the explicit and implicit consent of the public, have engineered their ideologies into the public schools, imposing their views of the "new-order society" on the next generation. Historically, schools have been used as the factory for assimilating immigrants, sorting students into career paths, preventing the rise of social diseases, creating stewards for the environment, managing population growth, or, more recently, controlling illegal aliens. The target of all of these ventures has been the curriculum. It is fitting that in this last chapter we also look to curriculum and the new curriculum reforms as reflecting social policy for the next century.

As we worked on this book—writing, reflecting, considering the authors' viewpoints—we kept coming back to a central theme: acceptance of difference. Throughout the curriculum reform agendas, "what is worth knowing" is couched in a reality checkpoint, namely, that curriculum changes have been designed to benefit greater and greater numbers of students, including those with disabilities. Even though there will still be children who will not "make it" to the same point in the academic curriculum, the message emerging from all of this is that *it is alright* to have diverse outcomes. What is emerging as *not* alright is the presentation of knowledge and skills that are not applicable, meaningful, or useful to students' lives and their futures.

For some educators, acknowledging that not all students will progress to the same point is troubling, if not flat-out heresy. For years schools have been heralded as the great equalizers of opportunity. The myth has been perpetuated that all children have equal access to society's golden egg

Curriculum Trends, Special Education, and Reform: Refocusing the Conversation. ISBN 0-8077-3562-0 (pbk), ISBN 0-8077-3563-9 (cloth).

through the schoolhouse doors, and suggestions to the contrary have fallen into that politically incorrect morass in which terms such as "elitist" are slung.

However, as current national trends illustrate, there is in fact some truth in challenging the premise that all individuals are alike. The new curriculum trends actually provide us with a legitimate and politically acceptable means for putting an end to the institutionalized sanctioning of failure that has permeated classrooms for decades—not only for children with disabilities, but for the large numbers of children generally labeled as "at risk." At the same time that we sympathize with the child with severe learning disabilities who worked hard and improved only to find that he still had not caught up to his classmates, the real question as it relates to curriculum is whether focusing on a goal that the student was literally unable to reach—that of trying to catch up or dealing with impossible adversity—was worth the time and effort. Was this a legitimate learning goal? The new curriculum thrusts provide us with a basis for renewing our faith in the right of every individual to fulfill her potential, demonstrate his unique talents, and chart her own course for learning into the future.

The message in this new wave of curriculum reform is that different students will learn the curriculum to different degrees. They will do so in different ways and use their learnings for different purposes. Not everyone (so the saying goes) is going to become a rocket scientist, so why design all curriculum around the needs of budding rocketeers? The challenge for educators is to facilitate a learning environment that teaches students fundamental learning-how-to-learn skills and encourages thinking, social, and communication skills, so that students can tackle new content in ways that better their current and/or future lives. The job of educators is to refrain from the philosophical debate that pits elitists against egalitarians and to stay focused on providing all students with a rich set of learnings—knowledge and skills—to enhance their eventual transition to becoming productive citizens.

Through these reforms, curriculum is being reframed to accommodate a diversity of learners and position them in the global economy in which they will find themselves upon graduation. Factory-line compliance skills have been replaced with skills deemed critical for success in service and information-based jobs—skills like communication, collaboration, problem solving, and higher-level thinking. Similarly, adding up the number of facts students have learned is being replaced with demonstrations of what they have learned *and* how they are applying those new learnings in meaningful contexts. The bottom line seems to be that curriculum content is only as valuable as its eventual use.

As the previous chapters demonstrate, reform in the academic curriculum is rich with possibilities to assist special educators in their quest for worthwhile school experiences for students with mild disabilities, and some common developments across them are readily apparent:

- Covering less material, but covering it in much greater depth
- Focusing on the meaning of what is learned rather than the facts and figures
- Teaching as the facilitation of student learning
- Linking ideas across subject matter
- Constructing rather than receiving knowledge; beginning where the students are and building on their prior knowledge
- Creating an authentic activity orientation for learning where students work as part of a classroom community
- Embedding the acquisition of basic skills into meaningful activities
- Engaging students in cooperative work and problem solving
- Closely aligning curriculum, instruction, and assessment

How well students with mild disabilities will negotiate the new curriculum remains to be seen. Obviously, conceptualizing and enacting curriculum based on these assumptions means a very different kind of schooling experience for them. Not all students now labeled as having mild disabilities will be successful given the new curriculum trends, nor will all students not so labeled. One of the real dangers we see in making the transition to a new view of curriculum in schools is the temptation to make a priori decisions about who will and will not be able to succeed given these new curricular expectations.

Implemented well, the new approaches to curriculum provide the long-awaited chance for students who previously have experienced failure in school to demonstrate that they can engage in meaningful school-related activities that lead to valuable learning. In this new curriculum context, making decisions about potential student success ought to be based on the demands of the new curriculum itself and the accomplishments students have made in it—and not on a set of expectations based on prior performance in the traditional, flawed curriculum. Authors of the various responses in this volume have identified a wide range of supports to accomplish this task. Some responses illustrate that despite their labels, children can indeed rise to new expectations given a solid, careful implementation of the new paradigm; others provide specific suggestions for making sure that strategies for implementation fully anticipate the learning difficulties children bring. Despite these varying entry points into curriculum reform efforts, one thing is certain. We need multiple opportunities to implement the new curriculum frameworks—in special education classrooms, in general education classrooms, and in classrooms where special and general education teachers share the work of teaching—without first saying, "Kids with disabilities will never be able to do that." Only then will we have a better understanding of what it is that children are capable of achieving. In such efforts, the job of special educators is to support students in taking the risk of letting go of the limited expectations people may have set for them based on the labels they carry—and to monitor and set free their own expectations and those of their general education colleagues as well.

In achieving this goal, some challenges may be more difficult to deal with than others because they involve hard questions that cut to the very heart of how special education traditionally has been conceptualized and how the education field in general views students with disabilities. Other challenges may be easier to address because they are problems faced by special and general educators alike and, once a common ground is set, can be addressed as a collaborative enterprise. In the end, if there is to be congruence between reforming the curriculum and reforming special education, it is vital to begin a sustained dialogue on how to bridge the differences and face the challenges.

FACING CURRICULUM CHALLENGES WITHIN SPECIAL EDUCATION

What are these "hard questions" that special education must grapple with in relationship to redesigning curriculum and why is it particularly important to address them now? In general, they represent internal issues that have persistently been problematic in the field but have never been resolved satisfactorily. With the advent of the current inclusion debates, the basic assumptions on which special education is founded are under scrutiny—both from within the field and from without. At this point, it is not altogether clear which assumptions will continue to undergird special education practice and which may be altered or dropped altogether, but some assumptions have major implications for the "hard questions" that stand at the intersection of special education and curriculum reform.

General educators look to special education for guidance in how to instruct students with disabilities. If special education has not considered adequately the most difficult issues it faces, there may be confusion about how to proceed together to create a more responsive curriculum for all students. At the same time, special and general educators have a mutual responsibility to come to terms with the larger, sociocultural role special education has come to play in the schools. General educators have gotten used to having special education around as a place to send students they are not entirely comfortable teaching, while special education has gotten used to being the large, separate bureaucracy it is. Collectively addressing curriculum reform means keeping this larger picture in mind and being honest about what it really means to the structure of schooling and the day-to-day dynamics of teaching. How will we include students who really have never been accepted as full, participating members of the school community? As a precondition to collective action, special education must, at the very least, address the following issues.

Hard Question 1: Can curriculum reform affect the persistent problem of defining which students special education ought to serve? For decades the debate regarding overlabeling of students in categories of mild disability has been troublesome to special educators (Dunn, 1968; Heller, Holtzman, & Messick, 1982). It has yet to be resolved. As special educators in mild disabilities commonly assert, if general education were as strong as it should be (i.e., if all teachers were prepared to teach more diverse groups of students), far fewer students would need special education. One has only to look in the recent inclusion literature (Kauffman & Hallahan, 1995) and at the recent attempts to add new categories of mild disability (see Hocutt, McKinney, & Montague, 1993; Reid, Maag, & Vasa, 1994) to observe that a traditional approach to disabilities is still considered to be an acceptable state of affairs. The trend actually may be a movement away from reducing the numbers of students so labeled.

Many special educators (e.g., Gartner & Lipsky, 1987; Stainback & Stainback, 1984) recoil at the idea of adding more students to the ranks of special education, particularly those with mild learning and behavioral disabilities. The fundamental question is still whether special education is justified in removing students when the reason for their placement may lie more in ecological than individual characteristics (Dunn, 1968). The simultaneous press for inclusion and the competing desire to protect special education as a construct have the potential to create gridlock in special education reform with respect to students with mild disabilities; curriculum reform creates the possibility of breaking up this gridlock.

In the context of curriculum, the conflict can be cast somewhat differently. Those who advocate continuing separate programs for students with mild disabilities tend to argue that few general education classrooms have made adequate instructional adjustments to ensure student success (Keogh, 1988). We would ask whether it is fair to blame general education teachers totally for not making the curriculum more accessible to students with disabilities. If the *curriculum* is designed to weed out those individuals who cannot learn at a fast pace, who have difficulty processing visual and/or auditory input, or who do not see its value, then there is little even master teachers can do from an instructional perspective to overcome such a hopeless predicament. Clearly, the general education curriculum has not been particularly responsive to a wide range of student needs. For the most part, the general education program has relied on tracking to address the divergence between what is offered in the curriculum and the abilities of students to master it (Oakes, 1985). The traditional secondary school curriculum is a prime example, with its college preparation track, vocational education track, and special education track (the latter two carrying with them stigmas that many treat as a necessary evil).

From a curriculum perspective, the problem with separate programs for students with mild disabilities is that rarely, if at all, do we hear claims that the curriculum itself works to minimize students' disabilities. The special education curriculum for students with mild disabilities, for example, does not differ significantly from that of the general program. Unlike traditional vocational education, where Shakespeare and calculus have been replaced as curriculum goals with the study of car engines and construction tools, seldom has there been such a notable difference in the reading and mathematics that students learn in classes for the mildly disabled compared with their peers in general education. What we find is an even greater emphasis on basic skills (to support entry or re-entry into the general education curriculum) and an emphasis on helping the students complete "some" aspect of what their general program peers are learning. In special education, curriculum tends to end there. Most special education teachers do not teach science or social studies, or, as Curtis points out in his response, when they do, the content that is taught bears little resemblance to the content of the standard curriculum.

In other words, neither general nor special education has succeeded in creating a curriculum that maximizes learning for the largest number of students and that minimizes the inappropriate labeling of students. Within special education, placement and instruction have dominated as interventions. A third option exists, however. Special educators could recognize that some disabilities are in fact a function of the existing curriculum, take a careful look at what students are being asked to do in the first place, and then ask whether it is worth doing. Here we see the dialogue ripe for special and general educators to explore what is possible for students to achieve and to forge a common ground for making curriculum decisions that will serve the greatest number of students well. Poised on the brink of reforms that demand new approaches to schooling, the potential exists to distinguish between what is and is not a disability and to reduce the numbers of students who do not master the unreasonable set of expectations in the traditional curriculum and thus end up in special education. As part of its involvement in curriculum reform efforts, special education must be willing to take a strong stand on the identification issue, which in mild disabilities is, among other things, also largely an issue related to minority overrepresentation (Pugach, 1995b).

Hard Question 2: What are special education students really capable of doing? Current curriculum trends demand, perhaps more than ever before, that students engage in much more complex forms of thinking. As the authors of the responses collectively point out, not all students will reach this goal easily. At the very least, a set of structured experiences will need to be implemented to foster such achievement. The structures used, for example, in the "We-Search" case presented by Morocco and Zorfass, or in the guidelines offered by Kameenui, Chard, and Carnine for mathematics, do not need to be based on drill and practice to be appropriate for students with disabilities or for other students who are not succeeding. With those structures, real progress can be noted toward achieving more complex forms of thinking.

The inclusion of special education students in general education classrooms stands to challenge teachers to provide the best curriculum and instruction available, while at the same time raising the question of whether all students ought to be expected to achieve the same level of academic performance. If special educators' answer to this question is that for some students the goal of highly complex thinking may not be entirely realistic, the immediate, crucial issue becomes how to construct and implement a curriculum that is flexible enough to accommodate all students. It also must provide the greatest possible challenge for those who do not in actuality have a disability—no matter what label they may have carried in the past.

The real question boils down to whether special education really knows what it wants for "its kids" and how far special educators think their students can advance. This concern is intimately tied to the issue of how students are identified in the first place. It could be argued fairly that special education programs have actively sheltered many students from having to face complex intellectual activities. Some critics would state that most special education students never have been exposed to a robust, motivating curriculum, nor have they been helped in pursuing the goals such a curriculum offers. Unfortunately, these past practices inhibit our understanding of what the current population of special education students is capable of accomplishing. In Englert and Tarrant's (1995) study of early literacy, the expectations that special education teachers held for their students' learning steadily increased as students demonstrated their competence as readers and writers under new curriculum frameworks for literacy. Similarly, descriptions like the one offered by Anderson and Fetters in this volume illustrate that even at the secondary level, where specialization increases, students with disabilities can "think like scientists"—given the appropriate curriculum, instructional supports, and expectations. Whether the students they followed grow up to be scientists is another issue, but exposing them to the possibility through authentic scientific activity seems to be a worthy goal indeed. Whether special educators on the whole will be comfortable allowing—even pushing—students who now are labeled as having mild disabilities to achieve more than has been expected in the past is only starting to be understood, and is clearly dependent on curriculum choices.

Hard Question 3: How strong is the commitment to behaviorism? The curriculum trends described in this volume are decidedly a move away from the behavioristic philosophy that special education has promoted in its own programming. For many special educators, a behavioral approach to the teaching of basic skills is the mainstay of their educational belief system. Further, basic skills are to be taught before anything else, as the teacher's early comments in Klenk and Palincsar's study of Randy so clearly illustrate.

Whether special educators are willing to shift from a behavioral to a more child-centered approach to curriculum based on a belief in children's construction of knowledge—or, as Reid, Kurkjian, and Carruthers (1994) question, whether teacher education practices are sophisticated enough to prepare special education teachers to develop the skills needed for constructivist teaching—remains to be seen. Despite the close philosophical ties between early childhood education and early childhood special education portrayed so accurately in Johnson and Carr's response, no such common ground or close ties link special and general education at progressively higher levels of the educational ladder. Protecting young children from the press of decontextualized academics is a fight that early childhood education has fought on a unified front with early childhood special education, with the developmental perspective as the philosophical glue. Whether constructivism will emerge as a point of agreement is unclear, but it is clear that, for some special educators, constructivism is seen as an ill-structured instructional alternative whose activity orientation is sure to handicap special education students even further (e.g., Fuchs & Fuchs, 1994).

The issue is not whether constructivism is the panacea, but instead whether special educators are willing to learn enough about how curricula based on a constructivist philosophy work and use the resulting insights as part of their curriculum reform efforts. Increasingly there are specific examples of special educators who are successfully demonstrating how to use a constructivist approach to working with students who have mild disabilities (see, for example, Ruiz & Figueroa, 1995; for a social constructivist approach, see Englert, Raphael, & Mariage, 1994; Klenk & Palincsar, this volume), and who also retain an unwavering commitment to improving educational practice for students who are the most difficult to teach. Within special education, a truce needs to be called so that discussions of method do not deteriorate into discussions about who is willing to protect special education as it has always been practiced and who wishes to dismantle it, but rather focus on how to work together to improve educational opportunities for students.

Special education may have an important role to play in ensuring that these new curriculum trends are implemented in a way that guarantees that basic skills are adequately embedded in these activity frameworks as means, not ends. However, unless special educators understand the principles of constructivism and strive to gain expertise in how curriculum works from this perspective—as well as a tolerance for those who use it well—they may not feel confident enough to practice. In short, to paraphrase W. B. Yeats, is special education only slouching toward constructivism, while general education is advancing at an increasingly speedy trot?

Hard Question 4: From a curriculum perspective, what are special education's expectations for inclusion? Tension continues to escalate regarding whether inclusion is good special education policy. Respected professionals line up on both sides of the debate, equally concerned about the future of students with disabilities. At the core of the pro-inclusion position is the belief that without it children will be deprived of their just place in society and the benefits that come with participation in the normative school experience. At the core of the anti-inclusion position is a deep-seated desire to protect special education as a separate entity in the schools (and, we might observe, in the power and resource structure of the educational establishment). Dominating the rhetoric is the question of place (Kauffman, 1993): *Where* is it that students with disabilities will be educated?

Despite a long-standing preference for educating students with disabilities in general education classrooms, inclusion continues to be debated from the perspective of place and, by extension, the limited degree to which general education seems capable of changing in the eyes of special education (Pugach, 1995a). Protecting place means protecting what special education does that general education cannot seem to do; given this focus, dialogue about fundamental curriculum reform simply has not been part of the debate about inclusion. *In its recent history, special education has never mounted a sustained curriculum discussion;* it has not had that discussion internally so that special educators might generalize their thinking to general education curriculum reform, nor has it participated directly with its general education colleagues in a discussion of curriculum.

To clarify the expectations they hold for inclusion, special educators first need to get beyond arguing about who is for or who is against it. Internally, continuing to cast the arguments in such an adversarial manner precludes honest conversation about classrooms and the capacity of the general education system to change. Worse, it has created within general education a sense that place is all that deserves attention, and has pressed many of its now fearful general education colleagues into taking sides about inclusion as well—all in the absence of substantive discussion about curriculum. Whatever the outcomes of the internal debates about inclusion, curriculum reform will have to be an essential part of the conversation if special education wishes general education to accommodate students with disabilities to any degree. Whether special education service delivery evolves in a fully inclusive manner or a partially inclusive one, the standard curriculum needs to change. If full inclusion occurs, curriculum in general education needs to be addressed as a collaborative effort. If partial inclusion continues and special education programs akin to resource rooms persist, curriculum has to be dealt with in decisions about what special education teachers do in those special classrooms *and* in decisions about what general education teachers do, since general education is where most students now labeled as having mild disabilities still receive their education.

The answer to this hard question, then, is that we have not yet had the conversation about what special educators' curricular expectations are for inclusion. We know the curriculum has to be accommodating to meet children's needs, but we often talk about accommodation without describing the *curriculum* context in which that accommodation will be taking place. The internal challenge for special education is to move beyond finger-pointing and take an honest look at where special education's resources can best contribute to significant curriculum reform and implementation—in general education and special education classes alike. Then the question of how much inclusion is good special education policy can be addressed from a position of curricular strength.

FACING CURRICULUM CHALLENGES TOGETHER

Resolution of the challenges special education faces internally will not be enough. There are also many challenges that special and general educators must face together in order to enact fundamental curriculum reform in schools.

The Demanding Nature of Curriculum Work

Shifting curriculum philosophies and learning appropriate instructional methods to enact those philosophies is not easy work—for either special or general education professionals. Although some teachers may make important curricular changes on their own out of sheer desire for improved practice and self-renewal, many practicing teachers will need strong, interactive structures for professional development to support the skillful implementation of new curriculum frameworks. Some may believe that curriculum work is the province of curriculum specialists and is too difficult for an individual teacher to undertake alone. How much teachers will want to invest in making such changes is not easy to predict, especially since the power to determine classroom curriculum varies across classrooms and districts.

For many special educators, participating in curriculum reform may seem like double work: learning the curriculum issues and acting on them, and simultaneously figuring out how all of this relates to greater integration of students and new roles for special education teachers. Although we have argued that these two goals are intertwined and that one supports the other, active efforts to make those connections will be needed. Special educators will have to participate in school and district curriculum redesign efforts, as both learners and, as illustrated by Englert and Tarrant (1995), knowledgeable leaders.

In reality, the curriculum trends described here represent new roles for all teachers; everyone will have to come to grips with what it means to facilitate knowledge growth rather than dispense knowledge, to take a problem-solving stance, to integrate knowledge and skills across subject areas, and to use the exemplary technological advances described, for example, by Montague and by Mastropieri and Scruggs. The situation may be especially threatening for special educators; if they throw out the traditional curriculum, they also throw out all the known roles special educators are used to playing—roles associated, as we argued in Chapter 1, with curriculum and instructional adaptation, and not with curriculum reform. Whether they are in special or general education, all teachers will be supported in these change efforts only to the extent that the professional norms at their schools foster professional growth. For this to occur, the most contemporary approaches to staff development (e.g., Lieberman & Miller, 1991) and the creation of collegial workplaces (Rosenholtz, 1989) are essential. At the same time that they learn how to do the daily work of teaching from a new curriculum perspective—for example, how to implement Davis and Maher's "new view" of school mathematics—teachers need to have time and space to talk about how their daily efforts relate to the larger curriculum framework. The overarching question, "Why teach this way?" needs to be posed regularly as a means of self-monitoring and needs to be incorporated in the professional dialogue that Rosenholtz (1989) reminds us characterizes self-renewing schools. Dialogue like this applies no less to special than to general education teachers.

The Universal Need for Vocational Education Reform

In secondary education, the relationship of the academic curriculum to the reform of vocational education is an important issue that has major implications for special education reform as well. Vocational education, usually dealt with in special education under the rubric of transitional programming, has always been one of the mainstays of special education practice (see Rusch & Phelps, 1987). For special and general education alike, the challenge is how to create vocational programs that are respectable alternatives to the college track and that provide appropriate intellectual challenges related to vocational preparation (e.g., *IVAE Connection,* 1995). The practice of sorting students into college-bound or vocational tracks is slowly changing with the introduction of efforts to integrate academic materials in courses like English, mathematics, and science with the knowledge and competencies actually used in workplace settings (O'Neil, 1994). One specific curriculum challenge is how to invest vocational education programs with a serious, contemporary grounding in the academic foundations of those vocations based on the trends described by the authors here. Another is how to link vocational preparation with the surrounding communities.

Within special education, community-based vocational programs have long been a distinguishing characteristic of transitional programming. This is an area in which special education could contribute much to curriculum reform. Another aspect of the vocational question that has to be confronted is where vocational goals for students with disabilities might diverge from those for nondisabled students. Even if vocational programming is redesigned radically so that it becomes a serious "subject" in school, some students, likely those with moderate to severe disabilities, will continue to need more functional approaches to a vocationally oriented curriculum.

Keeping a Fix on Curriculum While Instructional Methods Change

The general curriculum trends described in this volume signify new directions for the practice of curriculum in the schools that are becoming evident in general education classrooms across the country. Teachers like Ms. Carrese in the science class described by Champagne, Newell, and Goodenough are experimenting with changes that are beginning to be reflected in the textbook adoption process, in the activities teachers choose, and in how subject areas are related to each other.

As new curriculum ideas emerge, they are accompanied by new instructional practices. For the most part, methods and instructional techniques tend to resonate best with teachers, rather than more philosophical and technical questions about what principles should form the basis of their efforts. Given that most teachers have practiced their craft with little or no input into curriculum renewal teams or curriculum framework projects, this is not an unexpected situation.

The new curriculum trends require systemic, far-reaching changes in how knowledge is learned and taught. Unlike new methods that come onto the scene to support the status quo, the methods that accompany these new curriculum trends represent a different framework, as Schug and Hartoonian point out in their description of improving instruction in geography and economics education.

A solid understanding of new organizational strategies for delivering the curriculum also is needed. For example, integrating the curriculum is currently a highly favored way to reduce fragmentation and irrelevance—two concerns reflected in the subject area reform agendas (Aschbacher, 1991; Beck, Copa, & Pease, 1991; Drake, 1991; Fogarty, 1991; Jacobs, 1989; Zorfass, Morocco, Persky, Remz, Nichols, & Warger, 1991). The need for curriculum integration is based on the assumption that situations in which people apply learning to solve problems—or make decisions or discover answers—*rarely* are subject specific (Beane, 1991). As Maxwell noted in her chapter, an integrated approach to curriculum organization has had a long tradition in early childhood education (see also Katz, 1988; Katz & Chard, 1990; National Association of Elementary School Principals, 1990), but extending the sound use of integration is a progressively greater challenge as academic content gets more complex at the elementary, middle, and secondary levels (Brandt, 1991; Hurd, 1991; Parker, 1991; Smith, 1991). Likewise, service learning is receiving wider attention as an organizational strategy for creating curricula with authentic and meaningful content (Conrad & Hedin, 1991; Warger & Zorfass, 1994) by drawing on the identification and resolution of community problems. Special and general education teachers need to work together in forging new partnerships for developing integrated curriculum units or service learning projects that are consistent with the overarching curriculum frameworks from which their use emanated.

There is a real danger that the new curriculum goals may be overshadowed by these new and often highly motivating instructional approaches and delivery strategies. The emphasis on new modes of instruction, activities, and organization might obscure the broader reasons these innovations were introduced in the first place. Teachers may be seduced into thinking that they are implementing new curriculum frameworks when in reality they merely are slicing off one method and failing to place it in the larger curriculum context—perhaps without understanding the curriculum frameworks from which the activities emerged.

For special educators, this poses a dilemma. Partly because of the isolation from curriculum matters, not to mention their traditional reliance on instructional techniques to accommodate problems with learning, special educators could be placed in a vulnerable position when asked to assist students with "new" activities. When told that a student is having difficulty with cooperative learning, will they know whether it is because the student is having difficulty with the curriculum content or with the cooperative learning activity being used to teach the content? Just as special educators have analyzed traditional instructional formats (e.g., large-group instruction, discussion, lab work, drill, and practice) in order to anticipate potential student difficulties, they will need to be skilled in sorting out new instructional techniques from the new curriculum goals so that they can relate the two. Further, they will need to develop intensive instructional structures that are consistent with the general curriculum philosophy that is adopted and that also make sense in terms of providing the kind of small-group and individual support students will need. This will mean a complete reconceptualization of what it means to provide small-group instruction in the first place, and of how it can be structured so as not to violate the sense of learning community on which so many of the new curriculum trends rely (Pugach, 1995b).

Shifting Assessment Philosophies

High-stakes testing is quickly being joined by what are known as authentic forms of classroom-based assessment. The term "authentic" is used to convey the idea that performance assessments should engage students in applying knowledge and skills in ways that are used in the real world (McTighe & Ferrara, 1994; Wiggins, 1993). Rather than wait until the end of a semester or unit to test students' knowledge, with performance assessment teachers apply multiple sources to assess students' understanding throughout each lesson. Classroom-based performance assessment is used *over time* to improve learning and inform teaching—not simply to sort and grade students (Bartz, Anderson-Robinson, & Hillman, 1994; Hiebert, Valencia, & Afflerbach, 1994).

As many of the authors noted, the new curriculum reforms require an emphasis on performance-based assessment. As Lovitt observed in his response, a close alignment between curriculum and assessment is useful only to the extent that the curriculum itself is worthwhile. Curriculum, instruction, and assessment are seen as congruent, with assessment reflecting what has been taught and learned. It makes little sense to test memory of multiple choice facts when the curriculum and the instructional program focus on problem-solving skills. Beyond paper-and-pencil tests, teachers are turning to performances, products, demonstrations, and discussions to determine what students know and are able to do.

Relative to special education reform, assessments for determining accountability and for measuring student progress have had long histories. Classroom-based assessment has long been promoted in the special education literature as curriculum-based measurement (CBM) (Deno, 1985; Fuchs, Deno, & Mirkin, 1984). These assessments, although tied to the curriculum, typically are based on the measurement of very discrete units of learning that complement a basic-skills philosophy. From a basic-skills orientation, special educators have closed the gap between curriculum, instruction, and assessment. However, transferring such an approach to more complex forms of learning represented by the new curriculum trends presents a substantially more difficult challenge. In the end, CBM may not be well suited as an assessment framework for the new curriculum trends, although it remains a significant tool for assessing basic skills.

With Chapter 1 legislation that includes language promoting performance assessment, and major curriculum groups such as the International Reading Association and the National Education Association pushing for an expanded view of classroom-based performance assessment, the opportunity exists for special and general educators to join together in learning to utilize strategies for bringing assessment into line with the new curriculum trends. However, similar to the need for a sound understanding of the curriculum framework before implementing new instructional methods, teachers likewise need to be careful to relate new assessment methods, like portfolios, to a sound overall strategy for a new philosophy of assessment.

Preparing New Teachers for Active Curriculum Roles

Preservice teacher education pays little attention to curriculum as a framework, either from the perspective of theory or in terms of the various approaches to curriculum planning. As a field of study, curriculum is usually thought of as graduate-level work. Most of us recognize that, despite a lack of formal attention to curriculum issues, teachers make curriculum decisions all the time. Teachers continuously interpret and revise curriculum goals as they plan and implement lessons and units of study. As we noted earlier, without a broad curriculum framework in place, teachers may implement one small aspect of a curriculum philosophy as a new activity but miss the full power of that activity as a means to a particular curriculum end.

In elementary and secondary teacher preparation, curriculum typically is addressed in the form of methodological study of the various content areas, with some attention paid to how to link those areas in interdisciplinary units of study. Only in early childhood education and more recently in the middle school literature is interdisciplinary curriculum a given. Certainly there is variation across programs, and some may deal with curriculum as a broad concept more than others. As a general rule, however, prospective teachers begin their careers thinking about curriculum less as a philosophical framework and more as the sum of the various content areas. In contrast, the preparation of special education teachers does not have this curriculum content basis upon which to build. Most preservice special education students are not required to have concurrent certification in general education, and only a minority of teacher education programs have offered dual certification in general and special education (Kearney & Durand, 1992).

No matter what degree of inclusion is practiced in a given school or district, special education teachers need to be knowledgeable about the regular curriculum and its implications for students who have difficulty achieving in school. This is one of the most compelling reasons to build integrated teacher education programs where the general education curriculum forms the basis for specialized preparation. Otherwise, prospective special education teachers will continue to learn to adapt the curriculum (in, for example, literacy and mathematics) without knowing what the purpose and content of the standard curriculum were in the first place. Or, we may teach prospective special education teachers that the basis of collaboration is individual student problem solving and rarely guide them to consider the larger curriculum picture as a point of departure for intervention (Warger & Pugach, 1993).

Calls for integrating the preparation of special and general education teachers are not new (Pugach, 1992; Pugach & Lilly, 1984; Stainback & Stainback, 1989), and some real progress has been made in specific programs as a result of the great press for teacher education reform in the past decade (Blanton, Griffin, Winn, & Pugach, in press). It is with respect to curriculum issues that the distance between special and general education is at its greatest. Dual certification may mean preparation in two unrelated programs of teacher education, one in general and one in special education. In such programs, the issue of curriculum—like many other issues—may be dealt with in parallel tracks and from conflicting philosophical perspectives. Preparation for collaboration may occur in the special education portion of the program but not in the general education portion. Bridging the curriculum gap necessitates an integrated, not a parallel, approach to joint teacher preparation in which special and general teacher educators are knowledgeable about curriculum from the outset and can come to terms with their differences and develop a unified perspective on what is worth teaching.

PRACTICAL GUIDELINES FOR PARTICIPATING IN CURRICULUM REFORM

Curriculum reform takes place on many levels: state, district, building, and grade, as well as in individual classrooms. We believe that teachers need to take an active role in curriculum reform at each of these levels, but specifically in their own buildings and classrooms, where they have the most control over what goes on and exert the greatest influence in creating learning environments that are responsive to the differing needs of students. The challenges outlined in this chapter will need to be addressed directly if curriculum reform is to get beyond lists of standards and broad philosophical statements. How to assist every teacher to be worried about the question, "What's worthwhile about what we are teaching?" as a foundation for curriculum action is a formidable task. The practical suggestions we offer here apply equally to special and general education teachers; they are meant to provide a set of concrete next steps to bridge the wide curriculum gaps that preclude the real integration of students with disabilities and the creation of motivating educational frameworks for all students, whether they have disabilities or not.

1. Become knowledgeable about curriculum. The trends described in this volume in many ways are just that—trends. Although educational practice is moving toward this vastly different set of curriculum goals, the change is in progress and many schools are still functioning under older conceptions of curriculum. One of the most fundamental challenges for all teachers—whether in special or in general education—is to learn about the content and purpose of these new curriculum frameworks so they can participate in the dialogue from an informed perspective. This is likely to be a much greater challenge for special educators, since a curriculum perspective is not commonly taken in their planning of educational programs. So the first practical step educators can take if they wish to foster improved programs for all students, including those with disabilities, is to agree to participate actively in curriculum redesign in the first place.

On a practical level, getting up to speed on curriculum issues may mean reading new journals, talking with new professional colleagues, or attending a different set of district or professional meetings. It may mean venturing a bit beyond your current comfort zone and asking questions about issues with which you are unfamiliar. It also may mean asking yourself a new set of questions, starting with, "How do I think about curriculum?" and ending with a built-in periodic questioning of the value of what you choose to do in your classroom or program. Developing a "curriculum consciousness," keeping it, and using it as a benchmark against which to measure your own practice are vital tools for educators interested in improving schooling.

2. Choose a specific curriculum basis for your work. A second practical step is to choose one curriculum area in which to develop some extensive expertise. If you are in special education, chances are you do most of your work in literacy and mathematics. These may be logical starting points for expanding your understanding of the content area—but do so from the perspective of the most contemporary curriculum trends in the field. Reaching this goal may require collaborating with a partner in general education who is an expert in one of these fields.

If you are in general education, chances are you already have a favorite subject and may have developed extensive expertise in current curriculum trends; in this case, you are an important resource for your special education colleagues. If you are a special education teacher interested in team teaching, another way to define a new area of expertise is to choose a content area where your general education partner is an expert and tackle that first. Your partner can provide the support needed to try (and fail in a safe place) new approaches; it is a natural way to get ongoing feedback (Pugach & Wesson, 1995).

As you begin to develop new curricular expertise, keep three things in mind. First, your best sources for curriculum leadership may be right in your building or district; if they are not, you may want to look to a local university for someone who is current in a particular field and is willing to engage in ongoing collaborative dialogue and support around curriculum implementation. Second, start slowly and tackle one field at a time. Most people are not experts in all of the curriculum fields, and they do not have to be; there is simply too much to know. By grounding your knowledge in one area, you can consider how trends there relate to new trends across content areas—a way of supporting a shift to interdisciplinary curriculum design. Third, embarking on a new venture may at first seem daunting; to support your efforts, find trustworthy colleagues and create networks among teachers who are interested in the same content areas and questions. Setting up computer networks in various subject areas is one efficient way of connecting people who are committed to implementing new curriculum philosophies.

3. Set up curriculum redesign teams to include both general and special educators. If curriculum redesign or renewal teams are being formed or exist in your district or building, urge representation from special education if it is not already represented. Initially the logic of this move may escape some individuals. As a tool for expanding curriculum consciousness across the district, it is an excellent opportunity that must not be lost.

The role of special educators on such teams will, of course, vary with their individual expertise. What they bring is the potential to consider the total range of students as curriculum decisions are made.

Specifically, curriculum redesign teams need to:

- Identify curriculum trends
- Determine the impact of trends on curriculum
- Review scope and sequence
- Identify goals that are representative of curriculum trends
- Review goals in relation to student characteristics
- Identify potential areas of mismatch
- Identify instructional strategies to support goals
- Identify assessment techniques to measure mastery of goals

Glatthorn (1990) suggests that curriculum development should be a main focus for cooperative professional development activities with teams of special and general education teachers, but that it will take extra effort to go beyond special education's traditional concern with "the basics" and how to adapt curriculum. He urges such teams to broaden their focus to include questions about long-term goals of content-specific programs and the kind of knowledge that needs to be emphasized. In this way, general and special educators can talk and work together in an effort to improve the curriculum for all students.

4. Introduce curriculum into discussions/policy setting for inclusion. As a corollary, the issue of curriculum needs to be introduced into plans for greater inclusion of students with disabilities. As schools and districts enter into discussions about whether more integration is desirable, curriculum must not be ignored. Instead, curriculum reform can be seen as one fundamental way of creating educational environments that support the whole range of students in schools and it should be interjected regularly into the dynamics of inclusion from an organizational as well as a classroom perspective.

A second benefit of introducing a curriculum perspective into discussions of inclusion is that it broadens ownership of what is now considered special education. Once special educators raise curriculum as a central issue for inclusion—and can talk about it from an informed viewpoint—then the investment in school improvement ceases to be a function of special education alone. One of the persistent problems in special education reform is that it often is seen as a parochial set of interests. Curriculum may be one of the most powerful links in broadening an understanding of the goals of special education reform—on the part of both special and general educators. Linking curriculum reform and inclusion also extends to other organizational and professional reforms—for example, staff development efforts cited earlier, that produce opportunities for lasting change. Planning for inclusion needs to be a joint effort across general and special education and should not be limited to discussions of structure and location.

5. Introduce curriculum as a new perspective for collaboration. Special and general education no longer exist in isolation from one another; in the past decade, collaboration between the two has grown exponentially, largely as a function of new philosophies of special education service delivery. As a growing commitment on the part of special education, collaboration has been based on the need for individual problem solving; the most frequent goal has been to create individual interventions, often in management or adaptations.

With the growing desire for more integration, the question of special education's role in the wider arena of school reform is a prominent one, and collaboration is a natural way to foster such relationships. One way to build such linkages is to refocus collaboration away from the student as the traditional source of the problem and onto the curriculum. Then, the content of collaborative interactions will directly address how the curriculum might be redesigned. A curriculum-centered, problem-solving model for collaboration might look something like that shown in Figure 7.1 (Warger & Pugach, 1993, 1996).

In the first stage of the curriculum-centered model, participants establish rapport and set expectations for collaboration. This is the time for the special educator to become familiar with the curricular goals and outcomes for students in classrooms, before jumping into developing solutions. In the next stage, the problem is identified in terms of the curriculum. As new goals, instructional techniques, and assessment strategies are discussed, the rationale for the goals, the way the instructional strategies selected support them, and how the assessment authentically measures progress toward them should guide the discussion. Another consideration at this stage is the match or mismatch between student characteristics and the new curriculum goals. Instead of assuming that the student will have difficulties, it will be important to determine what "hidden" prerequisites, if any, exist for a specified goal and which ones may lead to problems for the student. This ap-

Figure 7.1 Curriculum-Centered Problem-Solving Model

Stage One: Establish Initial Rapport & Negotiate Contract

Stage Two: Problem Identification

- Identify new curriculum goals, instructional strategies, & assessment techniques
- Identify new relationships among student, curriculum, teacher, & peers
- Discuss potential mismatch with student characteristics
- Presentation of relevant data
- Statement of potential difficulty area

Stage Three: Intervention

- Brainstorm suggestions: curriculum, instruction, assessment
- Select strategies
- Identify support practices for students and/or teachers
- Develop & implement plan

Stage Four: Evaluation & Closure

Source: Reprinted from *LD Forum,* Summer 1993.

proach helps teachers to see each new curriculum goal as either an opportunity or a difficulty for a given student.

Once new curriculum goals are in place, teachers can develop ideas for expanding, modifying, or enhancing the curriculum for all students. They can identify specific support strategies that might be needed for a specific student. Finally, teachers need to establish a plan for determining how well students are able to achieve the curriculum outcomes, how students responded to new instructional strategies, and how well the assessment in use captured student learning. Always, at the end of such a cycle of collaboration, teachers should ask themselves the "big" curriculum question: What did the students learn, and how well?

Shifting the focus of collaboration to the curriculum increases the opportunity to contribute to the general improvement of schooling. Together with general education teachers, special educators can directly support the creation of a more challenging, motivating curriculum for all students. With curriculum reform as the goal of the collaboration, both sets of participants are afforded the opportunity to consider problems in light of educational goals, or "what's worth knowing," rather than by reference to the seemingly intractable problems of individual students. This is not to minimize the specific problems children might have, but rather to maximize the potential for addressing the broadest range of problems possible through a curriculum perspective.

CURRICULUM AND SPECIAL EDUCATION: STRANGE BEDFELLOWS NO MORE?

Professionals in special and general education have several choices with respect to the current curriculum reform movement. The most important choice, we believe, relates to how special education wishes to negotiate the whole issue of curriculum with its general education colleagues. Special education can continue to do things the way it has always done them, by working *around* the curriculum, or it can stop, take stock, and use the unique opportunity offered by the current reform context to look at the reform picture from an entirely new perspective, the perspective of curriculum, and enter into a long-needed dialogue with general education about the fundamental purpose of schooling.

Special educators can participate in curriculum reform at two levels. First, they can continue using the model of modification and adaptation, but in relationship to the new curriculum trends described in this volume. This approach would, at the least, help special educators gain an important understanding of what the new curriculum will demand of students. However, it would not place special educators in a position of parity with their general education colleagues in terms of building schools based on a new conception of curriculum. It is at this second level that we hope special and general educators will form a new partnership.

This second, deeper level of curriculum partnership is pivotal because it provides the most direct way of addressing the quality of education no matter where it occurs—in special or general education classrooms. By transcending the argument over place, we squarely face the reality that curriculum reform is needed across the board, in special and in general education, and that no matter where children are educated in schools, they deserve the best possible approaches to curriculum. A true curriculum partnership also places special and general education teachers in close proximity with respect to what general education teachers have always worried most about, namely, what is taught and how it is taught—but from a perspective of concern for students who in the past have been least likely to succeed. We are not so naive as to think that reforming the curriculum will happen quickly or easily for either special or general educators. Given the wide range of possible entry points into reform, curriculum provides the clearest focus for making the changes that affect children most directly, namely, what their teachers do in the classrooms of America's schools, and, most important, why they do it.

As we hope this volume demonstrates, curriculum reform is an ideal focal point for the collective energy of special and general educators. It forms a natural bridge between general concerns for the improvement of schooling and specific concerns about how best to work with students who have had persistent problems in the conventional curriculum. As the authors have shown, curriculum trends are converging to present a unified sense of what may be our best current philosophy of curriculum and accompanying instruction for the greatest range of students.

If we listen to these authors, they are telling us that there indeed may be a more effective way of defining what it is that is worth knowing, and thus what is worth teaching, in school. Helping students now labeled as having mild disabilities will continue to be a challenge. With the new curriculum philosophies firmly in place, many of the problems encountered in the decontextualized, bits-and-pieces approach to curriculum may be overcome. Minimizing problems by creating a more responsive, sensible approach to curriculum will occur only to the extent that all the players participate in that reform and design flexible implementation plans that do not violate basic curriculum understandings about what is worth knowing. Our hope is that special and general educators will take on this task together, with a sense of mutual responsibility for all the children and youth they teach.

REFERENCES

Aschbacher, P. R. (1991). Humanitas: A thematic curriculum. *Educational Leadership, 49*(2), 16–19.

Bartz, D., Anderson-Robinson, S., & Hillman, L. (1994). Performance assessment: Make them show what they know. *Principal, 73*(3), 11–15.

Beane, J. (1991). The middle school: The natural home of integrated curriculum. *Educational Leadership, 49*(2), 9–13.

Beck, R. H., Copa, G., & Pease, V. (1991). Vocational and academic teachers work together. *Educational Leadership, 49*(2), 29–32.

Blanton, L. P., Griffin, C. C., Winn, J. A., & Pugach, M. C. (in press). *Teacher education in transition: Collaborative programs to prepare general and special educators.* Denver, CO: Love.

Brandt, R. (1991). The outcomes we want. *Educational Leadership, 49*(2), 3.

Conrad, D. E., & Hedin, D. (1991). School based community service. *Phi Delta Kappan, 72*(10), 743–749.

Deno, S. L. (1985). Curriculum-based measurement: The emerging alternative. *Exceptional Children, 52,* 219–232.

Drake, S. M. (1991). How our team dissolved the boundaries. *Educational Leadership, 49*(2), 20–23.

Dunn, L. M. (1968). Special education for the mildly retarded—Is much of it justifiable? *Exceptional Children, 35,* 5–22.

Englert, C. S., Raphael, T. E., & Mariage, T. V. (1994). Developing a school-based discourse for literacy learning: A principled search for understanding. *Learning Disability Quarterly, 17,* 2–32.

Englert, C. S., & Tarrant, K. L. (1995). Creating collaborative cultures for educational change. *Remedial and Special Education, 16,* 325–336.

Fogarty, R. (1991). Ten ways to integrate the curriculum. *Educational Leadership, 49*(2), 61–65.

Fuchs, D., & Fuchs, L. S. (1994). Inclusive schools movement and the radicalization of special education reform. *Exceptional Children, 60,* 294–309.

Fuchs, L. S., Deno, S. L., & Mirkin, P. K. (1984). The effects of frequent curriculum-based measurement and evaluation in pedagogy, student achievement, and student awareness of learning. *American Educational Research Journal, 21,* 449–460.

Gartner, A., & Lipsky, D. K. (1987). Beyond special education: Toward a quality education for all students. *Harvard Educational Review, 57*(4), 367–395.

Glatthorn, A. A. (1990). Cooperative professional development: Facilitating the growth of the special education teacher and the classroom teacher. *Remedial and Special Education, 11*(3), 29–34.

Heller, K. A., Holtzman, W. H., & Messick, S. (Eds.). (1982). *Placing children in special education: A strategy for equity.* Washington, DC: National Academy Press.

Hiebert, E. H., Valencia, S. W., & Afflerbach, P. (1994). Definitions and perspectives. In S. W. Valencia, E. H. Hiebert, & P. Afflerbach (Eds.), *Authentic reading assessment: Practices and possibilities* (pp. 6–21). Newark, DE: International Reading Association.

Hocutt, A. M., McKinney, J. D., & Montague, M. (1993). Issues in the education of students with attention deficit disorder: Introduction to the special issue. *Exceptional Children, 60,* 103–106.

Hurd, P. D. (1991). Why we must transform science education. *Educational Leadership, 49*(2), 33–35.

IVAE Connection. (1995). Quarterly newsletter of the Center on Education and Work, *1*(1). Madison, WI: Center on Education and Work.

Jacobs, H. H. (1989). *Interdisciplinary curriculum: Design and implementation.* Alexandria, VA: Association for Supervision and Curriculum Development.

Katz, L. G. (1988). Engaging children's minds: The implications of research for early childhood education. In C. Warger (Ed.), *A resource guide to public school early childhood programs.* Alexandria, VA: Association for Supervision and Curriculum Development.

Katz, L. G., & Chard, S. C. (1990). *Engaging children's minds: The project approach.* Norwood, NJ: Ablex.

Kauffman, J. M. (1993). How we might achieve the radical reform of special education. *Exceptional Children, 60,* 6–16.

Kauffman, J. M., & Hallahan, D. P. (Eds.). (1995). *The illusion of full inclusion.* Austin, TX: PRO-ED.

Kearney, C. A., & Durand, V. M. (1992). How prepared are our teachers for mainstreamed classroom settings? A survey of postsecondary schools of education in New York State. *Exceptional Children, 59*(1), 6–11.

Keogh, B. K. (1988). Improving services for problem learners: Rethinking and restructuring. *Journal of Learning Disabilities, 21*(1), 19–22.

Lieberman, A., & Miller, L. (Eds.). (1991). *Staff development for education in the '90s* (2nd ed.). New York: Teachers College Press.

McTighe, J., & Ferrara, S. (1994). *Assessing learning in the classroom.* Washington, DC: National Education Association.

National Association of Elementary School Principals. (1990). *Early childhood education and the elementary school principal.* Alexandria, VA: Author.

Oakes, J. (1985). *Keeping track: How schools structure inequality.* New Haven, CT: Yale University Press.

O'Neil, J. (1994). Preparing students for work: Greater ties sought between academic, vocational content. *ASCD Update, 36*(9), 4–5.

Parker, W. (1991). Social studies: Goals and trends. In Association for Supervision and Curriculum Development (Ed.), *Curriculum handbook* (pp. 6.17–6.40). Alexandria, VA: ASCD.

Pugach, M. C. (1992). Unifying the preservice preparation of teachers. In W. Stainback & S. Stainback (Eds.), *Controversial issues facing special education* (pp. 255–269). Boston: Allyn & Bacon.

Pugach, M. C. (1995a). The failure of imagination in inclusive schooling. *The Journal of Special Education, 29,* 212–223.

Pugach, M. C. (1995b). Twice victims: The struggle to educate children in urban schools and the reform of special education and Chapter 1. In M. C. Wang & M. C. Reynolds (Eds.), *Making a difference for students at risk: Trends and alternatives* (pp. 27–60). Thousand Oaks, CA: Corwin Press.

Pugach, M. C., & Lilly, M. S. (1984). Reconceptualizing support services for classroom teachers: Implications for teacher education. *Journal of Teacher Education, 35*(5), 48–55.

Pugach, M. C., & Wesson, C. L. (1995). Teachers' and students' views of team teaching of general education and learning-disabled students in two fifth-grade classes. *Elementary School Journal, 95*(3), 279–295.

Reid, D. K., Kurkjian, C., & Carruthers, S. (1994). Special education teachers interpret constructivist teaching. *Remedial and Special Education, 15*(5), 267–280.

Reid, R., Maag, J. W., & Vasa, S. F. (1994). Attention deficit hyperactivity disorder as a disability category: A critique. *Exceptional Children, 60,* 198–214.

Rosenholtz, S. J. (1989). *Teachers' workplace.* New York: Teachers College Press.

Ruiz, N. T., & Figueroa, R. A. (1995). Emerging outcomes from research on learning handicapped classrooms with Latino students: The Optimal Learning Environment (OLE) project. *Education in Urban Society, 27,* 463–483.

Rusch, F. R., & Phelps, A. L. (1987). Secondary special education and transition from school to work: A national priority. *Exceptional Children, 53,* 487–492.

Smith, C. (1991). Integrated language arts. In Association for Supervision and Curriculum Development (Ed.), *Curriculum handbook* (pp. 3.17–3.29). Alexandria, VA: ASCD.

Stainback, S., & Stainback, W. (1989). Facilitating merger through personnel preparation. In S. Stainback, W. Stainback, & M. Forest (Eds.), *Educating all students in the mainstream of regular education* (pp. 121–128). Baltimore: Brookes.

Stainback, W., & Stainback, S. (1984). A rationale for the merger of special and regular education. *Exceptional Children, 51,* 102–111.

Warger, C. L., & Pugach, M. C. (1993). A curriculum focus for collaboration. *LD Forum, 18*(4), 26–30.

Warger, C. L., & Pugach, M. C. (1996). Forming partnerships around curriculum. *Educational Leadership, 53* (5), 62–65.

Warger, C. L., & Zorfass, J. (1994). *Breaking away: Extending curriculum into the community.* Newton, MA: Education Development Center.

Wiggins, G. (1993). Assessment, authenticity, context, and validity. *Phi Delta Kappan, 75*(3), 200–225.

Zorfass, J. M., Morocco, C. C., Persky, S., Remz, A. R., Nichols, J., & Warger, C. L. (1991). *Make it happen! Inquiry and technology in the middle school curriculum.* Newton, MA: Education Development Center.

About the Editors and the Contributors

Charles W. (Andy) Anderson is Associate Professor in the Department of Teacher Education, Michigan State University. He began his educational career as a middle school science teacher; he received his Ph.D. in science education from the University of Texas at Austin. Dr. Anderson's primary research interest is using research on student learning to improve classroom science teaching.

Douglas W. Carnine, Professor of Education at the University of Oregon, is Director of the National Center to Improve the Tools of Educators. His interests include curriculum analysis, instructional design, and school reform as they affect diverse learners.

Victoria W. Carr is Research Associate and Coordinator of Evaluation and Consultation, Arlitt Child and Family Research and Education Center at the University of Cincinnati, where she coordinates center evaluation and research activities for a fully inclusive preschool program that serves culturally and economically diverse children and their families. She developed and taught early childhood courses and assisted in designing the undergraduate and graduate Interdisciplinary Early Childhood Education Programs at Northern Kentucky University, with a focus on unifying early childhood and early childhood special education. She is currently a doctoral candidate at the University of Cincinnati where her research and writing interests involve play, assessment, and collaboration.

Audrey B. Champagne is Chair, Department of Educational Theory and Practice, and Professor of Chemistry and of Educational Theory and Practice at the State University of New York at Albany. She also chairs the Working Group on Assessment of the National Science Education Standards Project.

David J. Chard is Assistant Professor in the Department of Special Education at Boston University. He earned his undergraduate degree in math and science education from Central Michigan University and his doctorate from the University of Oregon. His current interests include legal advocacy for students with disabilities and research on reading acquisition and instructional design.

Charles K. Curtis is Associate Professor in the Department of Social and Educational Studies at the University of British Columbia, where he coordinates the Social Studies Program. He received his Ed.D. from Utah

State University. For the past several years his research interests have been primarily concerned with attitude change toward persons with disabilities.

Robert B. Davis is Professor of Mathematics Education at Rutgers University. Professor Davis received a Ph.D. in mathematics from MIT and has published widely on research in mathematics. His recent work focuses on the teaching and learning of mathematics.

Marcia K. Fetters is Assistant Professor in the Department of Curriculum and Instruction at the University of North Carolina at Charlotte. Dr. Fetters was previously a high school science teacher. She received her Ph.D. in science education and teachers' professional development from Michigan State University.

Jacqueline M. Goodnough teaches tenth- and eleventh-grade chemistry and biology at Mohonasen Central School in Rotterdam, New York. Her special interests are authentic assessment and integrating mathematics, science, and technology courses.

H. Michael Hartoonian is Professor in the Graduate School and Director of the Carey Center on Ethics, Economics, and Education at Hamline University. He received his Ph.D. from the University of Wisconsin–Madison in Curriculum and Instruction—History and the Social Sciences. He is a member of the Board of Directors and President of the National Council for the Social Studies, is past president of the Council of State Social Studies Specialists, and serves on the Executive Board of the Social Science Education Consortium.

Lawrence J. Johnson is Associate Dean for Research and Development and Director of the Arlitt Child and Family Research and Education Center at the University of Cincinnati. He is the co-author of four books, *Meeting Intervention Challenges: Issues from Birth to Three; Collaborative Practitioners, Collaborative Schools; Educating Young Black Gifted Children;* and *Anticipating the Needs of Special Education Students;* he is also the co-author of a curriculum and assessment instrument, *Coordinating Assessment with Preschool Programming.*

Edward J. Kameenui is Associate Director for the National Center to Improve the Tools of Educators and Associate Dean for the Division of Learning and Instructional Leadership in the College of Education at the University of Oregon. His interests include instructional design, reading research, learning disabilities, and curriculum development.

Laura Klenk is Assistant Professor of Reading in the Graduate School of Education at the State University of New York at Buffalo. She teaches courses in literacy acquisition, corrective reading, and research in literacy. Her research interests include literacy acquisition in young children with learning disabilities and enhancing play centers to promote literacy development in early childhood classrooms.

Thomas C. Lovitt is Professor of Special Education at the University of Washington, where he is affiliated with the Experimental Education Unit, a division of the Child Development and Mental Retardation Center. Since 1982, Dr. Lovitt has been the principal investigator of five federally funded projects involving adolescents with mild disabilities who were mainstreamed into general education classes. He has written extensively in this area. His doctorate is from the University of Kansas.

Carolyn A. Maher is Professor of Mathematics Education at Rutgers University. Her research and practical work with teachers focus on how students construct mathematical ideas over time, from elementary school through college. She has been able to videotape the same students for as long as 7 consecutive years and thus follow their mathematical development over a considerable time. She co-edited the research monograph *Constructivist Views on the Teaching and Learning of Mathematics* and serves on the International Committee for the International Group for the Psychology of Mathematics Education.

Margo A. Mastropieri is Professor of Special Education in the Department of Educational Studies at Purdue University in West Lafayette, Indiana. Her research has emphasized effective learning and memory strategies and science education for students with disabilities.

Christine Burton Maxwell is Associate Professor of Early Childhood Education at the University of Wisconsin–Milwaukee. Her current research interests focus on the processes and outcomes of reform efforts to create family-centered approaches to public schooling for young children. As Co-Director of the Milwaukee Early Schooling Initiative, Dr. Maxwell has collaborated with two urban public schools to integrate family support throughout their educational programs.

Lisa E. Monda-Amaya is Assistant Professor in the Department of Special Education at the University of Illinois, Urbana-Champaign. She received her Ph.D. in Special Education from Florida State University in 1989. Professor Monda-Amaya was named Outstanding Undergraduate Instructor for the College of Education in 1992. She was presented with the CGSE Faculty Award for Excellence in Teaching, Advising, and Research in 1992. Since 1990, she has been responsible for the design and coordination of the Collaborative Resource Teacher Training Program.

Marjorie Montague is Professor of Special Education at the University of Miami, Coral Gables, Florida. She specializes in learning disabilities and emotional and behavioral disorders. Her research interests include cognitive strategy training for improving the academic performance of students with learning disabilities and cognitive-behavioral interventions for young children with behavioral disorders.

Catherine Cobb Morocco is Associate Director at the Education Development Center, Inc., where she directs projects focused on improving teaching and assessment, particularly in the areas of language arts and science. A current focus of her work is how teachers acquire a deep understanding of principles of active, inquiry learning. Dr. Morocco received her Ed.D. from Harvard University.

Sigrin T. Newell is on the faculty of Walden University in Minneapolis, specializing in teacher education and science education. She also coordinates the New York State Science Mentor Network and works with urban inservice science teachers.

Annemarie Sullivan Palincsar is Jean and Charles Walgreen Professor of Reading and Literacy in the School of Education at the University of Michigan. She teaches general and special educators in a program entitled Literacy, Language, and Learning Disabilities. Her research interests include understanding and enhancing how literacy is taught and used across the curriculum in the primary grades.

P. David Pearson is Professor in the College of Education at Michigan State University. He completed his Ph.D. in Education at the University of Minnesota. From 1989 to 1995, he was Dean of the College of Education at the University of Illinois, Urbana-Champaign. In 1989, he received the Oscar Causey Award for outstanding contributions to reading research, and in 1990, he was honored by the International Reading Association with the William S. Gray Citation of Merit for his contributions to theory, research, and practice.

Marleen C. Pugach (Editor) is Professor in the Department of Curriculum and Instruction at the University of Wisconsin–Milwaukee. Her major interests include collaborative programs of teacher preparation that link general and special education, building collaborative relationships between special and general education teachers, how inclusion and school reform intersect, and the specific role of curriculum trends in the reform of special education. She is specifically interested in these issues as they relate to urban schools.

Mark C. Schug is Professor of Curriculum and Instruction at the University of Wisconsin–Milwaukee and Director of the UW–Milwaukee Center for Economic Education. Dr. Schug has taught for 24 years at the middle school, high school, and university levels. For the past 9 years, he has been the editor of *The Senior Economist* published by the National Council on Economic Education and has co-authored two recent national programs—*Capstone: The Nation's High School Economics Course* and *United States History: Eyes on the Economy*—also published by the National Council on Economic Education. Professor Schug earned his Ph.D. from the University of Minnesota in 1980.

Thomas E. Scruggs is Professor of Special Education in the Department of Educational Studies at Purdue University in West Lafayette, Indiana. His research has emphasized effective science learning, test-taking, and memory strategies for students with disabilities.

Cynthia L. Warger (Editor) has been a classroom teacher, a university teacher educator, and a professional education and association executive, and is currently an educational consultant. She received her Ph.D. in Educational Psychology from the University of Michigan. She has published extensively, including books, manuals, and articles in the area of social skills, teacher collaboration, and addressing the behavioral needs of children and youth. Her work as editor of the professional journal, *Teaching Exceptional Children,* received national awards from the EDPRESS Association.

Judith M. Zorfass is Associate Center Director at the Education Development Center, Inc. She received her Ed.D. from Harvard University. She manages projects that focus on classroom-based research, the development of curriculum materials, professional development, and dissemination. She is particularly interested in the ways in which technology can support students with disabilities.

Index